High Street, Canterbury.

KENT

ORDNANCE SURVEY HISTORICAL GUIDES

KENT

Dr Felix Hull

GEORGE PHILIP
ORDNANCE SURVEY

First published in Great Britain in 1988 by
George Philip & Son Ltd,
27A Floral Street,
London WC2E 9DP
and Ordnance Survey
Romsey Road
Southampton
SO9 4DH

British Library Cataloguing in Publication Data

Hull, F.
Kent.—(Ordnance survey historic county guides).
1. Kent—Historical geography
I. Title II. Series
911'.4223 DA670.K3

ISBN 0-540-01134-7

Filmset by Tameside Filmsetting Ltd,
Ashton-under-Lyne, Lancashire
Printed by BAS Printers Ltd,
Over Wallop, Hampshire
Bound by Robert Hartnoll Ltd
Bodmin, Cornwall

Picture acknowledgements

The illustrations in this book are reproduced by kind permission of the following:
The Francis Frith Collection: pp 56, 75, 98, 102, 115
Kent County Libraries: pp 7, 35 (bottom), 38 (bottom), 42, 50 52, 81, 86, 107, 110, 125
Kent County Council, Archives Office: p 32
London Borough of Greenwich: p 28
Radio Times Hulton Picture Library: pp 1, 25, 60, 63, 74
The Sidery Collection of William Henry Boyer: p 58
Geoff Smith of Ronald White Ltd: pp 29, 35 (top), 39 (top), 43, 46, 57, 66, 80, 83, 84, 94, 106, 113, 123, 124

Endpapers: *Canterbury High Street at the turn of the century.*
Half title: *Typical Kentish oasts at Broomfield, used for drying hops.*
Frontispiece: *Chilham Square in 1903.*

Contents

Kent

A view of hop-pickers in East Kent, taken in 1898. This picture clearly shows how all ages were involved.

HE OPENING YEARS of the nineteenth century saw the development of a new form of map-making in this country which was to have a great effect on the way in which we look at our environment and the standard of accuracy which we expect from maps, whether used for business or for pleasure. In 1801 the first ever one inch to one mile Ordnance Survey map was produced in four sheets to cover the whole of the ancient county of Kent. This was followed in 1805 by a comparable map of Essex and, in each case, the surveyor directing the operation was Lieutenant-Colonel (later Major-General) William Mudge of the Royal Artillery.

Each map had been prepared during the previous decade by the use of drawings on scales to two inches and three inches to one mile and each had its origin in the fears of a French invasion following the Revolution and the subsequent activities of Bonaparte. Their publication, however, proved to be the beginning of a great series of maps and plans on various scales, but noted internationally for their accuracy and their clarity of style.

The present volume is based on the original work of Colonel Mudge, though the actual plates available are for the later editions of the 1801 map. After the original issue of a map of the whole county, various sections were published subsequently at different dates between 1816 and 1844 and the railways were inserted as became needful. The forty-seven plates each have a caption relating nineteenth-century Kent to that of today, and in six instances the large map is complemented by a copy of the modern Landranger map, reduced to one inch to a mile for ease of comparison. In addition, in the three special cases of Erith, Canterbury and Tunbridge Wells extracts from the 1:25,000 map are included. Where it has been considered appropriate, early and modern illustrations of special features have been added.

It is hoped, therefore, that this production will help in the realization that there is both remarkable continuity in our towns and countryside, just as there has also been striking change. It was perhaps good fortune that 1801 was the chosen year, for Kent, as it was at the start of the last century, would have been largely recognizable to a visitor from an earlier age, whereas by 1901 dramatic and often irreversible changes had taken place in population growth, transport and also in the structure of society, changes which have accelerated still further in the present century.

Many factors have gone into the making of Kent as we know it, some of which stem from human endeavour while others are the outcome of geological and geographical structure. Geology affected not only the agrarian and industrial pattern of the country, but also the nature of its settlement following the Saxon invasions of the fifth century.

Geography—notably the close association with the continent of Europe—has predetermined that Kent would often feel the brunt of invasion or attack, from prehistoric times when the land bridge still held, till the Second World War and the flying bomb. Similarly, the development of London as the capital of the realm has had a profound effect on the exploitation of Kent as a granary, a means of easy access from the coast and a dormitory area. Commuting by the thousand may be a recent phenomenon, but courtiers and governmental officials have had their houses and land in Kent for many centuries.

The position of Kent as the south-eastern corner of the land has resulted in a certain isolation although at the same time it has also offered a corridor constantly carrying men and their affairs to and from Europe and the heart of England. The Thames, on the north, continues the pattern of a water boundary and it is only in the west and south that there is a land border with Surrey and Sussex. Geologically the county is formed by a series of bands beginning with the alluvial marshes of the Thames shore in the north, followed southwards by the wide chalk belt of the North Downs and then the mixed soils of Holmsdale stretching from Westerham and the Surrey border as far as Ashford in the east, this vale, in turn, rising to the scarp of the ragstone ridge, which reaches over 800 feet in height at Brasted Chart west of Sevenoaks. Southwards of this range of hills lies the Weald, an ancient forested area partly on low, swampy and heavy clays and partly on lighter and higher sandy soils. Across this region in the west and centre of the county lies the valley of the Medway and its tributaries the Eden, Teise and Beult, the main stream cutting its way northwards through ragstone and chalk to reach the Thames estuary beyond Chatham. Finally come the marshes of Romney and of the river Rother, and also those lying between Thanet and the mainland. In historic times Thanet was separated from the rest of Kent by a wide stretch of tidal water represented now by the tiny Wantsum stream.

Early and Roman occupations are well attested to in all parts of Kent except the Weald. The megaliths of Kits Coty and Coldrum are evidence of our early settlers and Dover, Canterbury and Rochester were places of significance in Roman days. Watling Street (now more or less the line of the A2) was a primary artery from time immemorial and a principal element of the Roman road system. Another ancient road ran at the foot of the downs, along the spring line; it had its origin in Salisbury Plain, and ran to Winchester and from there to the coast with a branch to Canterbury. In the eighteenth century this track became known as the Pilgrims' Way, but it can never have been as significant as the road from London and Southwark immortalized by Chaucer in *The Canterbury Tales*.

The Romans developed significant defence works at Reculver and Richborough at either end of the Wantsum channel between Thanet and the mainland and also at Dover, where the pharos survives within the grounds of the castle. Caesar may have landed near Deal, but the Roman occupation, when it came, filled Kent with settlements and villas, notably the great villa at Lullingstone with its Christian church almost on the site of a later Saxon one, and also the villa at Eccles in the Medway valley. It is said that Jutish or Saxon sea pirates were invited to settle in Thanet by desperate Romano-British rulers anxious for allies in their internecine strife following the withdrawal of the Roman legions and that, in turn, these Saxons, led by Hengist, turned on their paymasters and swiftly conquered Kent and much land westwards besides. Aylesford, just north of Maidstone, may have been the site of one of the principal battles in 455, and certainly from about that time and for another 400 years Kent was a separate kingdom, though at times a vassal state to the midland kingdom of Mercia. Memories of this early independence lingered throughout the county's history and the occasional use of the word 'lathe', even today, is a reminder of pre-Conquest units of administration. Indeed the pattern of Saxon Kent is still with us, for our place names are remarkably homogeneous. Only a few names of rivers and of the county itself are certainly earlier than the Saxon invasions and, unlike Essex on the other side of the Thames, a mere handful of Norman lords has left patronyms as additions to the Saxon village names. Saxon Kent, however, was essentially the county north of the ragstone ridge. The Weald, to the south, was still largely impenetrable and was not fully colonized by the first Jutish settlers. Wealden parishes were formed much later, some after the Norman Conquest, but evidence of earlier infiltration is found in the many place-names which end with the suffix 'den', meaning a swine pasture. In the year 597 an occurrence took place which had a profound effect upon future Kentish history. This was the arrival of Augustine with a band of monks from Rome.

Aethelberht I was one of the more outstanding Kentish kings. He was married to a Christian princess for whose sake he welcomed the mission to Canterbury and the see was founded that year, to be followed by that of Rochester in 604. For the next thousand years Kent was dominated by the church and by ecclesiastics; monastic houses flourished and the archbishop, himself, held large estates across the county. In fact at least a third of Kent seems to have been owned by the church. Despite the failure of the Kentish royal line in the ninth century and the assumption of power by the kings of Wessex, Kent remained a highly developed and prosperous part of the country. The Danish and Norse invasions played only a small part in its story, though the monasteries at Minster in Thanet and Minster in Sheppey were sacked.

The Domesday account of Kent, while fully endorsing the adverse effect of the Weald on the pattern of settlement, is in some ways misleading and difficult to follow. For the purposes of the great survey entries were largely standardized, except where there was some very special reason. Thus there is some evidence for Dover having a special position in relation to the Crown and certain particular local laws are indicated, but the breakdown of the population into villeins, cottars, bordars and serfs is difficult to relate to what we know of late Saxon society in Kent, although it does suggest that there was a considerable number of families who were landless, if not slaves. The Conqueror was fully aware of the significance of this south-eastern corner of the country. His progress from Hastings to London was by way of New Romney—which he apparently burnt—Dover and Canterbury. From there he followed Watling Street to the capital, and legend has it that at Swanscombe near Dartford he was ambushed by the Kentings and persuaded to confirm their liberties, thus giving rise to the motto, 'invicta', the unconquered, which is still found along with the white horse of Hengist on the county arms. Whatever the truth of this old story, it is a fact that in the thirteenth century a body of local custom affecting Kent appears in early Statute books and that it had the force of law. Significantly this 'Custom of Kent' related to those who held their land in gavelkind, a form of tenure, only finally abolished in this century, whereby all the sons inherited, property being divided between them. Often enough, however, this system, known as partible inheritance, was overcome by means of financial settlements whereby money rather than land was divided, a pattern still to be found in the Channel Isles.

William I and his successors were very conscious of the needs of defence and over the years a number of castles were established both within Kent and in neighbouring Sussex. The great keeps of Dover, Canterbury and Rochester are witness to this building programme and to the first line of defence, but other castles were also built at Saltwood, Chilham, Leeds, Thurnham, Sutton Valence, Allington, Tonbridge and Eynsford. Moreover, the Norman kings and their immediate successors had considerable holdings in northern France, and it is during this period that arrangements were established for five towns, Hastings, Romney, Hythe, Dover and Sandwich, to provide the king with fifty-seven ships for fifteen days each year to act primarily as a ferry service to his duchy of Normandy and other lands in France. Gradually other towns in Kent and Sussex were associated with the Cinque Ports and, more particularly after the loss of Normandy in 1204, the ship service took on a specifically naval aspect and the Constable of Dover castle was given authority over the Ports as Lord Warden. In 1278, Edward I, who had been imprisoned by the portsmen during the Barons' War, and who after the death of Simon de Montfort had become Lord Warden for the remainder of Henry III's life, granted a detailed charter to the Cinque Ports, setting out their obligations and their privileges, notably freedom from national taxation and from the royal courts of justice. By a strange quirk of fate this codification of rights almost coincided in date with a series of storms which destroyed Old Winchelsea in Sussex, removed the river Rother from New Romney to Rye and, coupled with the eastward drift of sand and shingle along the Channel, gradually closed every one of the Ports except Dover, which only survived by means of constant dredging. By the fourteenth century the Ports, once the scourge of the French coast, were already in decline. The later medieval story of Kent is one of disturbance. The coast suffered from French attack, Sandwich being sacked as late as 1457, while the county as a whole played its part in the Peasants' Revolt of 1381 and in

Jack Cade's Rebellion of 1450. Nationally speaking the former was the more significant. Shrieval extortions, the death throes of serfdom, the aftermath of the Black Death in 1348–9, which may have killed one in three of the population, all led to disaffection. This was brought to a head by the poll tax of 1379 and by tales of the unseemly behaviour of tax collectors. Wat Tyler, one of the principal leaders of the revolt, was a man of Kent, possibly from around Staplehurst, and John Ball was a prisoner at Maidstone. Ball, sometimes referred to as 'the mad priest of Kent' was a kind of early socialist and is linked with the rhyme:

When Adam delved and Eve span,
Who was then the gentleman?

The Kent men met at Blackheath, a traditional meeting-place near London, and marched on the capital, but the death of Wat Tyler at Smithfield and the subsequent actions of the young king only resulted in further misery within the county. Yet, in fact, serfdom in Kent was already a thing of the past, and it is noteworthy that William de Septvans, who had been sheriff in the year of the rebellion, freed his remaining serfs in his will of 1408.

The Cade rebellion was a different matter. It was essentially Kentish in character, although with wider political overtones and the rebels were not, as Shakespeare would have us believe, 'a ragged multitude of hinds and peasants', but rather consisted of a remarkable cross-section of society: gentlemen, artisans, yeomen and husbandmen rose as a body so that the lists of pardons read like the hundredal militia of the day. Their complaints were principally the iniquities of the sheriff of the day and of his family, the difficulties of obtaining justice, and the long distances between east and west Kent which affected those attending quarter sessions. It was said that it took five days for someone from Westerham on the Surrey border to attend sessions at Canterbury and they asked that justice be done in west as well as east Kent. Few executions followed, although Cade himself was hunted down, but the perpetrators of extortion and bad justice were punished and arrangements were soon after made for sessions to be held at Maidstone as well as at Canterbury, a development which played a part in Maidstone's becoming the county town, although the old Shire Court was already held nearby at Penenden Heath. The dramatic changes resulting from the Reformation altered the social structure of Kent in Tudor times. The great ecclesiastical institutions of Canterbury and Rochester, the vast archiepiscopal estates and the holdings of a multitude of other religious houses may have represented between one third and one half of the land of Kent, and the power of the church led inevitably to a measure of anti-clericalism. The changes of the 1530s were, however, traumatic. Although the former priories of Christ Church, Canterbury and St Andrew, Rochester were abolished, the new capitular establishments were quickly re-endowed, but the holdings of the archbishop and of all the other great and small monasteries were taken by the Crown and ultimately came on to the land market. Not all were happy at what was taking place. While Henry VIII might be courting Anne Boleyn at Hever or Leeds, the 'Holy Maid of Kent', Elizabeth Barton of Court at Street near Lympne, was having visions with increasingly dangerous political overtones. Nevertheless, many, not least the gentry of Kent, benefited from the changes, and the accession of Mary in 1553 was once again the sign for a Kentish insurrection.

This time the leader was Sir Thomas Wyatt of Allington, near Maidstone, a brave leader related to the one significant noble house in Kent, that of Broke, Lords Cobham. This affair came near to success, but its failure is less important than that it tends to underline the social structure of Kent as a land of the lesser gentry. There is little doubt that the county was wealthy; a land of knights and esquires, of gentlemen, yeomen and merchants with considerable cross-fertilization between the classes of society. The contemporary jingle is a clear indication of the general opinion:

A knight of Wales,
A gentleman of Cales (Calais)
A laird of the north countree,
A yeoman of Kent, sitting on his penny rent,
Can buy them out, all three.

This social pattern also made the position of Lord Cobham the more significant as the only indigenous nobleman, and the equivocal William, Lord Cobham, who prevaricated during the Wyatt rebellion and thereby helped to destroy his kinsman, was later both Lord Lieutenant of Kent and Lord Warden of the Cinque Ports. The Marian reaction saw burnings of Protestants at Canterbury, Ashford and Maidstone and elsewhere and the Elizabethan church settlement was generally accepted, although there is evidence both for the infiltration of priests and of extreme reformers through Dover.

During the first half of the century the towns had suffered from a time of depression, but an influx of Walloon refugees to Sandwich, Canterbury and Maidstone helped to revitalize industry, especially in the cloth trade. This is, indeed, the period of the clothiers of the Weald, and their fine timber-framed hall houses in such villages at Headcorn, Biddenden and Smarden still delight the visitor.

Nor should it be overlooked that Kent played its part in the literary renaissance of the period. The father of the rebel, Wyatt, had been a poet, but he was outshone by Sir Philip Sidney, that paragon of knighthood and courtesy, whose home was at Penshurst. Still more important, Canterbury saw the birth of the playwright Christopher Marlowe, later to be killed in a brawl at Deptford at the other end of the county.

As in other ages, the defence of the south-east continued to give concern, culminating in the alarm of the Spanish Armada of 1588. The decline of the Cinque Ports as an effective force led to a different approach. As long ago as the reign of Edward III, in 1360, attention had been given to the defence of the Thames estuary, and the building of a castle at Queenborough in Sheppey, itself a new town, was an indication of this concern. In the early sixteenth century Henry VIII decided to build a series of castles or fortresses around the coast from Camber, near Rye, to Sandown, north of Deal. Of these Deal castle is now a museum and Walmer the official residence of the Lord Warden.

By the death of Elizabeth I, in 1603, there was already an indication of another social change, especially in West Kent. Families such as Sidney and Sackville, both courtiers and servants of the government, had acquired large estates at Penshurst and Knole. Sidney also had an interest in the Wealden iron industry, an indication that gentlemen were not averse to links with commerce, and other merchant families were buying land and building houses in the outer London areas of Greenwich and Woolwich. A lawyer such as the antiquarian, William Lambarde, who wrote the first local history of Kent, had his base in Greenwich and only later on purchased property in the Sevenoaks area. In the eastern half of Kent, local families, some of whom could trace their antecedents to the Conquest and beyond, were rising in status. Of such were Finch, Dering, Toke and Tufton. Although within a few years Sidney, Sackville, Finch and Tufton had all achieved noble status, there remained a remarkable homogeneity among the gentry of Kent, and much intermarriage. In the struggles of the Civil War many of these families sided with the King, though some were far from happy at the choice before them. The parliamentary leaders, however, realized that unless Kent was held, London would become untenable, and during 1642 they staged a take-over of the county by those lesser gentry who supported their cause. Most of the others joined the King at Nottingham or York, though the position of Robert Sidney, Earl of Leicester, was equivocal and his sons supported Parliament. Nevertheless, so effective was the action in 1642 that, apart from some local disturbance in 1643, the county was held quiet and the Cavalier supporters returned home to sequestrated estates and heavy fines. In 1648 a group of disaffected gentlemen hoped to stage a successful revolt supported by the navy, but the swift action by Fairfax, culminating in the battle of Maidstone, destroyed their hopes.

The Restoration saw the greater gentry once more in the ascendant and by the next century the Sackvilles, in the person of the Duke of Dorset, were dominant, at least in west Kent. The period was one of progress, despite the alarming appearance of the Dutch in the Medway in 1667 and the discovery of the fleeing James II at Faversham in 1688. Large estates were made larger, gardens were planned and agriculture was prosperous, although the gap between the rich and the poor tended to widen. But Kent was, in any event, an important agricultural county. It was a vital element in the London food market providing cereals from Thanet, fruit from north Kent and other parts of the county, hops from the Weald and from Holmsdale, cattle from the Thames marshes and sheep from every orchard as well as from the marshlands of Sheppey—Isle of Sheep—and Romney. The actual farms generally speaking were small, but their mixed economy proved a good source of wealth.

One reason behind the success of Kentish agriculture lay in the early enclosure of the county. From an early, if uncertain date, the agrarian pattern made it possible for very little of the county to be open-field, and from before the Reformation Kentish farmers benefited from the small enclosed fields which made up their farms. As early as the middle of the sixteenth century the topographer John Leland wrote that Kent was noted for 'fertility, wood, pasture, cattle, fish, fowl, rivers, havens with ships among the five ports most famous'. Whatever one must take from this eulogy to seek the truth, this was the public opinion of the 'garden of England'!

During the eighteenth century the population also grew, especially as a gradual appreciation of the significance of proper hygiene took effect. It can be estimated that Kent in the mid-seventeenth century, excluding the Cinque Ports and parts of Canterbury, had a population of around 132,000 persons. By 1801, the date of the first census, this had risen to approximately 309,000, a further indicator that the region and the period were prosperous, however much hardship and deep poverty there must still have been. One might say that at the time when Colonel Mudge and his men were surveying Kent, the county, rich and well populated, was waiting and prepared for the dramatic changes which were about to take place.

There is no question that the word most descriptive of Kentish development since 1801 is urbanization, for what was a predominantly agricultural county, well earning its soubriquet of 'the garden of England', became during the nineteenth and more especially the twentieth century an area in which local authorities are increasingly concerned to stem the tide of suburban sprawl.

Already in 1801 there were fifteen small chartered boroughs, almost all, except Maidstone and Canterbury, situated around the coast. Relatively speaking, until the 1950s, these did not grow disproportionately to the overall increase in population, but that rose from 309,000 in 1801 to 478,000 in 1831, 734,000 in 1861 and by 1921 had reached a total of 1,646,000 souls. If one examines the rural parishes, many of which suffered severe economic hardship in the early part of the last century, as the agricultural riots of 1830 and the Courtney riots of 1838 show, a rapid initial growth was followed by virtual stagnation. Neither these places nor the ancient towns can explain the full population growth. The answer lies in a number of places, principally in north Kent, which were little known in earlier years. Three, Deptford, Woolwich and Chatham, had been royal dockyard centres for many years, but expansion was also evident in Greenwich, Lewisham and Tunbridge Wells, the popular Kentish spa. The principal catalyst in the process of growth was the railway, which with the exception of the somewhat experimental line from Whitstable to Canterbury, entered the county in the 1840s. The excessive zeal and rivalry of the railway companies left Kent with a complex network of lines, few of which were truly profitable. It could be said that the Kentish lines went nowhere! Industry was largely lacking, for iron and cloth had died out a century before the iron horse and initially holiday and continental trade were limited. Nevertheless wherever the railway came in those early years towns grew, whether the outer London parishes, significant junctions such as Tonbridge or Ashford, with its railway works, or coastal centres like Margate and Folkestone. Many of these populated areas were totally unregulated and in 1832, 1849 and 1854 Tonbridge in particular suffered from outbreaks of cholera. A report of that last year warned: 'Although on each of these occasions the same locality has been attacked with the greatest virulence, and the more respectable inhabitants have, hitherto, comparatively escaped, it may not be so again.'

Better health control by public authorities, coupled with the railway network, brought about a vast alteration between 1860 and the end of the century. The first edition of the Ordnance Survey six-inch and twenty-five-inch maps still show metropolitan Kent criss-crossed with railways, but largely undeveloped, though already the earlier mansions of Greenwich were giving way to mean streets of standardized housing. The urbanization of Deptford, Greenwich, Woolwich and Lewisham, which were absorbed by the new London County Council in 1889, went on apace and was largely complete by 1870. Bromley, Bexley and Beckenham followed, the destruction of garden and parkland being lamented by the survivors of an earlier age. Beckenham, a village of 955 inhabitants in 1801, had a population of 31,709 by 1901; one private estate built up a hundred years earlier on the Erith marshes became in the 1860s the new town of Belvedere, and there was similar development elsewhere. At the same time the advantages of cheap and rapid travel to the coast were realized and places such as Herne Bay and Broadstairs grew out of all proportion both as holiday centres and as retirement towns.

Other local factors were also at work. The Thames shore and lower Medway valley provided the raw material for the cement industry; the streams of Kent had provided the stimulus for the family paper-maker, such as Whatman at Maidstone, and this industry now expanded at Dartford, in the Medway valley and near Sittingbourne. Finally, at the end of the century, after extensive exploration, the Kent coalfield was established, though this never achieved the growth originally hoped and the new town of Aylesham never became the metropolis intended.

At the same time, age-old agriculture remained. The depression of the 1880s saw an influx of Scottish farmers; hops were still a staple crop requiring a minor invasion of Londoners each autumn for the picking season. So significant was this element that strange single-track railways penetrated the Weald, relying on the annual flood of hop-pickers for their profit.

The pattern thus established continued into the present century, and indeed changes were few before the Second World War. Since 1945, however, a rapid further exploitation has affected Kent. The vast burgeoning of traffic, to and from the Continent, has led to a fresh network of motorways to supplement the overcrowded roads and the already present railway. The pressure for land has led to new villages being created; New Ash Green and Coxheath are two such, while the commuter demand has changed established villages such as Staplehurst and Headcorn into small dormitory towns. Along the old main line to the coast, Ashford has also been developed further as part of the London overspill scheme.

Romney Marsh, no longer the haunt of smugglers with the connivance of a fictitious Dr Syn, has been partially converted to arable farming, and at Dungeness the great bulk of the nuclear power station dominates. Villages such as Bearsted, situated near the larger towns, are absorbed and become dormitories while the coast is the haven for the retired.

During the last war Kent suffered severely, especially from the flying bombs, and both Canterbury and nearby Sturry were heavily bombed and badly damaged, while Dover once again endured shelling from across the narrow seas. The establishing of an airfield at Manston in Thanet finally obliterated a Saxon boundary still traceable on the third edition six-inch map of 1910, but the men of Kent acted as their distant ancestors when the little ships plied their way to the beaches of Dunkirk and the constraints of geography once more dominated human history.

So, despite suburbia, motorways and the possibility of the Channel Tunnel, there is a continuity seen in Kentish agriculture, in its place-names and also in its outlook which is still individual. Its timber-framed houses and converted oasts are also part of the older pattern not entirely lost despite vast alteration. The map of 1801 still lies beneath the brick, mortar and concrete of the past two centuries and there are still areas on the Downs or in the Weald or Romney Marsh where the picture represented by Mudge can be recognized even today nearly 200 years later.

It has been indicated already that the Mudge map was the first of its kind in the sense that it was the beginning of the Ordnance Survey series, but in another way it not only reveals the Kent of the early nineteenth century, but looks back to much earlier times. The south-east, because of its relative prosperity, its continental links and associations with London and the Court, appears to have assimilated the Renaissance art of map-making more readily than some remoter areas of the country. This art took three forms: coastal charts, of which understandably Kent was often the subject; plans of private estates and farms in which the local surveyor came into his own; and maps of whole counties or of county areas. The first real county atlas came from the work of Christopher Saxton in 1579 and includes a plan of Kent, Surrey and Sussex. This beginning was followed by similar county atlases, one of the most famous being *Speculi Britanniae Pars*, produced by John Norden, whose maps are still much sought-after. The chief feature of these early maps is that they tend to be copies one of the other with only marginal differences. In the same way, once a good map had been produced it was copied again and again in various editions so that there is little variation in style or content from the age of Elizabeth I to that of George II, and maps of Kent by the Dutchmen, Blaeu and Jansoon, and by the British cartographers, Norden, Speed, Morden and Bowen, follow this pattern, although the last named added extensive historical notes to his maps.

Kent, however, holds a special place of pride because one cartographer, Philip Symonson of Rochester, produced his own map of the county in 1596. This, although it followed Saxton in some ways, was a fine example of its kind, showing towns and villages, roads, rivers and hills. It, too, was copied from time to time and was used by Harris for his *History of Kent*, of which only one volume was issued in 1718. The lack of interest in real accuracy is shown when, with this late copy, a sketch of Dover was reversed because it fitted better into the space that way.

Towards the end of the eighteenth century, Andrews, Dury and Herbert issued a county map on the scale of two inches to one mile. Two editions were produced in 1769 and 1779 but their approach was dominated by the patronage possible from the gentle families, and much of the detail included was sketched in rather than surveyed. This somewhat archaic attitude towards map-making detracts from the value of their work and in any case they were overtaken by a new generation of cartographers with a new outlook. This fresh attitude is shown by the clear and competent maps of John Cary and later of C. and J. Greenwood. Indeed, C. and J. Greenwood produced maps in the early years of the last century which are, in their way, as fine as Mudge. Whether in fact they actually copied Mudge is not established, but the similarity is marked.

The significance of the Ordnance Survey map cannot be overstated. It established a new approach to map-making in which geographical accuracy was linked with clarity of fine detail. Although hachures were used to indicate relief, this was done with a sensitivity that provided a better portrayal of the countryside than had previously been possible. Moreover, although produced on the relatively small scale of one inch to one mile, it looked ahead to the future large-scale maps in its attempt to show the boundaries of fields and its indication of every building rather than the use of standard symbols for villages and towns.

The decision to reissue this fine example of British cartography is, therefore, to be welcomed, especially in Kent, for the map reveals the land as it was from time immemorial and just before those dramatic changes discussed above. The publication should enable us to appreciate better the roots of the environment in which we now live and how, although modern technology and population growth have greatly affected that environment, the age-old pattern of hills and rivers, woods, fields and settlements remains in much of the county of our choice.

Map Section

Tunbridge Wells in 1908, showing a view of the Pantiles from the northern or town end. The spring which gave rise to the spa is situated in the building immediately to the right of the stepped entrance and before the row of shops. This area is the original heart of Tunbridge Wells.

KEY TO ONE INCH MAPS

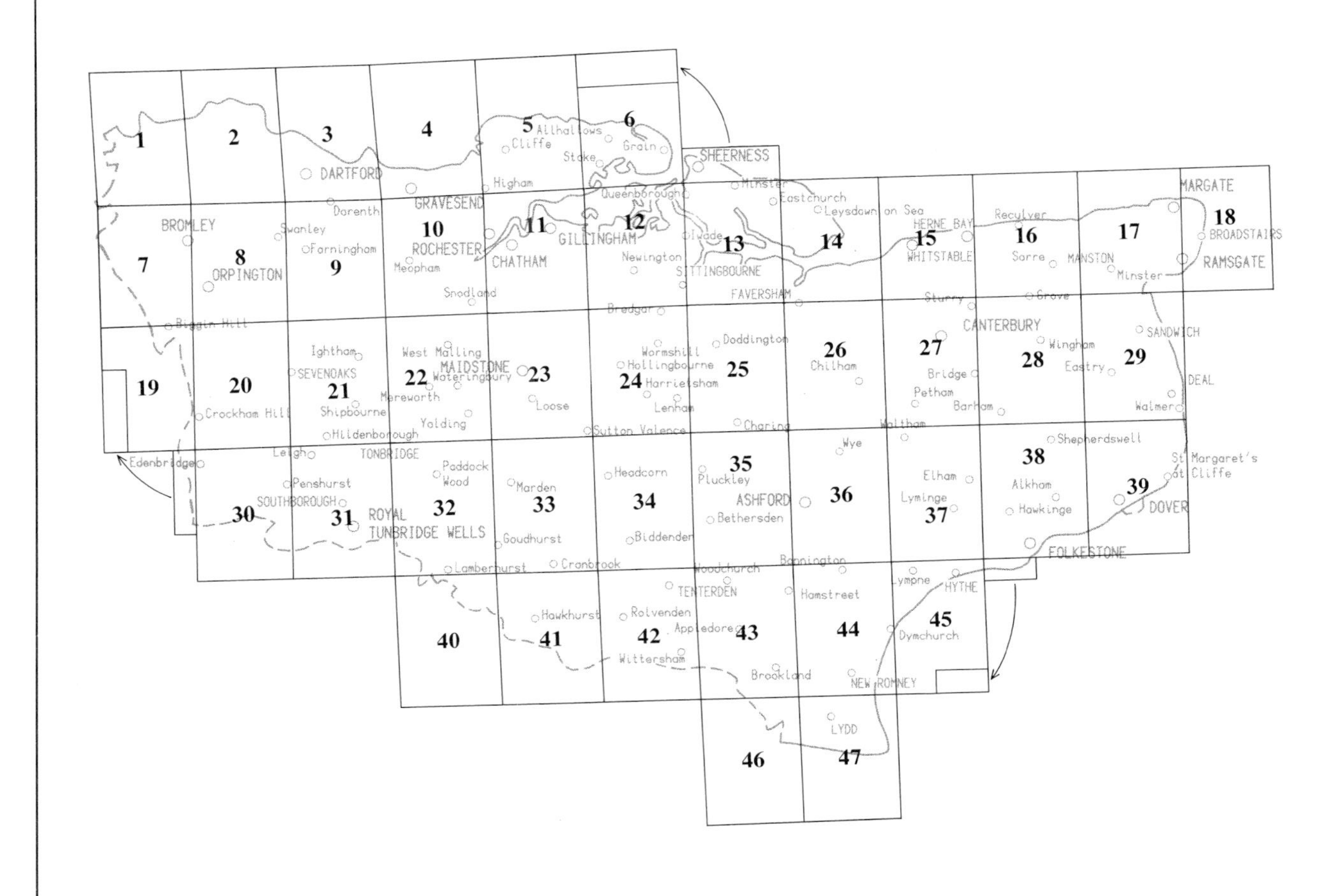

Map 1

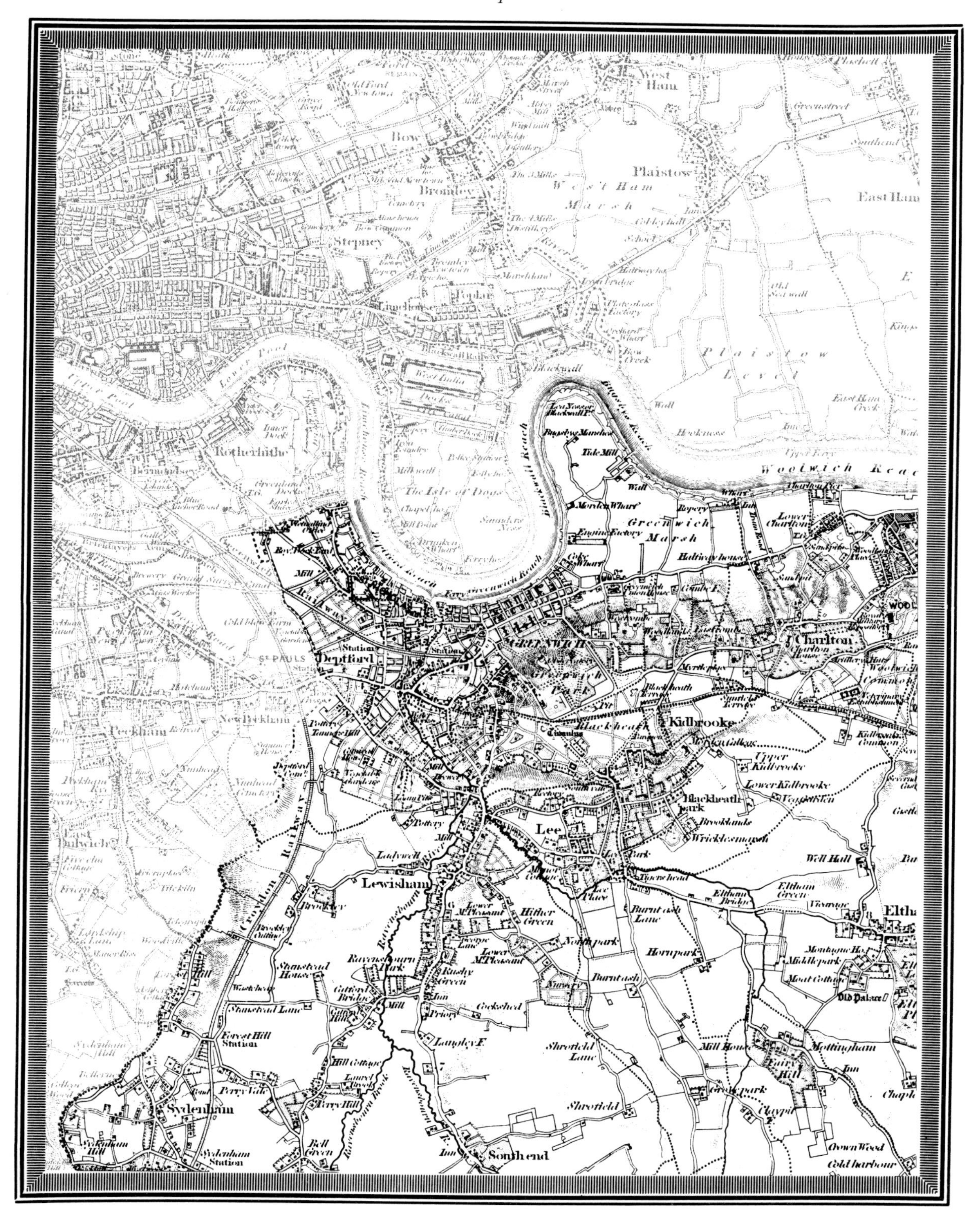

West Ham
Bow
Bromley
Stepney
Limehouse
Poplar
Plaistow
West Ham Marsh
East Ham
Plaistow Level
Blackwall
West India Docks
Rotherhithe
The Isle of Dogs
Woolwich Reach
Greenwich Marsh
Deptford
Greenwich
Greenwich Park
Charlton
Kidbrooke
Blackheath
Peckham
New Peckham
Lee
Lewisham
Blackheath Park
Brooklands
Upper Kidbrooke
Lower Kidbrooke
Well Hall
Eltham Bridge
Hither Green
Lower Mt. Pleasant
Ravensbourn Park
Rushey Green
Old Palace
Mottingham
Forest Hill Station
Sydenham
Sydenham Station
Perry Vale
Perry Hill
Bell Green
Southend
Shroffield
Croydon Railway
Lewisham
East Dulwich

Map 1 (previous page) Metropolitan Kent, comprising Deptford, Greenwich, Lewisham and Woolwich, was lost to London in 1889. In 1801 the area was one of villages with somewhat extended built-up areas at Deptford and Greenwich and round the dockyard at Woolwich. Woolwich Warren of 1801 became the site of Woolwich Arsenal. This district was an area of large houses for merchants and other London gentlemen whereas today it is almost entirely built over, except for Blackheath, Woolwich Common and Eltham Park. Expansion after 1801 was continuous; Lewisham grew from a population of 4000 to nearly 110,000 during the nineteenth century and it becomes almost impossible to relate the early map to that of the area today.

(Above) A view of Blackheath village in 1810 by W. Noble, with one of the mills in use at that time, looking south towards Lee, now a built up part of Lewisham. (Opposite) The same area today.

BARKING AND DAGENHAM L.B.
BARKING
DAGENHAM
AST HAM
Castle Green
Sand & Gravel Pit
Albyns Fm
South Hornchurch
DAGENHAM DOCK STA
Motor Works
Hornchurch Marshes
RAINHAM
Sewage Works
Creekmouth
Cross Ness
Beckton
Cyprus
Royal Albert Dock
King George V Dock
North Woolwich
Margaret or Tripcock Ness
Barking Reach
Thamesmead
Halfway Reach
Sewage Works
Power Station
Jenningtree Point
Frog Island
Rainham Marshes
Silt Lagoons
DANGER AR
Wennington
Silt Lagoon
Erith Marshes
Erith Reach
Aveley M
Coldharbour
Erith Rands
Subway
WOOLWICH
Abbey Wood
Lesnes Abbey Woods
Belvedere
Plumstead
Plumstead Common
Bostall Woods
West Heath
Lessness Heath
ERITH
Pier
Northumberland Heath
Woolwich Common
GREENWICH L.B.
Cemeteries
East Wickham
Crayford Marshes
Slade Green
North End
Shooters Hill
Eltham Common
Jackwood
Oxleas Wood
ROMAN ROAD
Welling
Barnehurst
Bexleyheath
Falconwood
BEXLEY
Danson Park
BEXLEY L.B.
Barnes Cray
CRAYFORD
Eltham Park
ELTHAM
Coll
Avery Hill
Blackfen
Hall Place
DARTFORD
Old Bexley
Bexley Woods
Bowmans
Palace
Children's Homes
Lamorbey Park
Coldblow
Dartford Heath
Maypole
Leyton Cross
New Eltham
Longlands
Mount Mascal Fm
Heath Side
SIDCUP
North Cray
Bunkers Hill
Joyden's Wood
Hook Green
Kemnal Manor
Manor Fm
Foxbury
Frognal Corner
Forest Walk
Chislehurst
DARENT

Map 2

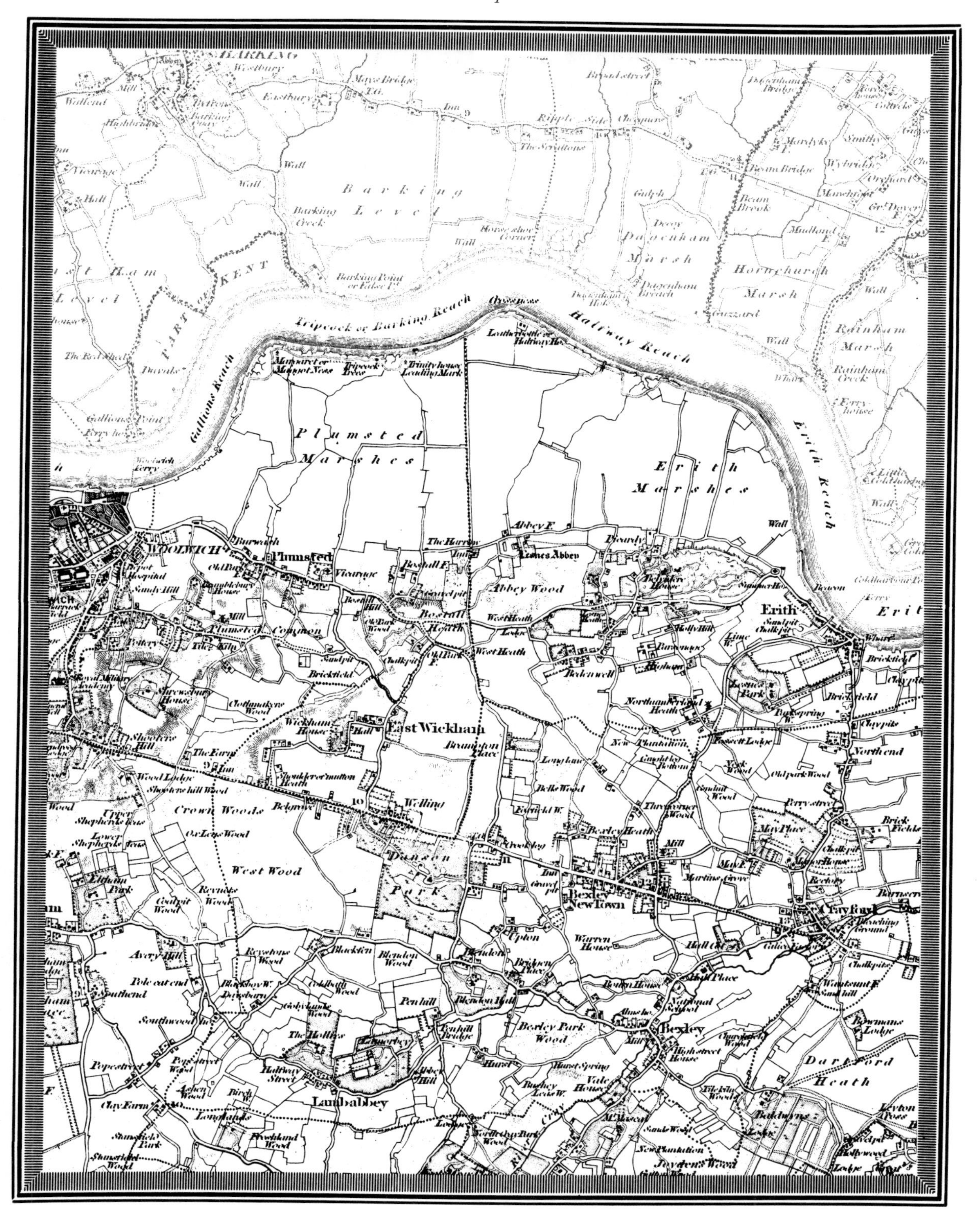

Barking
Westbury
Eastbury
Ripple Side
Broad street
Barking Level
Barking Creek
Dagenham Marsh
Hornchurch Marsh
Rainham Marsh
Rainham Creek
Dagenham Breach
Barking Point or False Pt.
Tripcock or Barking Reach
Halfway Reach
Gallions Reach
Erith Reach
Plumsted Marshes
Erith Marshes
Woolwich
Plumsted
Vicarage
Plumsted Common
Abbey F.
Lesnes Abbey
Abbey Wood
Bostall Heath
West Heath
Erith
Belvedere House
Lesness Park
Northumberland Heath
East Wickham
Wickham House
Shrewsbury House
Shooters Hill
Crown Woods
West Wood
Welling
Belgrove
Danson Park
Bexley Heath
Bexley New Town
Crayford
Blendon Wood
Blendon Hall
Upton
Warren House
Bexley
Bexley Park Wood
Dartford Heath
Eltham Park
Avery Hill
Southend
Lamorbey
Lamb abbey
Halfway Street
Vale House
Baldwyns

Map 2 and modern map 2 (previous page) The modern map on the left indicates the extent of change in this area, all of which west of the River Cray became the London Borough of Bexley in 1965. Erith on the Thames typifies the change. In 1841 it was still a small village of 2000 inhabitants when the census return included 200 harvest labourers, but it had grown to 25,000 by the end of the century and the Belvedere estate had by then been developed. In recent years the Erith marshes north of Abbey Farm have seen the growth of Thamesmead. Crayford and Bexley also grew in a similar fashion and Bexley Heath, a barren expanse in 1801, became a large town in its own right. There are few places where the rape of Kent is more evident than in this north-west corner of the county.

Detail map 2 (overleaf) The centre of Erith from the Thames southwards to the parish church in 1897. Already the former riverside village shows signs of the suburban development which completely changed its character.

A print of the riverside at Woolwich looking downstream with the royal dockyard in the foreground in about 1800. If the large building with a cupola beyond the principal vessel represents the royal arsenal then the print cannot date from before 1801 (see also page 35).

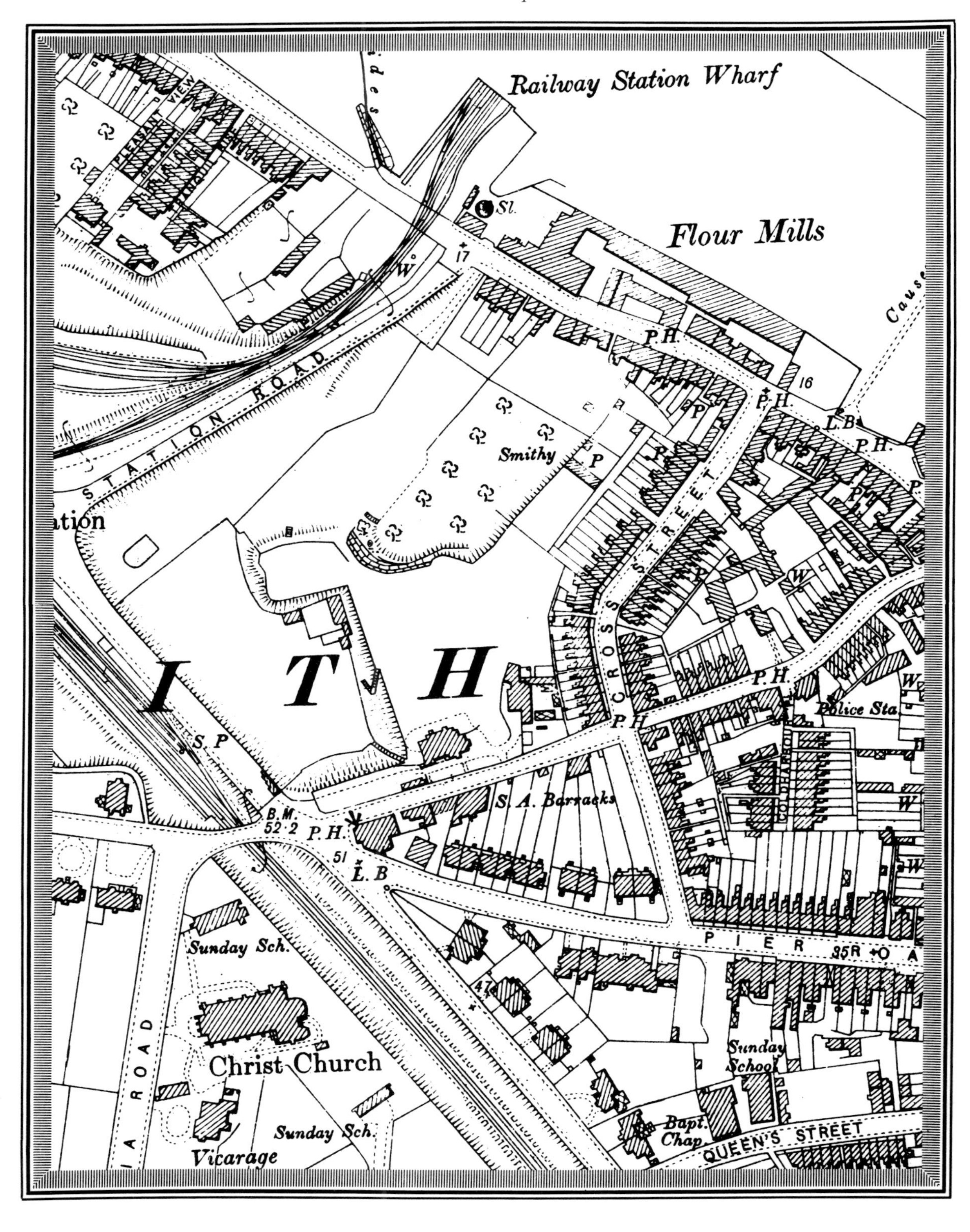
Railway Station Wharf
Flour Mills
Sl.
17
W
P.H.
16
L.B
Smithy
STATION ROAD
ation
CROSS STREET
I T H
S.P
P.H.
Police Sta
S. A. Barracks
B.M.
52·2
51
L.B
PIER ROA
Sunday Sch.
Christ Church
Sunday Sch.
Vicarage
Sunday School
Bapt. Chap.
QUEEN'S STREET
Cause

Present-day Woolwich with the ferry in the background (see also page 33).

Erith church and Belvedere house on top of the hill in about 1830 (below), from a print published in Tombleson's Thames and Medway. *Erith is now part of the London borough of Bexley, while Belvedere park was fully developed after the bankruptcy of Sir Culling Eardley Smith in 1860. Although the mansion was on the hill, much of the estate was low-lying and suffered severely in the floods of 1953.*
(Above) Riverside Erith today.

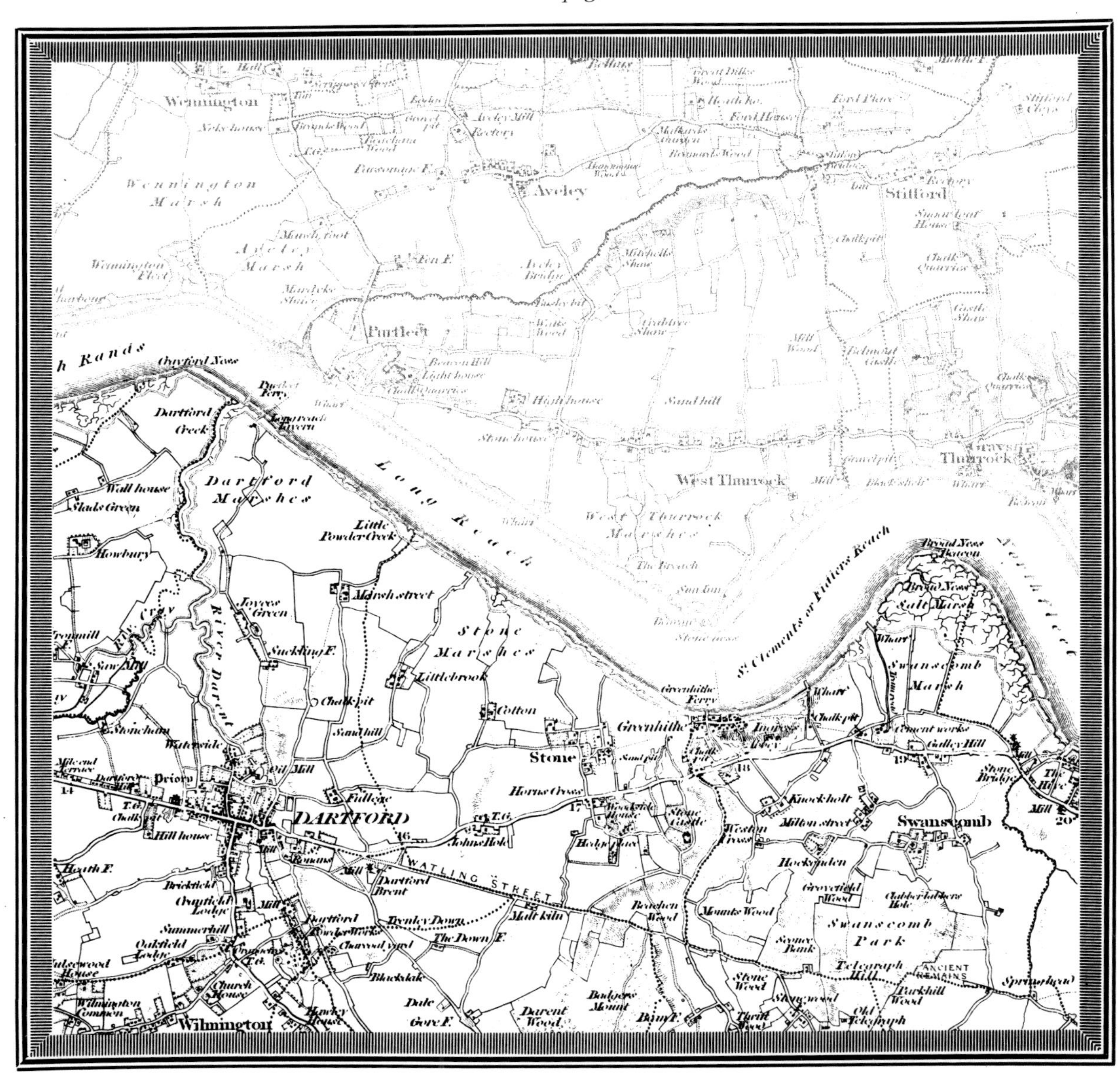

Map 3 This map shows the Thames shore area, crossed by Watling Street and including the four settlements of Dartford, Greenhithe, Stone and Swanscombe. The last reputedly saw the confrontation between William the Conqueror and the Kentings in 1066, and in recent years has become famous as the place where the 'Swanscombe woman', a fossilized pre-Neanderthal skull, was found in 1935. This area grew first because of industry, cement, paper and engineering, but is now an important commuter centre especially around Dartford. Springhead, in the bottom right corner of the map, has been identified as the Roman Vaginaciae.

Map 4 Gravesend is the point of embarkation both for the cross ferry to Tilbury and for the former long ferry to London, a safer and pleasanter way to enter Kent or the City than the tedious and sometimes dangerous Watling Street. Northfleet, a pleasant riverside village in 1801, became the local centre of the cement industry. All this area, except the marshes to the east, has been heavily developed both as a result of local industry and for commuter traffic. East of Gravesend the map would soon be altered by the building of the Thames and Medway canal, a failure ultimately taken over in part by the South-Eastern Railway.

The Old Leather Bottel inn at Northfleet hill at the present day and at the turn of the century. It is still recognizable although it has been modernized and much altered within.

Map 5

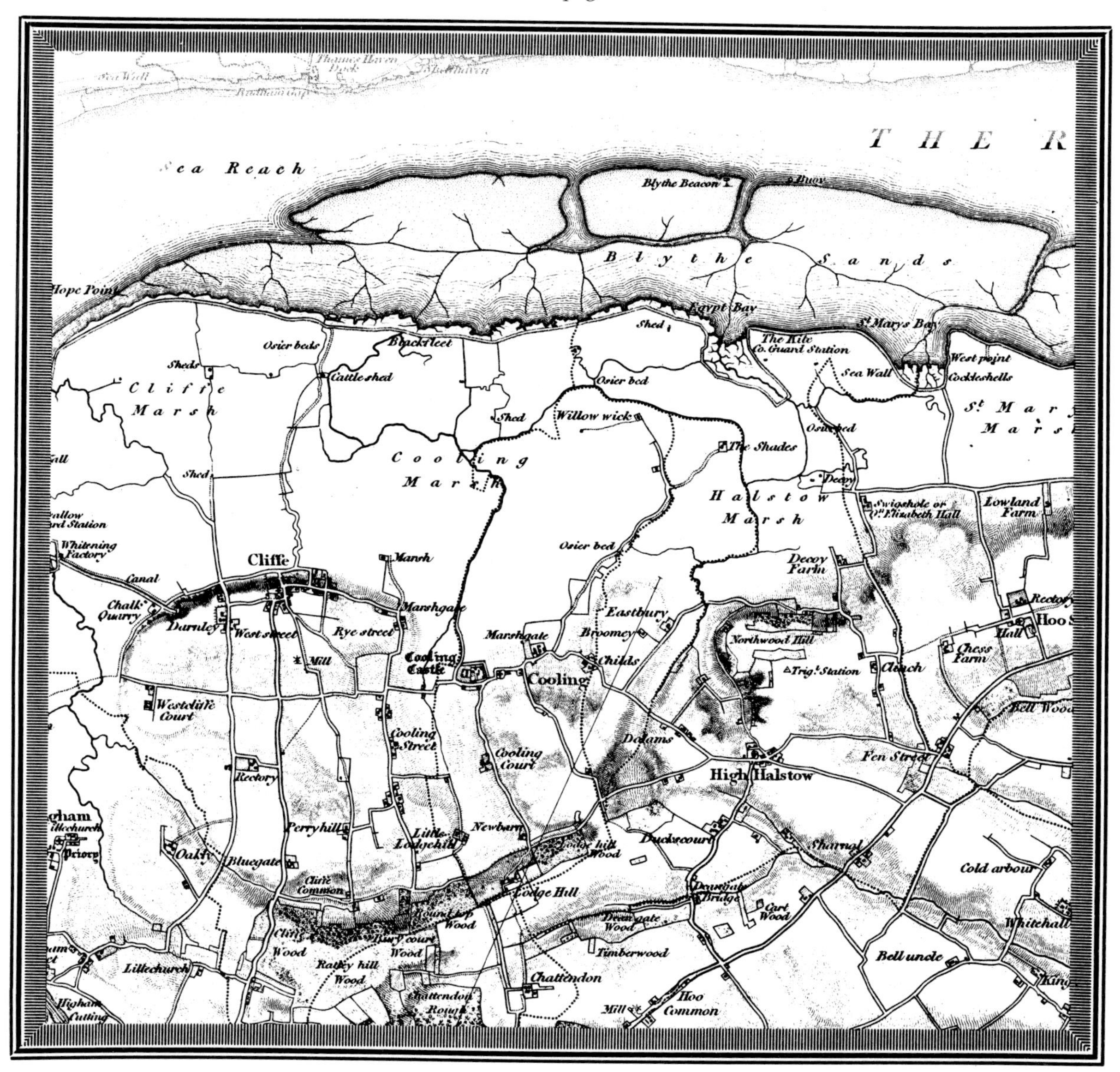

Map 5 The ancient settlement of Cliffe is shown here with the western part of the hundred of Hoo, a strange isolated area of Kent. Cliffe itself was the venue of Great Councils in the eighth and ninth centuries but during the last century the manufacture of explosives and cement have left their mark on the region. Cooling Castle in the centre of the map, noted for its gatehouse, was the home of the Lollard martyr, Sir John Oldcastle, and later of William, Lord Cobham, during the Wyatt rebellion against Mary Tudor in 1554.

Map 6 (overleaf) This part of the hundred of Hoo, and the country described by Dickens in *Great Expectations*, is a land of marshes and

Map 6

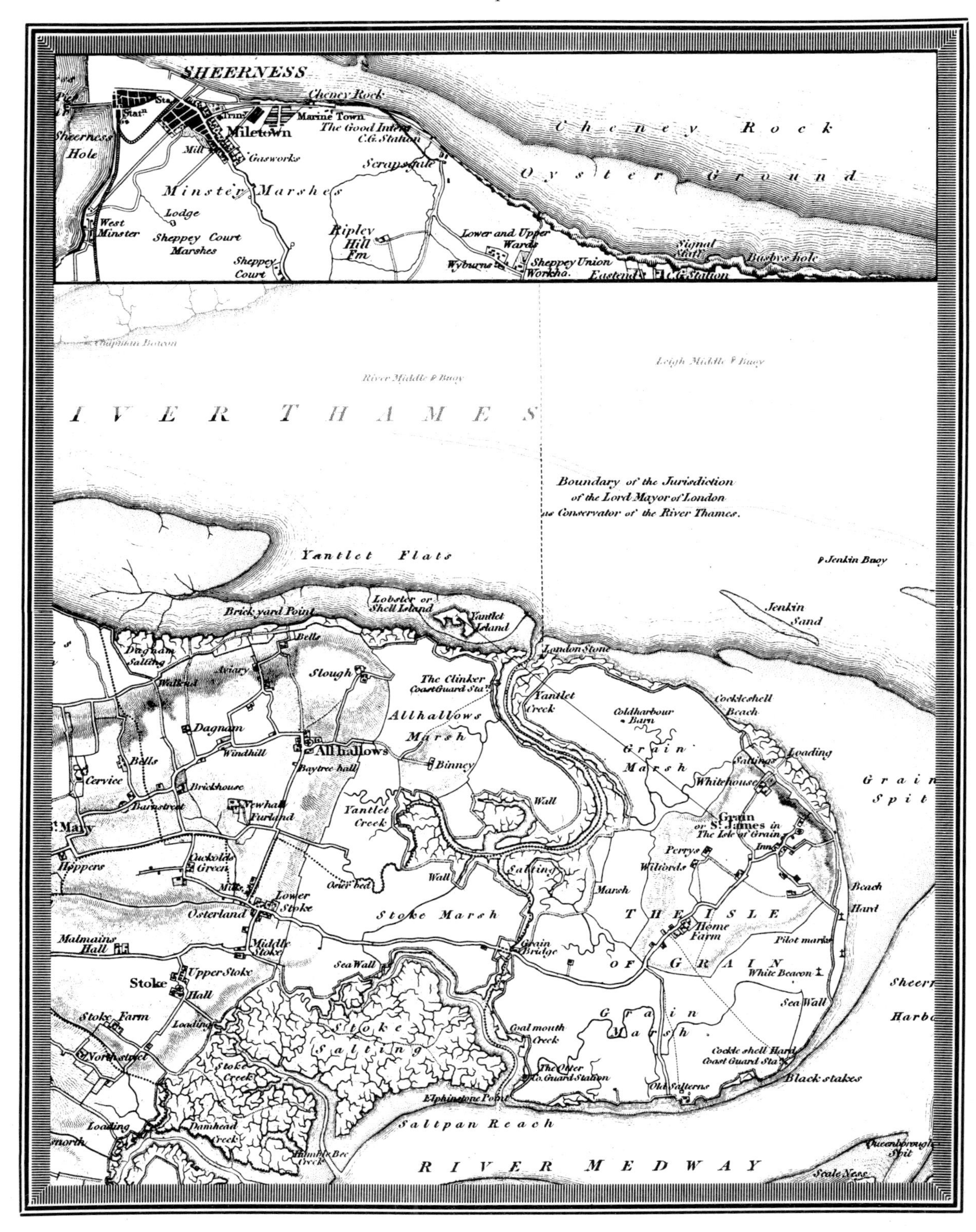
SHEERNESS
Cheney Rock
Marine Town
The Good Intent
C.G. Station
Miletown
Sheerness Hole
Mill
Gasworks
Minster Marshes
Scrapsgate
Cheney Rock Oyster Ground
West Minster
Lodge
Sheppey Court Marshes
Sheppey Court
Ripley Hill Fm
Lower and Upper Wards
Wyburns
Sheppey Union Workho.
Signal Staff
Busbys hole
Eastend
C.G. Station
River Middle Buoy
Leigh Middle Buoy
RIVER THAMES
Boundary of the Jurisdiction of the Lord Mayor of London as Conservator of the River Thames.
Yantlet Flats
Jenkin Buoy
Jenkin Sand
Brickyard Point
Lobster or Shell Island
Yantlet Island
London Stone
Dagnam Salting
Bells
Slough
The Clinker Coast Guard Sta.
Aviary
Allhallows Marsh
Yantlet Creek
Coldharbour Barn
Cockleshell Beach
Dagnam
Windhill
Allhallows
Baytree hall
Binney
Grain Marsh
Saltings
Loading
Whitehouse
Grain Spit
Bells
Cervice
Brickhouse
Barnstreet
Newhall Furland
Yantlet Creek
Wall
Grain or St. James in The Isle of Grain
Inn
St. Mary
Hoppers
Cuckolds Green
Mills
Orier bed
Wall
Salting
Perrys
Wilfords
Marsh
Beach Hard
Lower Stoke
Osterland
Stoke Marsh
THE ISLE OF GRAIN
Home Farm
Pilot mark
Malmains Hall
Middle Stoke
Grain Bridge
White Beacon
Sea Wall
Upper Stoke
Stoke Hall
Stoke Farm
Loading
Stoke Salting
Grain Marsh
Sea Wall
Sheerness Harbour
Coal mouth Creek
Cockle shell Hard Coast Guard Sta.
North street
Stoke Creek
The Otter Co. Guard Station
Old Salterns
Black stakes
Elphinstone Point
Saltpan Reach
Loading
Damhead Creek
Humble Bee Creek
RIVER MEDWAY
Queenborough Spit
Scale Ness

Map 7

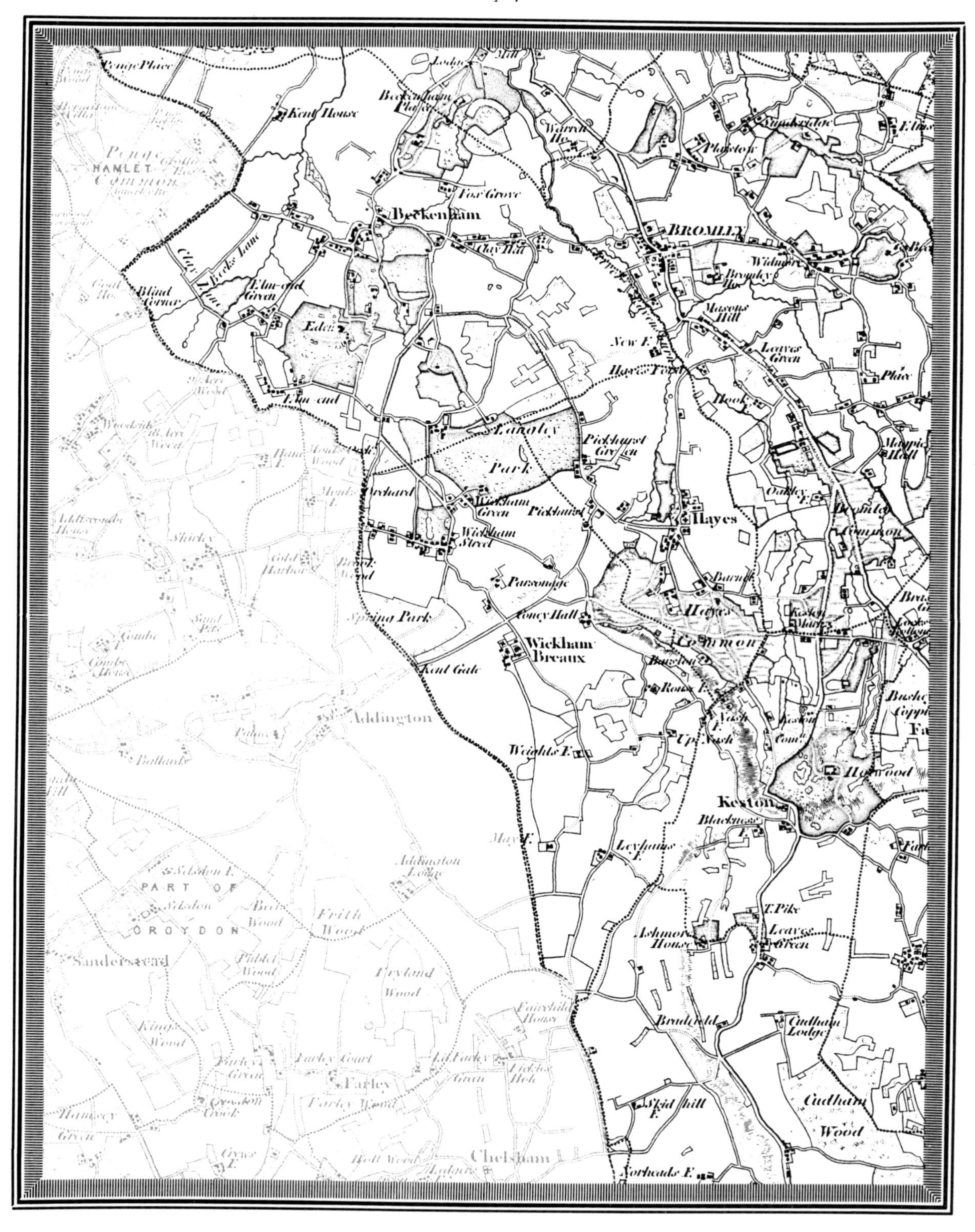
Penge Place
Kent House
Beckenham Place
Warren Ho.
Sundridge
Plaistow
HAMLET
Fox Grove
Beckenham
BROMLEY
Clay Hill
Widmore
Bromley Ho.
Clay Lane
Blind Corner
Elm-end Green
Eden
Masons Hill
New F.
Hayes Ford
Elm-end
Langley Park
Pickhurst Green
Hook
Magpie Hall
Wickham Green
Wickham Street
Pickhurst
Hayes
Oakley F.
Bromley Common
Shirley
Parsonage
Spring Park
Coney Hall
Hayes Common
Wickham Breaux
Kent Gate
Addington
Up. Nash
Weights F.
Holwood
Keston
Leyhams F.
PART OF
CROYDON
Frith Wood
Sanderstead
T. Pike
Leaves Green
Ashmore House
Fryland Wood
Fairchild House
Bradfield
Cudham Lodge
Kings Wood
Farley
Farley Wood
Cudham Wood
Chelsham

Map 6 cont

remote villages. Later a railway bisected the area and ran to Port Victoria on the Isle of Grain, now vanished, from where vessels plied to the Continent in the years before the First World War, so too it ran to Allhallows, a potential seaside resort which never developed. Until recently Grain was dominated by a large oil refinery and depot. Sheerness grew after a fortress and naval dockyard were established in the late seventeenth century. It remained a naval town until the 1960s, and since the closure of the dockyard has grown both in commercial significance and as a cross-channel port.

Map 7 (previous page) In 1965 the whole of this area was incorporated in the London Borough of Bromley, so that not only the densely peopled towns of Bromley and Beckenham came within the London area but so did the unspoilt villages of Keston and Downe, the latter with its Darwinian connections. The whole district developed rapidly after the coming of the railway and the possibility of quick and relatively cheap travel to the City. South of Bromley there is still an area of considerable beauty and of woodland and heath which lies within the Green Belt. Beckenham, in contrast, was a village of less than a 1000 souls in 1801 which had grown to 26,000 by 1901 and has continued to expand.

(Opposite and above) Bromley High Street as it was in 1898 before traffic congestion and the modernization of shops. The street is now at the very heart of the London borough.

Map 8 (overleaf) In the early nineteenth century this area consisted of a group of villages along the Cray, four taking the name of that river, and also of settlements at Chelsfield, Chislehurst (famed for its caves), Farnborough, Cudham and Halstead, as well as the larger centre of Orpington. Although some countryside persists, much is built over and the whole of the western part of this map lies within the London Borough of Bromley. The beautiful Darent Valley touches the south-eastern corner with the village of Shoreham, but this area is now crossed by the M25 motorway.

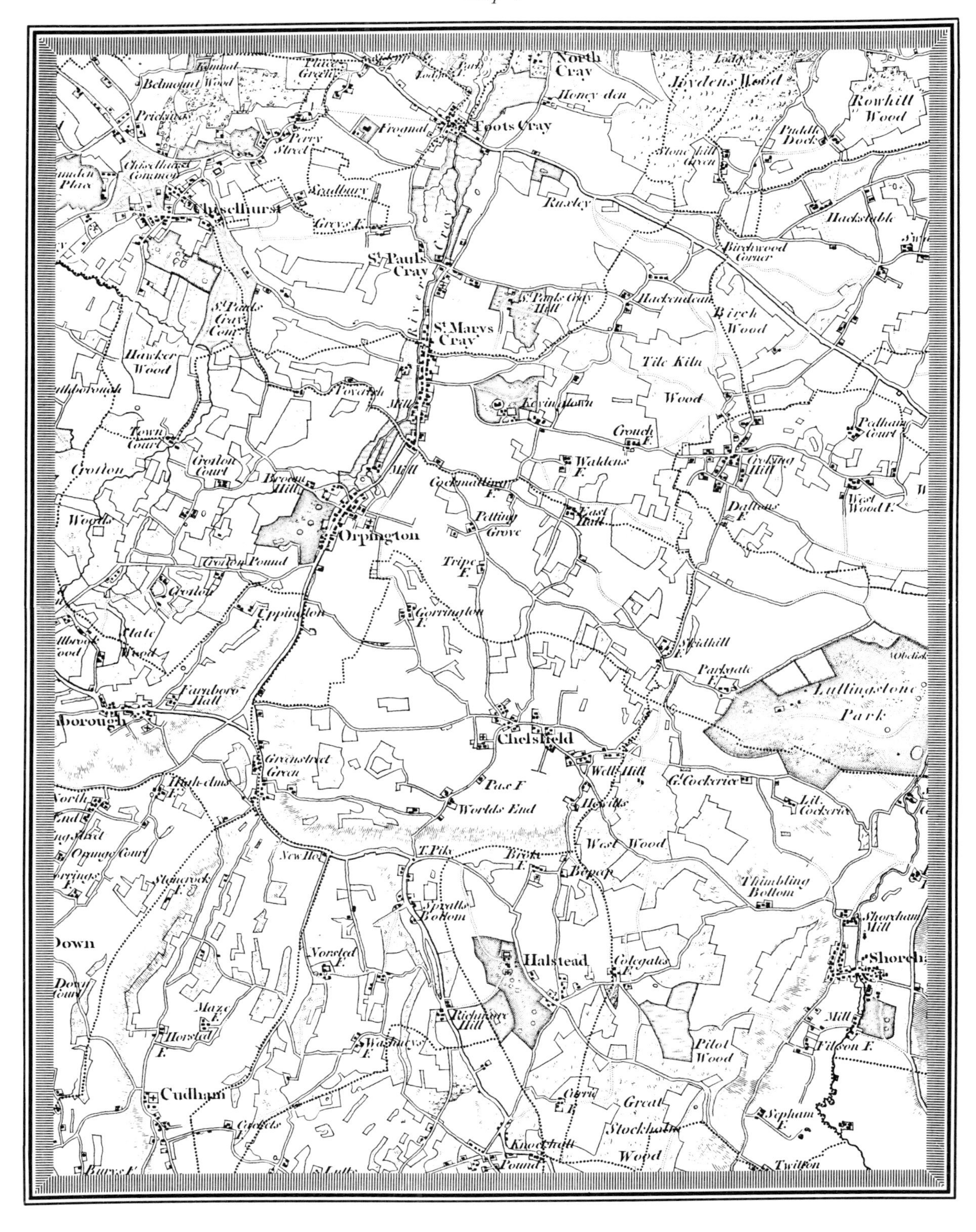
North Cray
Joydens Wood
Rowhill Wood
Belmount Wood
Foots Cray
Frognal
Perry Street
Chiselhurst Common
Chiselhurst
Ruxley
Hackstable
Birchwood Corner
St. Pauls Cray
St. Marys Cray
Birch Wood
Tile Kiln Wood
Hawker Wood
Town Court
Crofton
Crofton Court
Orpington
Crofton Pound
Petling Grove
Tripe F.
Gorrington F.
Uppington
Farnboro Hall
Crockens Hill
Daltons F.
Lullingstone Park
Chelsfield
Well Hill
Greenstreet Green
Worlds End
West Wood
Thimbling Bottom
Halstead
Colegates
Shoreham Mill
Pilot Wood
Filson F.
Cudham
Great Stockholm Wood
Knockholt Pound
Sepham F.
Horsted F.
Maze F.
Down

Map 9

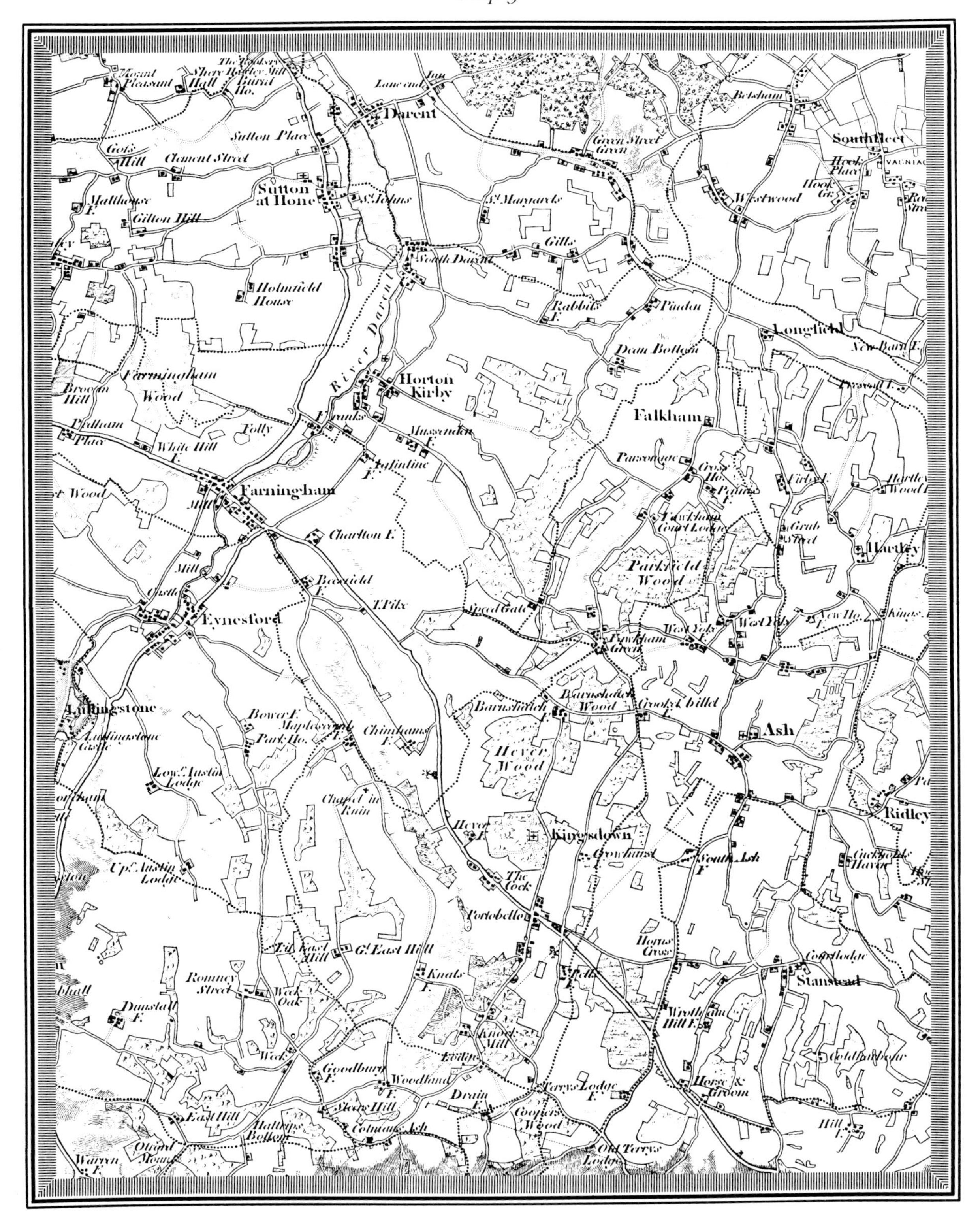

Mount Pleasant
Shore Hall
Darent
Belsham
Green Street Green
Southfleet
Sutton Place
Clement Street
Hook Place
Westwood
Sutton at Hone
St. Johns
St. Margarets
Malthouse F.
Gilton Hill
Gills
South Darent
Holmfield House
Rabbits F.
Pinden
Longfield
New Barn F.
Dean Bottom
River Darent
Farningham Wood
Horton Kirby
Falkham
Broom Hill
Franks
Mussenden F.
Pedham Place
White Hill F.
Folly
Parsonage
Farningham
Charlton F.
Grub Street
Hartley Wood F.
Hartley
Parkfield Wood
Mill
Eynesford
T. Pike
Speed Gate
Fawkham Green
West Yoke
New Ho.
Barnshatch Wood
Crooked billet
Lullingstone
Bower F.
Park Ho.
Chimhams F.
Ash
Lullingstone Castle
Low. Austin Lodge
Hever Wood
Chapel in Ruin
Hever F.
Kingsdown
Ridley
Growhurst
South Ash F.
Up. Austin Lodge
The Cock
Portobello
Horns Cross
Gt. East Hill
Lt. East Hill
Knats F.
Stansted
Romney Street
Week Oak
Dunstall F.
Wrotham Hill F.
Knock Mill
Week
Goodbury F.
Woodland
Terrys Lodge F.
Horse & Groom
Drain F.
Coopers Wood
Hill F.
East Hill
Colman Ash
Old Terrys Lodge
Warren F.

Map 9 (previous page) This outstanding district was saved by the Green Belt, even though it is traversed now by railways and motorways. Only the areas west of Farningham and Sutton-at-Hone have been heavily developed. It is a district of very early settlement with notable Roman remains at Lullingstone, the ruins of a Norman keep at Eynsford and later houses at St John's, Sutton-at-Hone and at Lullingstone Castle. On the other hand, in the east of the area new villages have been built in recent years, in particular at New Ash Green and, at West Kingsdown, the Brand's Hatch motor-racing circuit has been established.

Map 10 This area of downland is still in part agricultural as it was at the beginning of the nineteenth century. It is crossed by the scarp of the chalk hills and in the south-east reaches the lower Medway valley at Halling and Snodland. In recent years the area around Ifield has been developed as part of the commuter belt and the Medway valley has been industrialized by both paper and cement industries. Cobham Hall, now a school, was the home of the Broke family, Lords Cobham, and later of the Earls of Darnley. In the south-west corner by the Kentish Drover is the Trosley Towers Country Park on the edge of the Downs.

Map 11 and modern map 11 (overleaf) The ancient city of Rochester, with neighbouring Chatham and Gillingham, was surrounded by heavily wooded country in 1801, now largely built over. Rochester itself bears evidence of

Halling cement works, with the Medway behind.

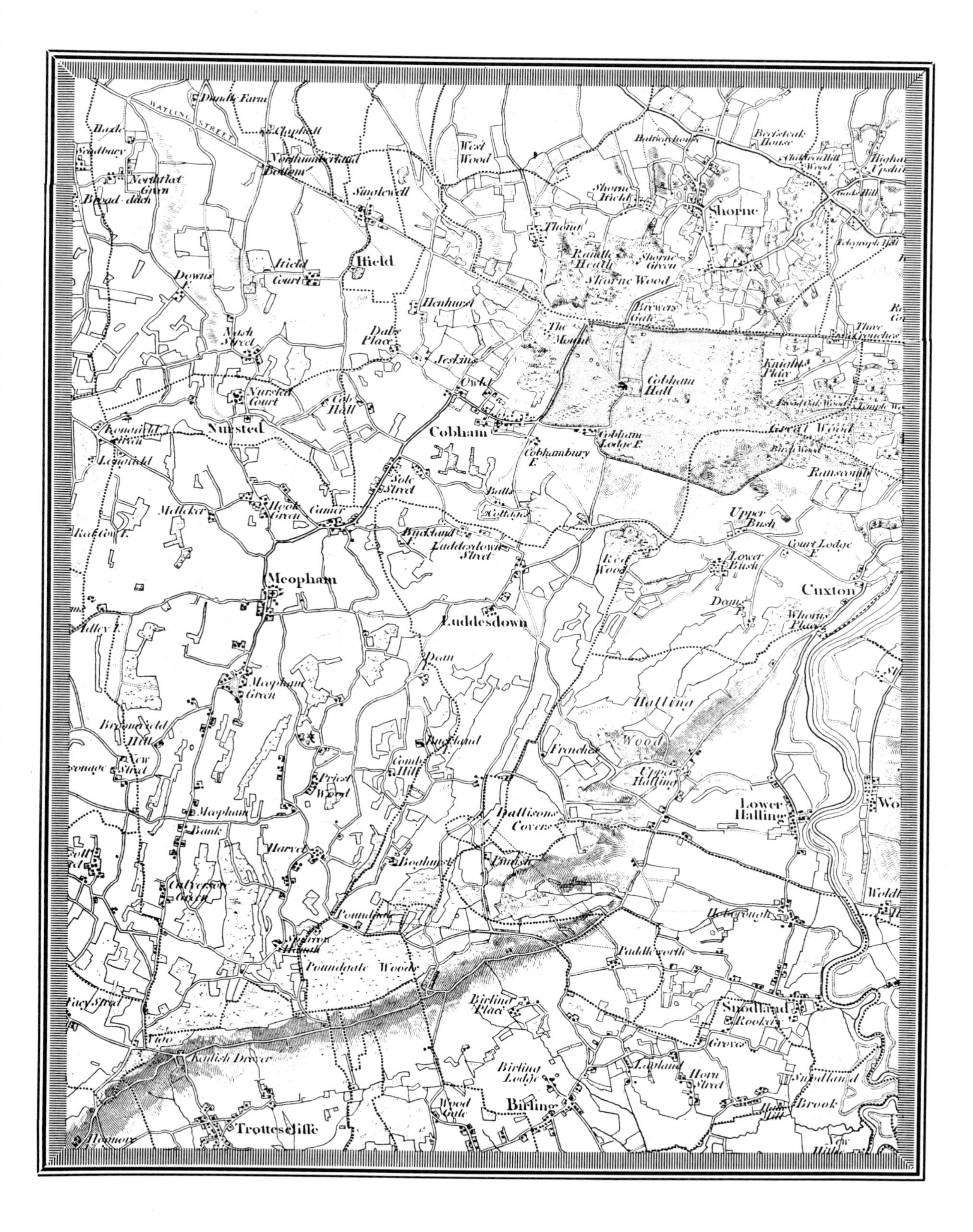

Watling Street
Northumberland Bottom
Northfleet Green
Singlewell
West Wood
Beefsteak House
Shorne Ifield
Shorne
Thong
Randle Heath
Shorne Green
Shorne Wood
Telegraph Hill
Ifield
Ifield Court
Downs
Henhurst
Brewers Gate
Nash Street
Dale Place
The Mount
Three Crouches
Knights Place
Jeskins
Cobham Hall
Nursted Court
Cob Hall
Nursted
Cobham
Great Wood
Cobham Lodge F.
Cobhambury F.
Ranscombe
Sole Street
Hook Green
Camer
Upper Bush
Court Lodge F.
Buckland F.
Luddesdown Street
Red Wood
Lower Bush
Meopham
Cuxton
Luddesdown
Dean
Meopham Green
Halling Wood
Broomfield Hill
New Street
Buckland F.
Frenches
Upper Halling
Comb Hill
Priest Wood
Meopham Bank
Lower Halling
Covert
Harvel
Bodhurst
Culverstone Green
Holborough
Poundgate
Poundgate Wood
Paddlesworth
Birling Place
Snodland
Rookery
Grove
Birling Lodge
Horn Street
Snodland Brook
Wood Gate
Birling
Trottescliffe

MEDWAY DISTRICT
Street
Little Oakleigh
Cliffe Woods
Depot
Deangate
Beluncle Fm
Lower Higham
King's Fm
Gore Green
Great Chattenden Wood
Tile Barn Fm
Wharf
Lillechurch Fm
Chattenden Fm
Higham Hall
HIGHAM STA
Lee Green
Stonebridge
Kingsnorth
Two Gates Fm
Hoo St Werburgh
White House Fm
Mockbeggar
Broad Street
Abbot's Court
Hill Fm
The Mount
Power Sta
Chy
The Knowle
Noke Street
Chattenden
Higham
Hoo Lodge
Jetty
Stone House Fm
Hillyfield
Beacon Hill
Saxon Shore Way
Hoo Flats
Long Reach
Wainscott
Lower Upnor
Marina
Darnet Fort
Gadshill
Pier
Short Reach
Castle
Upnor Reach
Pinup Reach
Little Hermitage
Hoo Salt Marsh
Hoo Fort
Hoo Ness
Schs
Tower Hill
Upper Upnor
Broom Hill
Gillingham Reach
Nor Marsh
Chapter Fm
Frindsbury
Piers
Sch
Bks
Copperhouse Marshes
Strood
Dockyard
The Strand
Chatham Reach
Limehouse Reach
Bridge Reach
Temple Manor
Mus
Brompton
Cemy
Grange
Castle
Cath
East Court Fm
Eastcourt Me Country P
ROCHESTER
DVROBRIVAE
Piers
Great Lines
Lower Twydall
Temple Marsh
Hospl
Meml
GILLINGHAM DISTRICT
Ranscombe
Merrals Shaw
Coll
Pump Fm
Bloors Pla
Wks
North Downs Way
Medway Br
Marina
Almshouses
GILLINGHAM
Foot/Cycle Path
TH
Twydall
Borstal
Schs
Hospl
Luton
HM Youth Custody Centre
Cemy
Wks
Wouldham Marshes
Nashenden Fm
Hale
Bks
Rings Hill Fm
CHATHAM
Darland
Rainham
North Halling
Starkey Castle Fm
H M Prison
Wayfield
Spekes Bottom
Ivy Cott
Capstone
New Town Halling
Ringshill Place
Wks
Rochester Airport
Coll
Princes Park
School Fm
ROMAN ROAD
Schs
Hempstead
Wigmore
Wouldham
Monk Wood
Sharsted Fm
Park Wood
North Downs Way
Bridge Woods
Burham Hill Fm
Buckmore Park
Walderslade
Gibraltar Fm
Scarborough
Walderslade Bottom
Elm Court
Blue Bell Hill
Lords Wood
Kemsley Street
Wks
Tunbury Wood
Burham Court
Burham
Lidsing
Bredhurst
D
Dunn Street
O
Snodland
Kit's Coty
Cossington Fields
Westfield Sole
Bredhurst Hurst
Little Culand
Resr
Little Halstead Fm
Scragged Oak
Hale Fm
Kit's Coty Ho
W
Monkdown Wood
Newlands Wood
Lower Street
Eccles
Little Kit's Coty Ho
Trackway
Motte
White Horse Stone
Grange Fm
Pollyfield
Rowe Place Fm
Harp Fm
N
New Hythe
Stockings Wood
Sand Pit
North Downs Way
Pratling Street
Boarley Fm
Tyland Fm
Boxley Ho
Pilgrim
Aylesford
Industrial Estate
Paper Mills
Mount Ho
Kent County Agricultural

Map 11

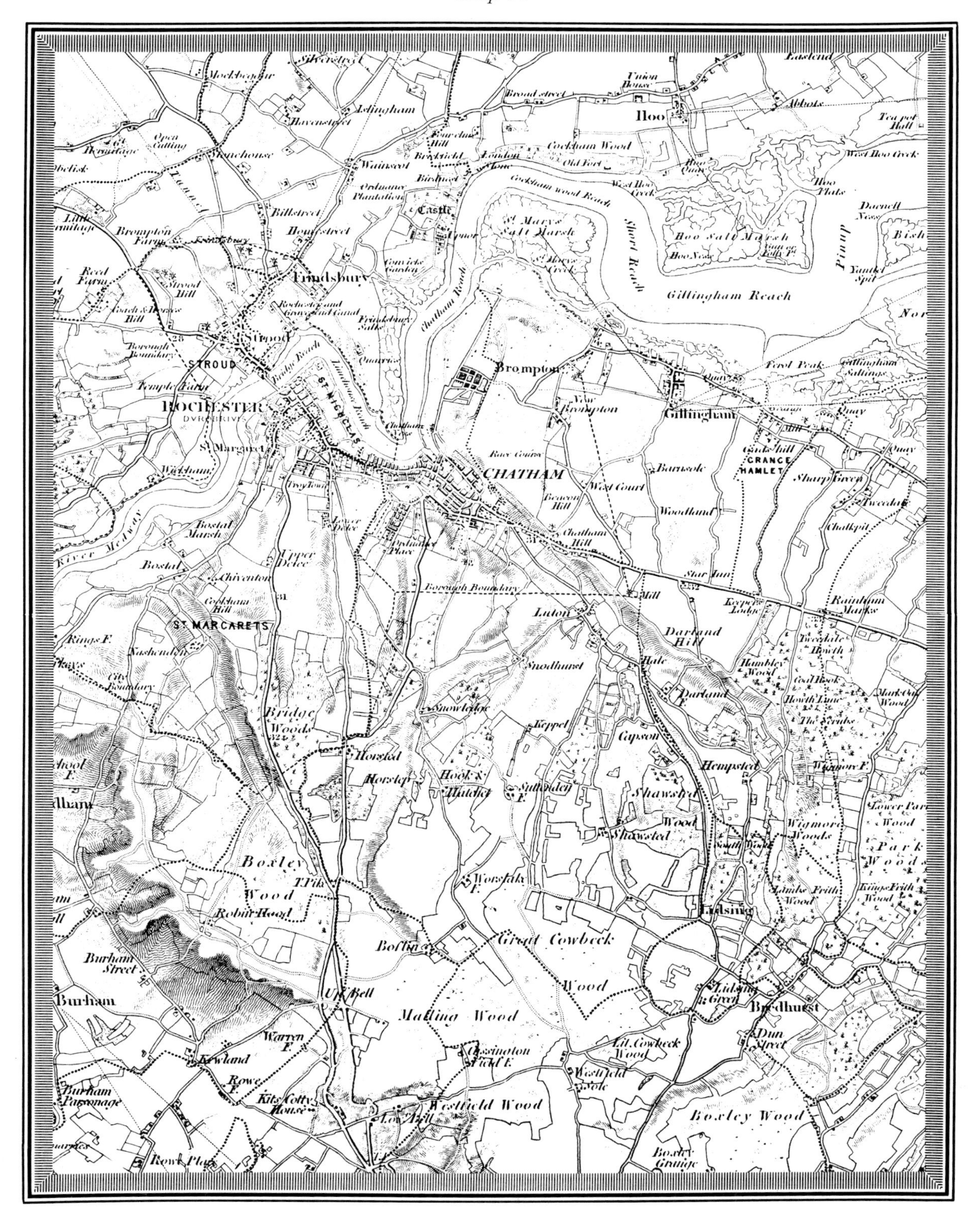

Silverstreet
Islingham
Havenstreet
Union House
Broad street
Hoo
Eastend
Abbots
Cockham Wood
Old Fort
Wainscot
Stonehouse
Open Cutting
Tunnel
Billstreet
Homestreet
Castle
Upnor
Ordnance Plantation
Cockham Wood Reach
Short Reach
St. Mary's Salt Marsh
Hoo Salt Marsh
Hoo Ness
Gillingham Reach
Brompton Farm
Reed Farm
Frindsbury
Strood Hill
Frindsbury Salts
Chatham Reach
Rochester and Gravesend Canal
Strood
Borough Boundary
STROUD
Bridge Reach
Quarries
Brompton
New Brompton
Gillingham
Temple Farm
ROCHESTER
DVROBRIVIS
ST. NICHOLAS
Limehouse Reach
St. Margarets
Race Course
CHATHAM
GRANGE HAMLET
Barnsole
Sharp Green
West Court
Beacon Hill
Woodland
Tweedale
Chalkpit
Chatham Hill
Star Inn
Wickham
River Medway
Bostal Marsh
Bostal
Upper Delce
Lower Delce
Ordnance Place
Chiventon
Cookham Hill
Borough Boundary
Luton
Mill
Keepers Lodge
Rainham Marks
ST. MARGARETS
Nashenden
City Boundary
Darland Hill
Hale
Snodhurst
Hambley Wood
Tweedale Howth
Darland F.
Bridge Woods
Snowledge
Keppel
Capson
Howth Lane
The Scrubs
Horsted
Hook
Hempsted
Wigmore F.
Lower Park Wood
Shawsted
Shawsted Wood
Wigmore Woods
Park Woods
Boxley
Wood
Robin Hood
Worstake F.
Lidsing
Lambs Frith Wood
Kings Frith Wood
Great Cowbeck
Wood
Bofflin
Burham Street
Burham
Upper Bell
Malling Wood
Lidsing Green
Bredhurst
Warren F.
Kewland
Lit. Cowbeck Wood
Dun Street
Rowe F.
Westfield Sole
Burham Parsonage
Kits Cotty House
Westfield Wood
Boxley Wood
Lower Bell
Boxley Grange

occupation from Roman times and has also a Norman castle and cathedral, and many memories of Charles Dickens and his works. The bridge at Rochester has been the responsibility of the Bridge Wardens for at least 600 years, but the present bridge, as did its immediate predecessor, lies further downstream than the medieval bridge still shown on the map. The naval dockyard at Chatham was founded in the sixteenth century and although now closed some of the historic buildings are preserved and are open to the public. Gillingham, from being a small village, is now a considerable town and borough in its own right and has absorbed nearby Rainham on the eastern edge of the map. Chatham has developed southwards into the area called Great Cowbeck Wood on the old map but

growth has been restricted by the line of the M2 road. Across the river at Upnor is the so-called castle, a minor defence work commanding the Medway passage.

A view down the river from Sun Wharf towards Gunwharf at Chatham in 1891, showing some of the dockyard buildings which have been preserved since the yard was closed. *(see also page 66).*

Rochester Castle gardens in 1891, with a fine view of the great keep and, to the left, the Cathedral as it was before the present short spire was added. The keep, 130 feet high, was begun by Bishop Gundulf of Rochester in the reign of Henry I (see page 66).

Map 12

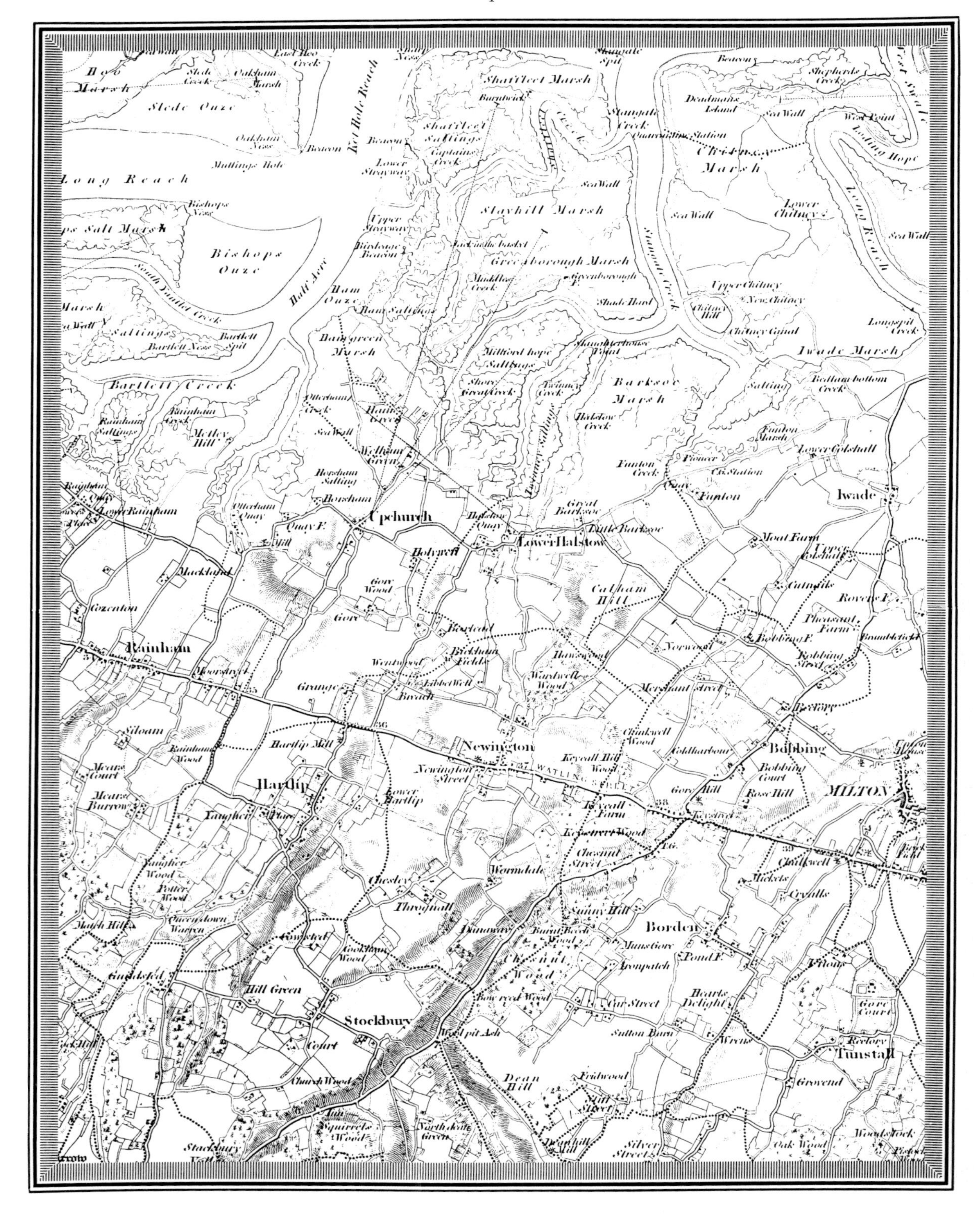

Hoo Marsh
Slede Creek
Oakham Marsh
Slede Ouze
Oakham Ness
Beacon
Kethole Reach
Muttings Hole
Long Reach
Bishops Ness
Bishops Ouze
South Yantlet Creek
Saltings
Bartlett Ness
Bartlett Spit
Half Acre
Bartlett Creek
Rainham Saltings
Rainham Creek
Motley Hill
Shakfleet Marsh
Barntwick
Shakfleet Saltings
Captains Creek
Lower Stray way
Upper Strayway
Stayhill Marsh
Sea Wall
Greasborough Marsh
Ham Ouze
Ham Saltings
Ham green Marsh
Milford hope Saltings
Shore Great Creek
Twinney Creek
Slaughterhouse Point
Stangate Spit
Stangate Creek
Quarantine Station
Deadmans Island
Beacon
Shepherds Creek
Chetney Marsh
West Point
Lodding Hope
Long Reach
Lower Chetney
Upper Chetney
New Chetney
Chetney Hill
Chetney Canal
Longspit Creek
Iwade Marsh
Barksoe Marsh
Halstow Creek
Bedlam bottom Creek
Salting
Funton Marsh
Lower Colshall
Funton Creek
Funton
Iwade
Ham Green
Otterham Creek
Horsham Salting
Horsham
Otterham Quay
Wetham Green
Upchurch
Halstow Quay
Great Barksoe
Little Barksoe
Lower Halstow
Moat Farm
Upper Colshall
Lower Rainham
Rainham Quay
Mackland
Holywell
Gore Wood
Gore
Callam Hill
Catmifs
Rovers F.
Pheasant Farm
Bramblefield
Cozenton
Rainham
Moorstreet
Bickham Fields
Wentwood
Libbet Well
Grange
Breach
Hawswood
Wardwell Wood
Norwood
Bobbing F.
Bobbing Street
Merchant street
Rectory
Siloam
Rainham Wood
Hartlip Mill
Newington
Newington Street
Watling Street
Keycoll Hill Wood
Chinkwell Wood
Coldharbour
Bobbing
Bobbing Court
Rose Hill
Gore Hill
Milton
Mears Court
Mears Burrow
Hartlip
Yaugher Place
Lower Hartlip
Keycoll Farm
Keycoll Wood
Keystreet
Chestnut Street
Chalkwell
Yaugher Wood
Potter Wood
Chesley
Wormdale
Mickets
Crouths
Queendown Warren
Thrognall
Sunny Hill
Borden
Danaway
Burnt Beech Wood
Cookham Wood
Chestnut Wood
Aronpatch
Pond F.
Hill Green
Stockbury
Court
Bowered Wood
Car Street
Hearts Delight
Gore Court
Wrens
Rectory
Tunstall
Sutton Barn
Well pit Ash
Church Wood
Dean Hill
Fridwood
Growend
Squirrels Wood
North dane Green
Stockbury Vall
Deanhill Mill
Silver Street
Oak Wood
Woodstock
Pistock Wood

Map 13

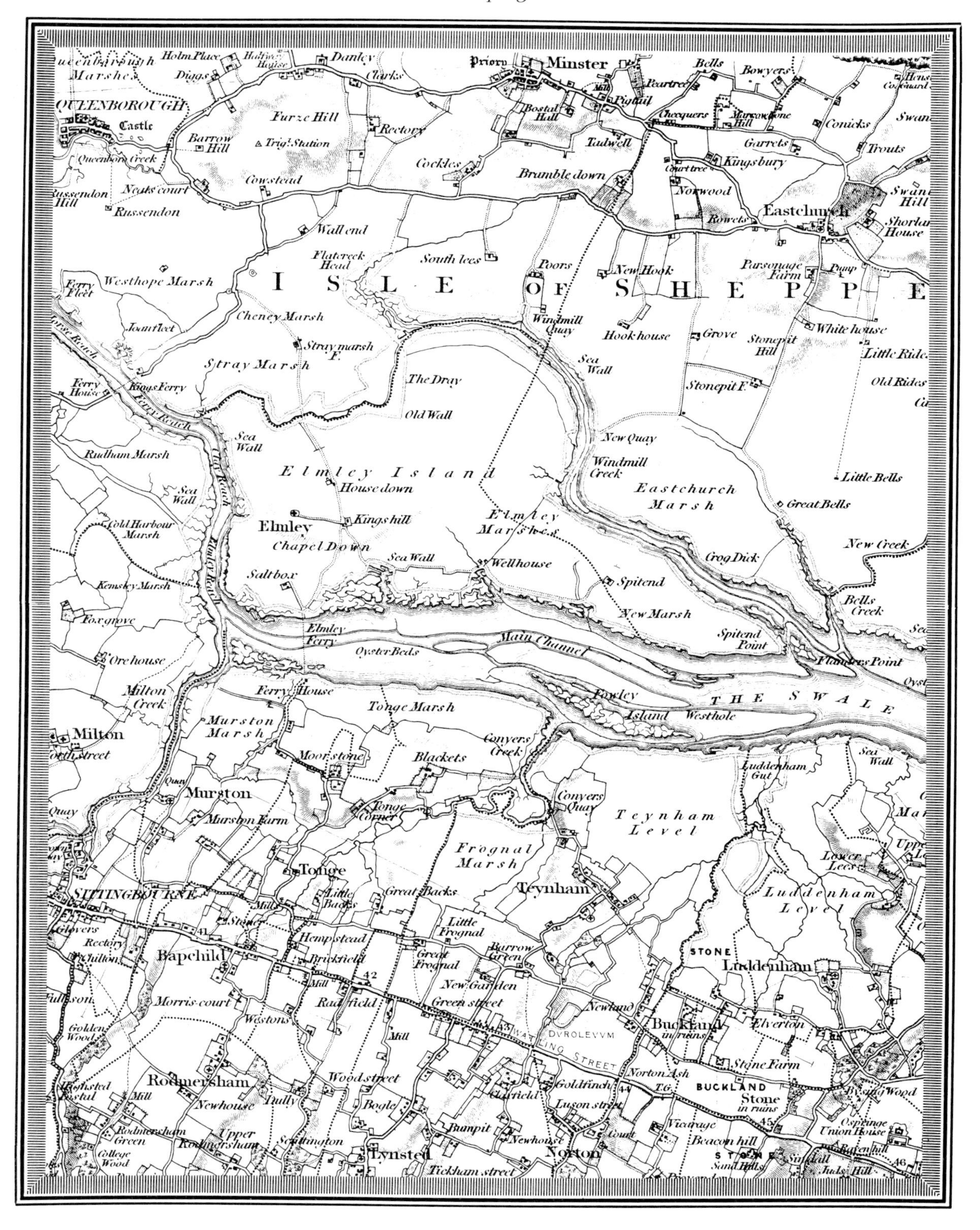
Holm Place
Diggs
Danley
Clarks
Priory
Minster
Bells
Bowyers
QUEENBOROUGH
Castle
Furze Hill
Rectory
Bostal Hall
Pigtail
Partree
Chequers
Conicks
Swan
Barrow Hill
Trig! Station
Tadwell
Garrets
Trouts
Queenboro Creek
Cockles
Bramble down
Court tree
Kingsbury
Russendon Hill
Neats court
Cowstead
Norwood
Swan Hill
Russendon
Eastchurch
Rowets
Shorland House
Wall end
Flatcreek Head
South lees
Poors
New Hook
Parsonage Farm
Pump
Ferry Fleet
Westhope Marsh
ISLE OF SHEPPEY
Cheney Marsh
Windmill Quay
Hook house
Grove
White house
Joantfleet
Stonepit Hill
Little Rides
Stray marsh F.
Stray Marsh
Sea Wall
Kings Ferry
Ferry House
The Dray
Stonepit F.
Old Rides
Old Wall
Sea Wall
New Quay
Rudham Marsh
Windmill Creek
Elmley Island
House down
Eastchurch Marsh
Little Bells
Sea Wall
Great Bells
Cold Harbour Marsh
Elmley
Kings hill
Elmley Marshes
Chapel Down
New Creek
Sea Wall
Wellhouse
Grog Dick
Saltbox
Kemsley Marsh
Spitend
Bells Creek
Fox grove
New Marsh
Elmley Ferry
Spitend Point
Main Channel
Ore house
Oyster Beds
Flanders Point
Milton Creek
Ferry House
Fowley Island
Westhole
THE SWALE
Tonge Marsh
Murston Marsh
Milton
Moorstone
Blackets
Conyers Creek
Sea Wall
Luddenham Gut
Murston
Conyers Quay
Teynham Level
Murston Farm
Tonge Corner
Quay
Frognal Marsh
Lower Lees
Tonge
SITTINGBOURNE
Great Backs
Teynham
Luddenham Level
Little Backs
Mill
Glovers
Little Frognal
Rectory
Hempstead
Barrow Green
Bapchild
Brickfield
Great Frognal
STONE
Luddenham
Mill
42
New Garden
Morris court
Radfield
Green street
Newland
Buckland in ruins
Elverton
Weston
Golden Wood
Mill
43
DVROLEVVM
WATLING STREET
Stone Farm
Norton Ash
Rodmersham
Wood street
Goldfinch
44
T.G.
BUCKLAND
Stone in ruins
Newhouse
Bogle
Luson street
Mill
Rodmersham Green
Upper Rodmersham
Bunpit
Vicarage
Beacon hill
45
Ospringe Union House
College Wood
Lynsted
Newhouse
Norton
STONE
Sand Hills
46
Tickham street

Map 12 (page 54) This is an area of marshland and orchards crossed by the Roman road of Watling Street, with its villages of Rainham (now part of Gillingham) and Newington. The marshes at Upchurch were the site of a significant Roman pottery. Apart from the district developed as part of Gillingham this is still a region of agriculture with dry valleys leading deep into the downland in the south and with fresh and salt marshes crossed by numerous creeks and channels to the north.

Map 13 (previous page) Although much of this area is still marshland, it is part of Kent which has seen considerable change. The old borough of Queenborough in Sheppey was founded in 1368 by Edward III in honour of his Queen, Philippa, and was also the site of a noble castle, now wholly vanished. In the late nineteenth century Queenborough was used as a port for continental traffic but its pier was abandoned after 1945. Sittingbourne itself, linked with the important Saxon centre of Milton Regis, grew partly as a result of the railway and partly from the Bowater paper works at Kemsley on the Swale, near Foxgrove on the early map. More recently it has grown as a commuter town. Minster was the mother church of Sheppey, and like its fellow in Thanet, is the site of a Saxon nunnery destroyed by the Danes. The north coast of Sheppey is composed of soft sandy cliffs which suffer severely from winter gales, but the south of the island is low-lying and marshy. The Isle

(Left) West Street, Faversham looking away from the corner of Abbey Street, in 1891. Today (above) the saddlery is a restaurant and the cobbles have given way to the blocks of a pedestrian precinct.

of Elmley, formerly approached by a separate ferry and for a short time in the last century a flourishing community, is now a nature reserve controlled by the Royal Society for the Protection of Birds. Kingsferry, the direct entry into Sheppey, was not bridged until 1856 and the present road bridge was opened in 1960.

Map 14 (overleaf) Faversham in the south-western corner of the map remains a beautiful small country town with fine houses in Abbey Street and an outstanding guildhall. It was a limb of the Cinque Port of Dover and its creek is still in use for small vessels. The area eastward is one of open marshland, with much of it severely flooded as recently as 1953. The

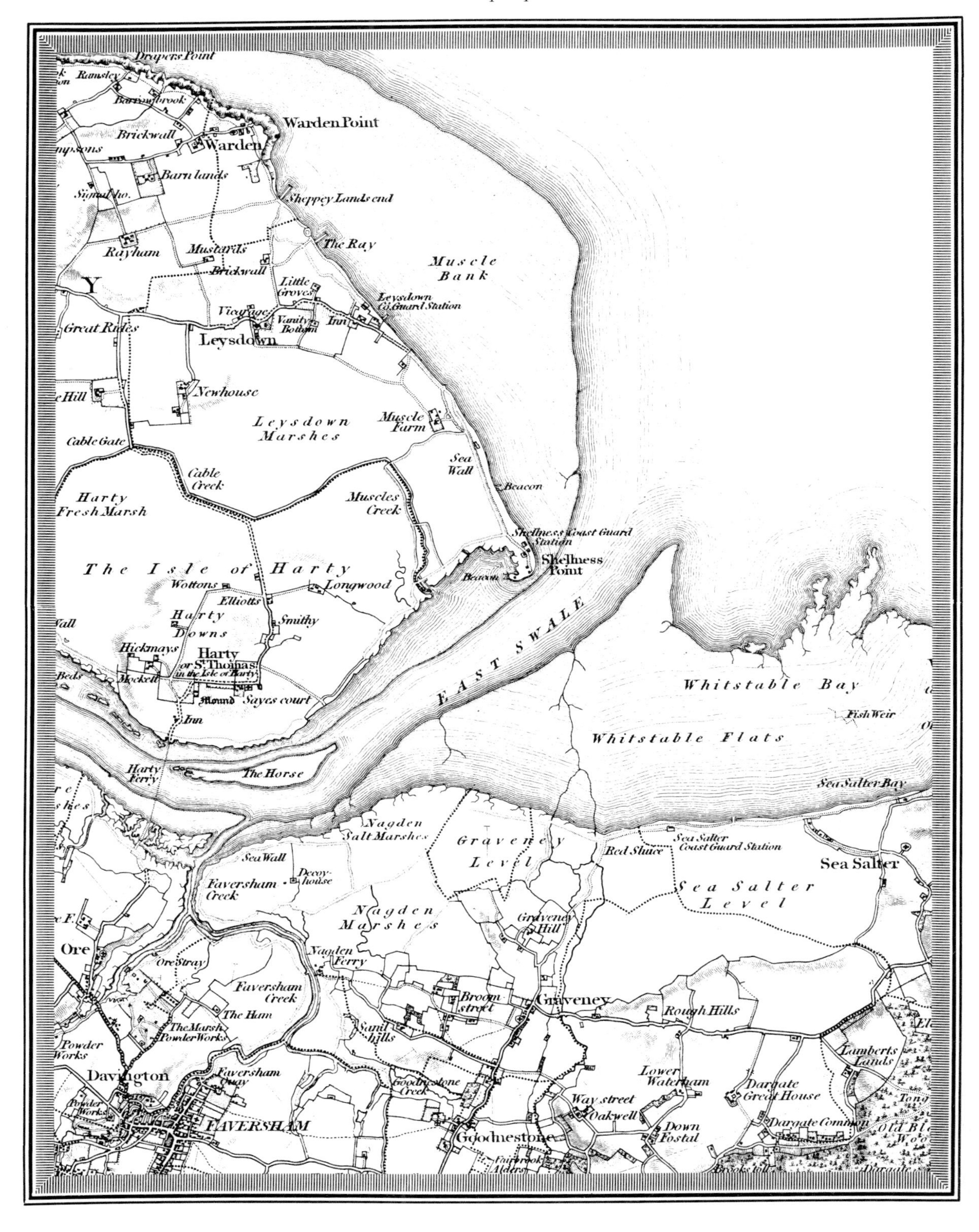
Drapers Point
Ramsley
Barrowbrook
Warden Point
Brickwall
Warden
Barn lands
Signal ho.
Sheppey Lands end
The Ray
Rayham
Mustards
Brickwall
Muscle Bank
Little Groves
Leysdown Co. Guard Station
Vicarage
Vanity Bottom
Inn
Great Rides
Leysdown
Newhouse
Leysdown Marshes
Muscle Farm
Cable Gate
Cable Creek
Sea Wall
Beacon
Harty Fresh Marsh
Muscles Creek
Shellness Coast Guard Station
Shellness Point
Beacon
The Isle of Harty
Wottons
Elliotts
Longwood
Harty Downs
Smithy
EAST SWALE
Hickmays
Harty or St. Thomas in the Isle of Harty
Mockett
Mound
Sayes court
Inn
Whitstable Bay
Fish Weir
Whitstable Flats
Harty Ferry
The Horse
Sea Salter Bay
Nagden Salt Marshes
Graveney Level
Red Sluice
Sea Salter Coast Guard Station
Sea Salter
Sea Wall
Decoy-house
Faversham Creek
Sea Salter Level
Nagden Marshes
Graveney Hill
Ore
Ore Stray
Nagden Ferry
Faversham Creek
Broom street
Graveney
Rough Hills
The Ham
The Marsh Powder Works
Sand hills
Powder Works
Lamberts Lands
Davington
Faversham Quay
Goodnestone Creek
Lower Waterham
Dargate Great House
Powder Works
Way street
Oakwell
FAVERSHAM
Down Fostal
Dargate Common
Goodnestone
Fairbrook
Alders
Dargate

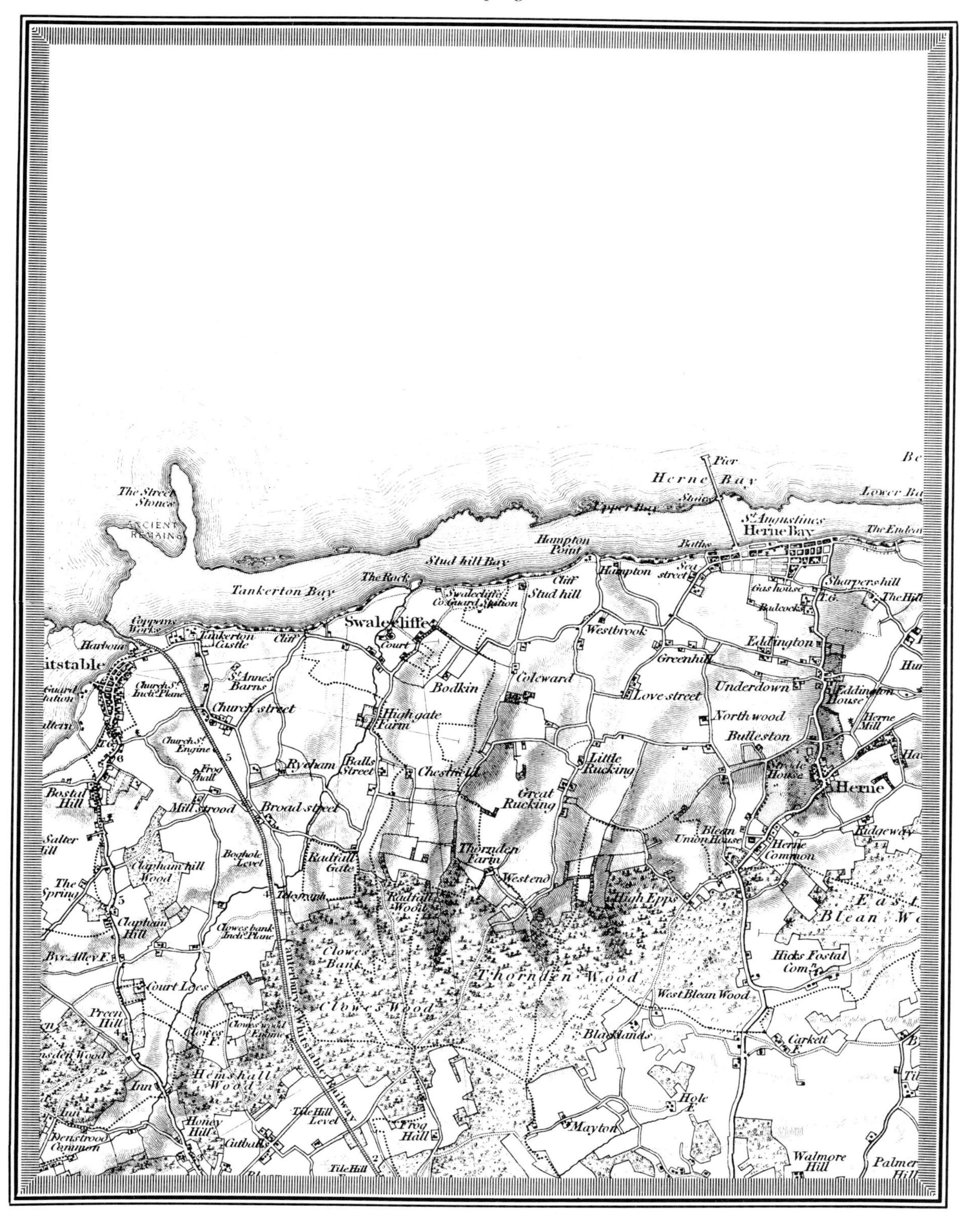
Herne Bay
Pier
Upper Bay
Lower Bay
St. Augustines
Herne Bay
The Street Stones
Ancient Remains
Hampton Point
Stud hill Bay
The Rock
Tankerton Bay
Hampton
Sea street
Stud hill
Swalecliffe
Tankerton Castle
Westbrook
Eddington
Greenhill
Coleward
Bodkin
Love street
Underdown
Church street
High gate Farm
Northwood
Bulleston
Ryeham
Balls Street
Chestfield
Little Rucking
Great Rucking
Herne
Broad street
Mill strood
Bostal Hill
Salter Hill
Clapham hill Wood
Radfall Gate
Thornden Farm
Westend
Herne Common
Ridgeway
High Epps
Radfall Wood
Clapham Hill
Clowes Bank
Thornden Wood
Blean Wood
Hicks Fostal Com.
West Blean Wood
Clowes Wood
Court Lees
Preen Hill
Blacklands
Carkett F.
Hemshall Wood
Hole F.
Mayton
Frog Hall
Tile Hill Level
Cutballs
Honey Hill
Denstrood Common
Walmore Hill
Palmer Hill
Tile Hill
Canterbury & Whitstable Railway

Map 14 cont
eastern end of Sheppey has been partially developed as a holiday camp area around Leysdown on Sea and Warden, although Shell Ness has become a nature reserve and the Isle of Harty remains a place of isolated scattered farms.

Map 15 (previous page) This map shows part of the north Kent coast from Seasalter to Herne Bay, including Whitstable which was famous in the past for oysters and as the collier port for Canterbury. In 1830 a railroad, partly manipulated by a stationary engine, was constructed between the two for the coal trade but it was closed after the Second World War. The modern Tankerton, here indicated by copperas works, was developed first as a private estate in the nineteenth century. Herne Bay, from being a small fishing village linked with Herne, two miles inland, grew rapidly after the railway arrived in 1861 and is now both a commuter and a retirement centre. To the south lie the woods of the Forest of Blean, an untamed area in 1801 and still much wooded.

Map 16 The Wantsum and Chislet marshes were formerly taken up with the Wantsum channel, said to have been three miles wide. At Sarre there was a ferry crossing in medieval times, the main route into Thanet. At the north-western corner of the map lies Reculver, one of the Roman forts of the Saxon shore and

Herne Bay after 1884. The pier, which was over half a mile in length and the second longest in Britain, was the pride of Herne Bay. Its pavilion was destroyed by fire in 1970 and the remainder demolished ten years later.

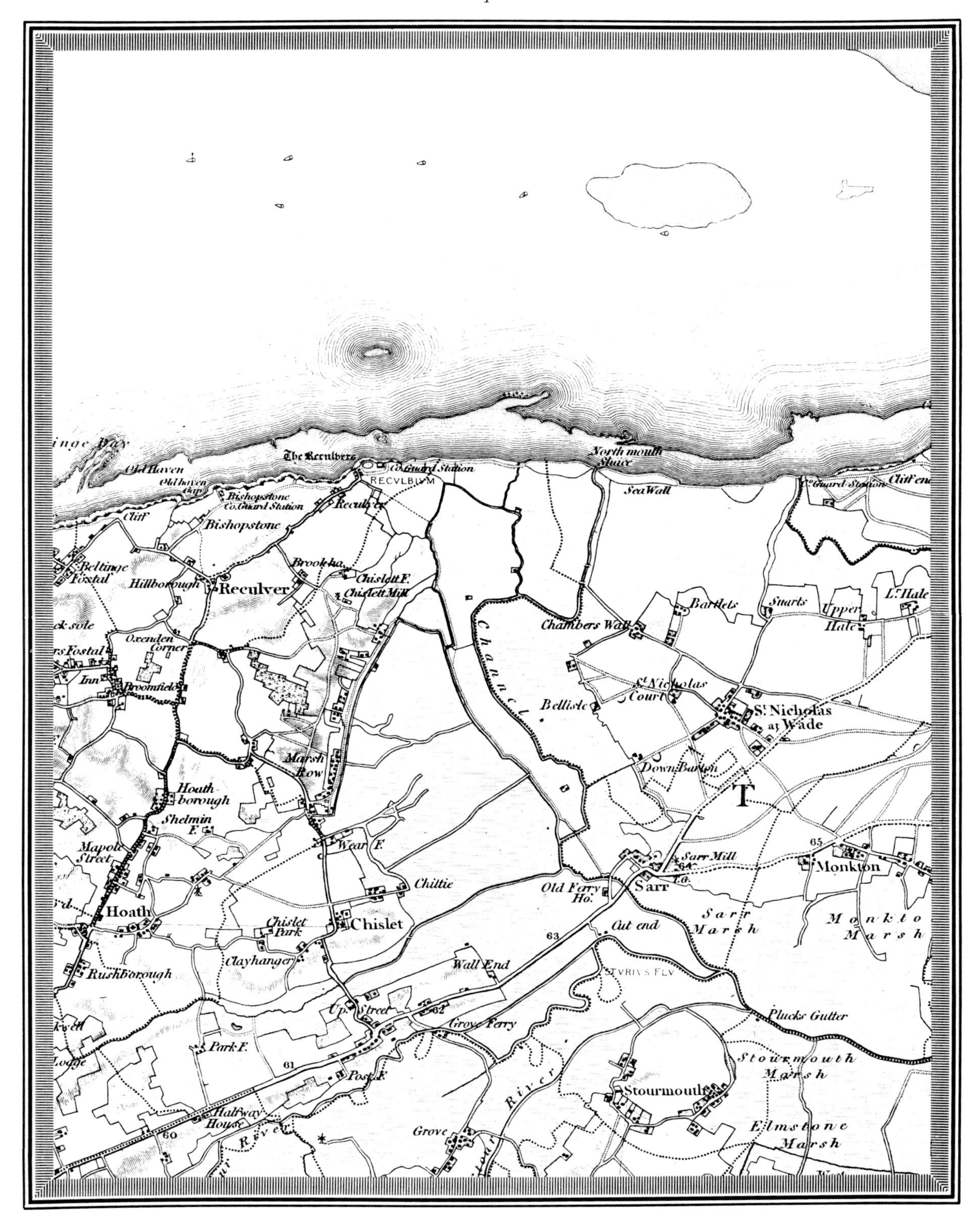
The Reculvers
Co. Guard Station
RECVLBIVM
Old Haven
Old haven Gap
Bishopstone Co. Guard Station
Reculver
Cliff
Bishopstone
Beltinge Fostal
Hillborough
Reculver
Brookha
Chislett F.
Chislett Mill
North mouth Sluice
Sea Wall
Co. Guard Station
Cliff end
Bartlets
Snarts
Upper Hale
L. Hale
Chambers Wall
Channel
Oxenden Corner
Inn
Broomfield
St. Nicholas Court
Bellisle
St. Nicholas at Wade
Down Barton
Marsh Row
Hoath borough
Shelmin F.
T
Mapole Street
Wear F.
Sarr Mill
65
Monkton
Chittie
Old Ferry Ho.
Sarr
Hoath
Chislet Park
Chislet
63
Cut end
Sarr Marsh
Monkto Marsh
Clayhanger
Rushborough
Wall End
STVRIVS FLV
Up. Street
62
Grove Ferry
Plucks Gutter
Park F.
61
Post F.
River
Stourmouth Marsh
Stourmouth
Halfway House
60
River
Grove
Elmstone Marsh

Map 17

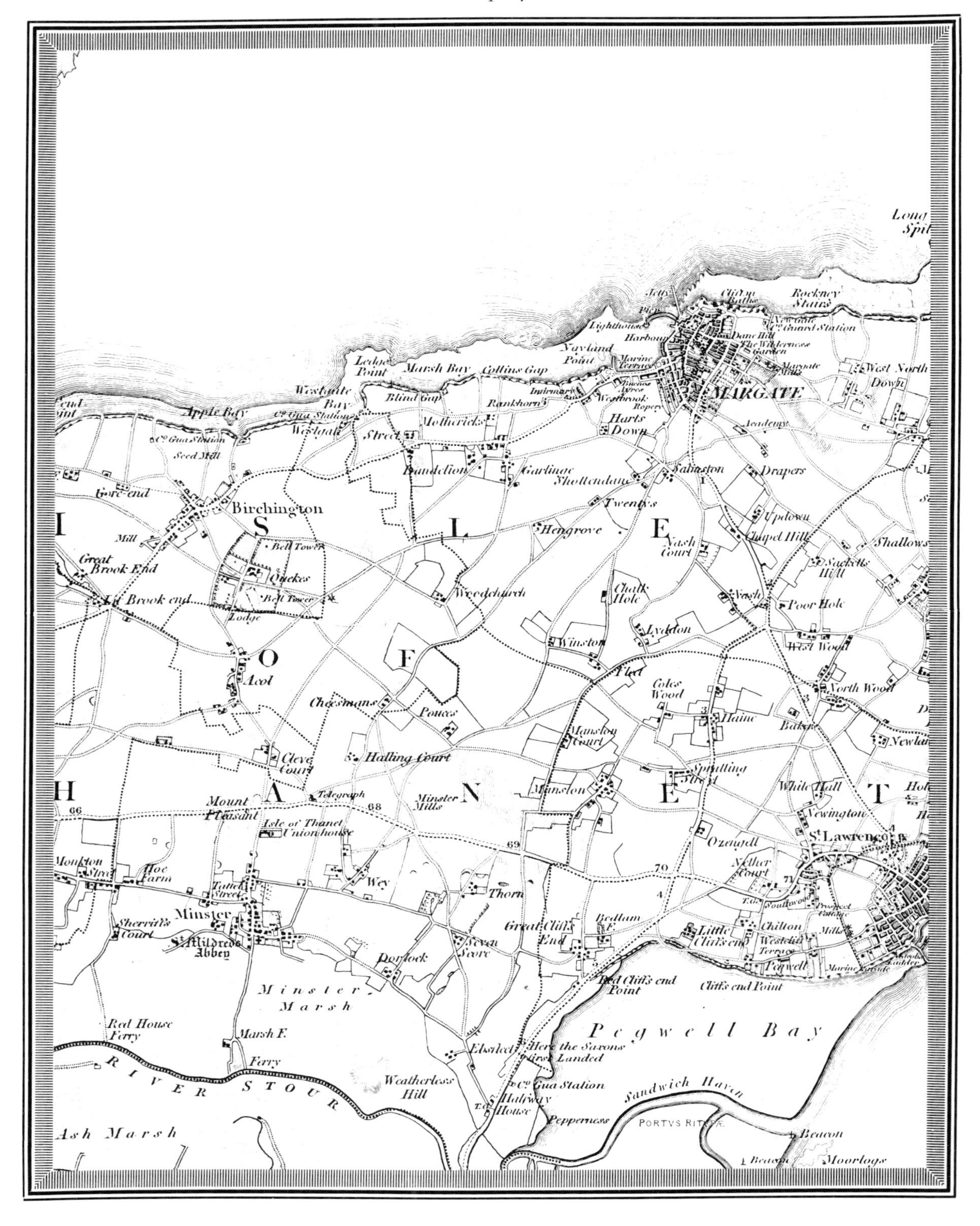

Long Spit
Rockney Stairs
Jetty
Lighthouse
Harbour
Nayland Point
Marine Terrace
Ledge Point
Marsh Bay
Collins Gap
Blind Gap
Westgate Bay
Apple Bay
Cº Gua Station
Westgate
Seed Mill
Street
Motherick's
Rankshorn
Infirmary
Westbrook
Ropery
MARGATE
New Gate
Cº Guard Station
Dane Hill
The Wilderness Garden
Margate Mills
West North Down
Academy
Harts Down
Dandelion
Garlinge
Shottendane
Salmston
Drapers
Gore end
Birchington
Twenty's
Updown
Chapel Hill
I S L E
Mill
Bell Tower
Hengrove
Nash Court
Shallows
Sacketts Hill
Great Brook End
Quekes
Little Brook end
Lodge
Woodchurch
Chalk Hole
Nash
Poor Hole
Lydden
Winston
West Wood
O F
Acol
Flet
Coles Wood
North Wood
Cheesmans
Pouces
Manston Court
Haine
Baker
Newlands
Cleve Court
Halling Court
Spratling Street
H A N E T
Mount Pleasant
Telegraph
Minster Mills
Manston
White Hall
Newington
66
68
69
70
Isle of Thanet Union house
Ozengell
St. Lawrence
Monkton Street
Hoe Farm
Tatter Street
Wey
Thorn
Nether Court
Minster
Sherriff's Court
St. Mildred's Abbey
Seven Score
Great Cliffs End
Bedlam F.
Little Cliffs end
Chilton
Westcliff Terrace
Pegwell
Prospect Cottage
Mills
Marine Parade
Dorlock
Red Cliffs end Point
Cliffs end Point
Minster Marsh
Pegwell Bay
Red House Ferry
Marsh F.
Ferry
Ebsfleet
Here the Saxons first Landed
RIVER STOUR
Weatherless Hill
Cº Gua Station
Halfway House
Sandwich Haven
Pepperness
PORTVS RITVPA
Beacon
Moorlogs
Ash Marsh

a member of Sandwich in the Cinque Ports Confederation. It controlled the northern entrance to the Wantsum and is still famous for the ruins of St Mary's church with its twin towers, which are already depicted as a landmark on a map drawn before 1414.

Map 17 This map shows the heart of the Isle of Thanet from Birchington and the older part of Margate in the north to the Stour marshes south of Minster and Pegwell Bay, traditional site for the landing of Hengist in the fifth century AD and also of St Augustine in 597. In the centre of the map lies Minster with its fine church and monastic remains. The monastery, destroyed by the Danes, was founded in about 670 by Ermenburga, daughter of a Kentish king and mother of St Mildred. The whole of the north coast is now developed as a holiday area with Margate as the principal centre, although it was for centuries the outport of the Thames and the final port of call for ships plying to and from London. In 1791 the Royal Sea Bathing Hospital was founded and from a small town of 4800 inhabitants in 1801 it grew to 46,500 by 1921. Between Margate and Minster, the great agricultural region of Thanet, there now lies Manston air station which came to fame during the Battle of Britain in the Second World War.

Map 18 and modern map 18 (overleaf) This area contains the well known resorts of Cliftonville, Broadstairs and Ramsgate. The last named

Ramsgate in 1910. Trams no longer run past the harbour on their way to the West Cliff, nor is the harbour filled with fishing vessels since it became a marina.

Map 18

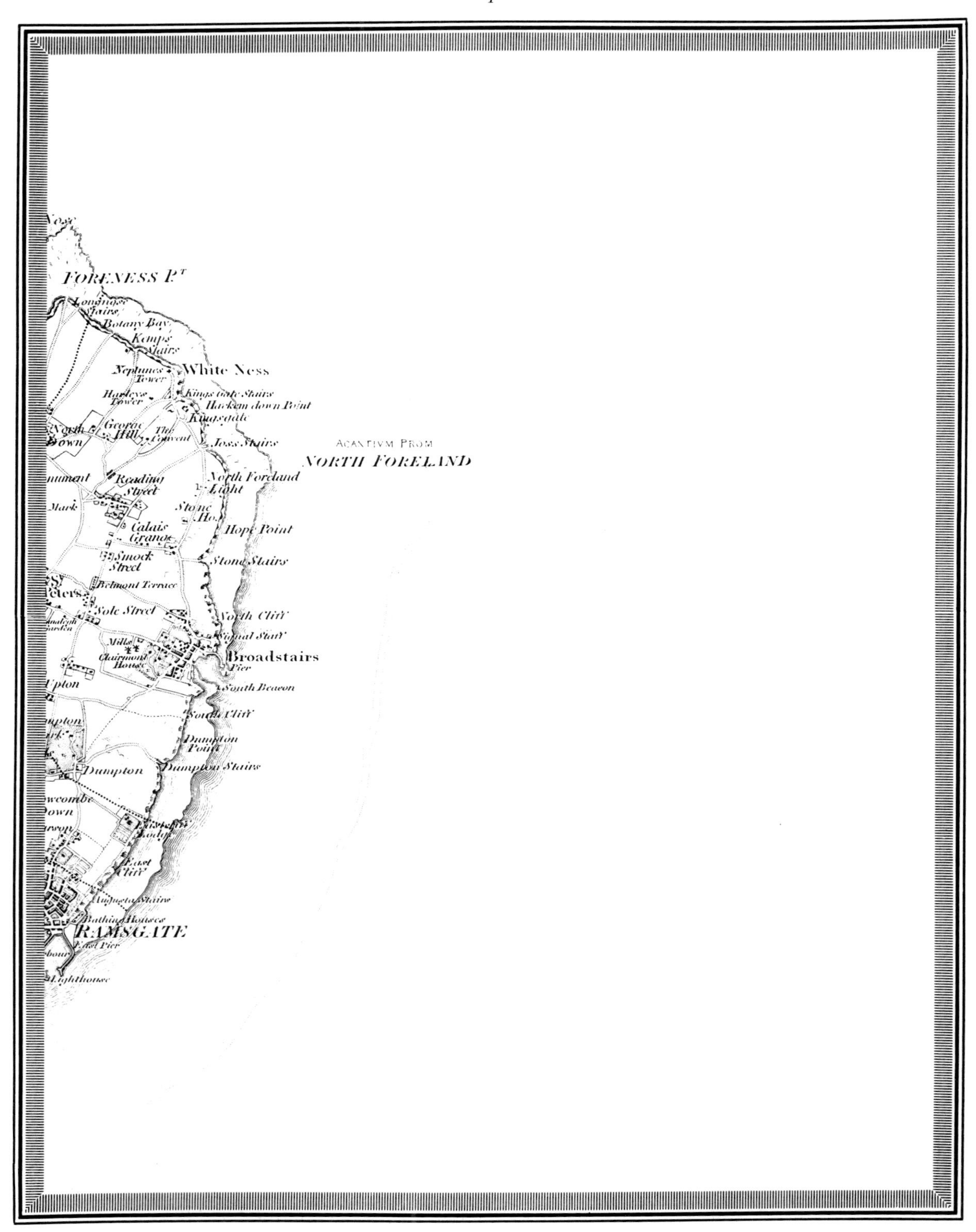

FORENESS P^T
Longnose Stairs
Botany Bay
Kemps Stairs
Neptunes Tower
White Ness
Harleys Tower
Kings Gate Stairs
Hackem down Point
Kingsgate
George Hill
The Convent
North Down
Joss Stairs
ACANTIUM PROM
NORTH FORELAND
Reading Street
North Foreland Light
Stone Ho.
Calais Grange
Hope Point
Smock Street
Stone Stairs
Belmont Terrace
St Peters
Sole Street
North Cliff
Signal Staff
Mills
Clairmont House
Broadstairs
Pier
South Beacon
Upton
South Cliff
Dumpton Point
Dumpton
Dumpton Stairs
East Cliff
Augusta Stairs
Bathing Houses
RAMSGATE
East Pier
Lighthouse

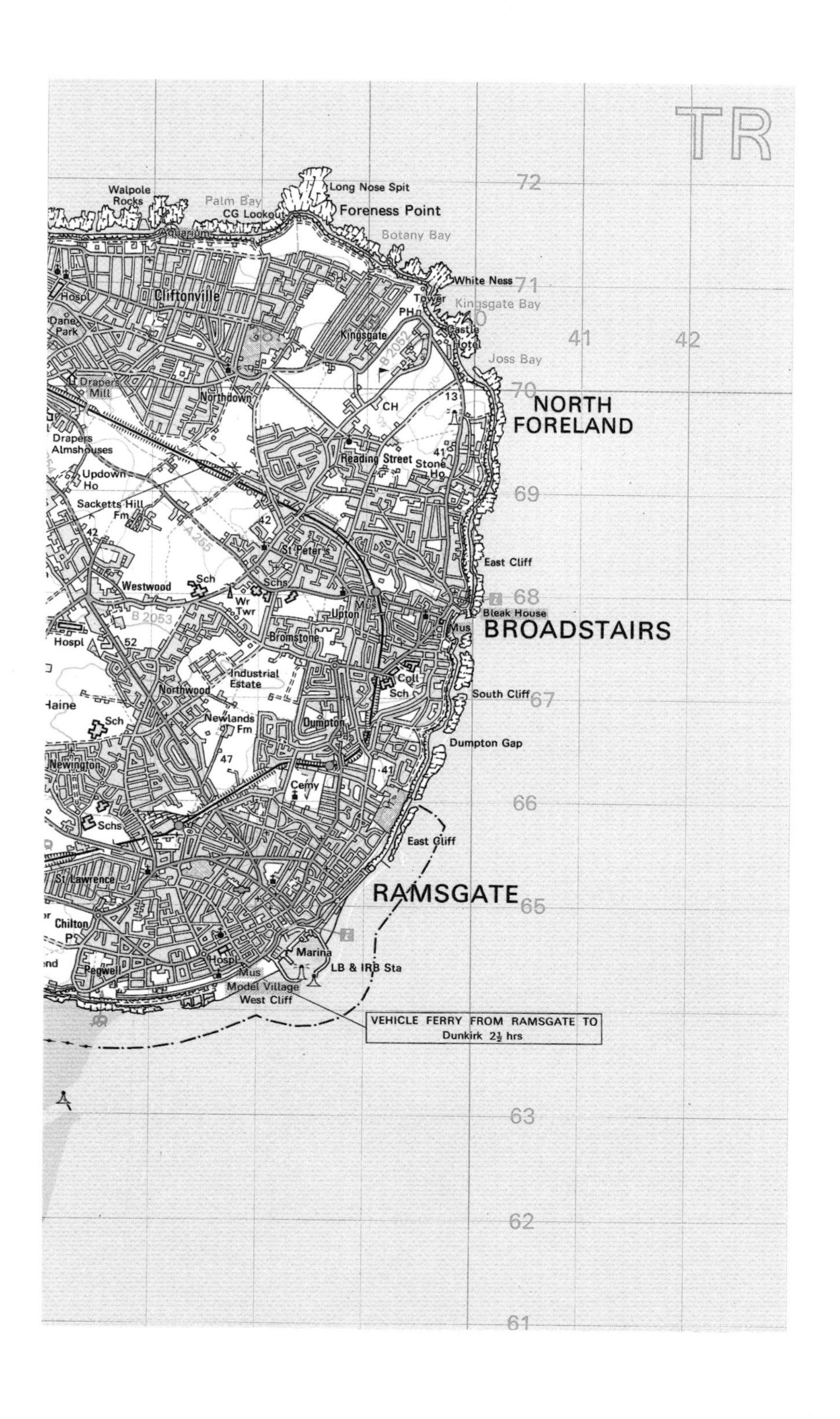
TR
Walpole Rocks
Palm Bay
CG Lookout
Long Nose Spit
Foreness Point
Botany Bay
White Ness
Kingsgate Bay
Castle Hotel
Joss Bay
Cliftonville
Hospl
Dane Park
Kingsgate
Drapers Mill
Northdown
NORTH FORELAND
Drapers Almshouses
Reading Street
Stone Ho
Updown Ho
Sacketts Hill Fm
St Peter's
East Cliff
Westwood
Wr Twr
Upton
Bleak House
Mus
BROADSTAIRS
B 2053
B 2052
A 255
Bromstone
Industrial Estate
Coll
Sch
South Cliff
Northwood
Newlands Fm
Dumpton
Dumpton Gap
Newington
Cemy
Schs
East Cliff
St Lawrence
RAMSGATE
Chilton
Marina
Pegwell
Hospl
LB & IRB Sta
Model Village
West Cliff
VEHICLE FERRY FROM RAMSGATE TO Dunkirk 2½ hrs
72
71
70
41
42
69
68
67
66
65
63
62
61

Pleasure craft moored near Chatham (see page 51).

Rochester Castle gardens in 1987 (see page 52).

Map 19

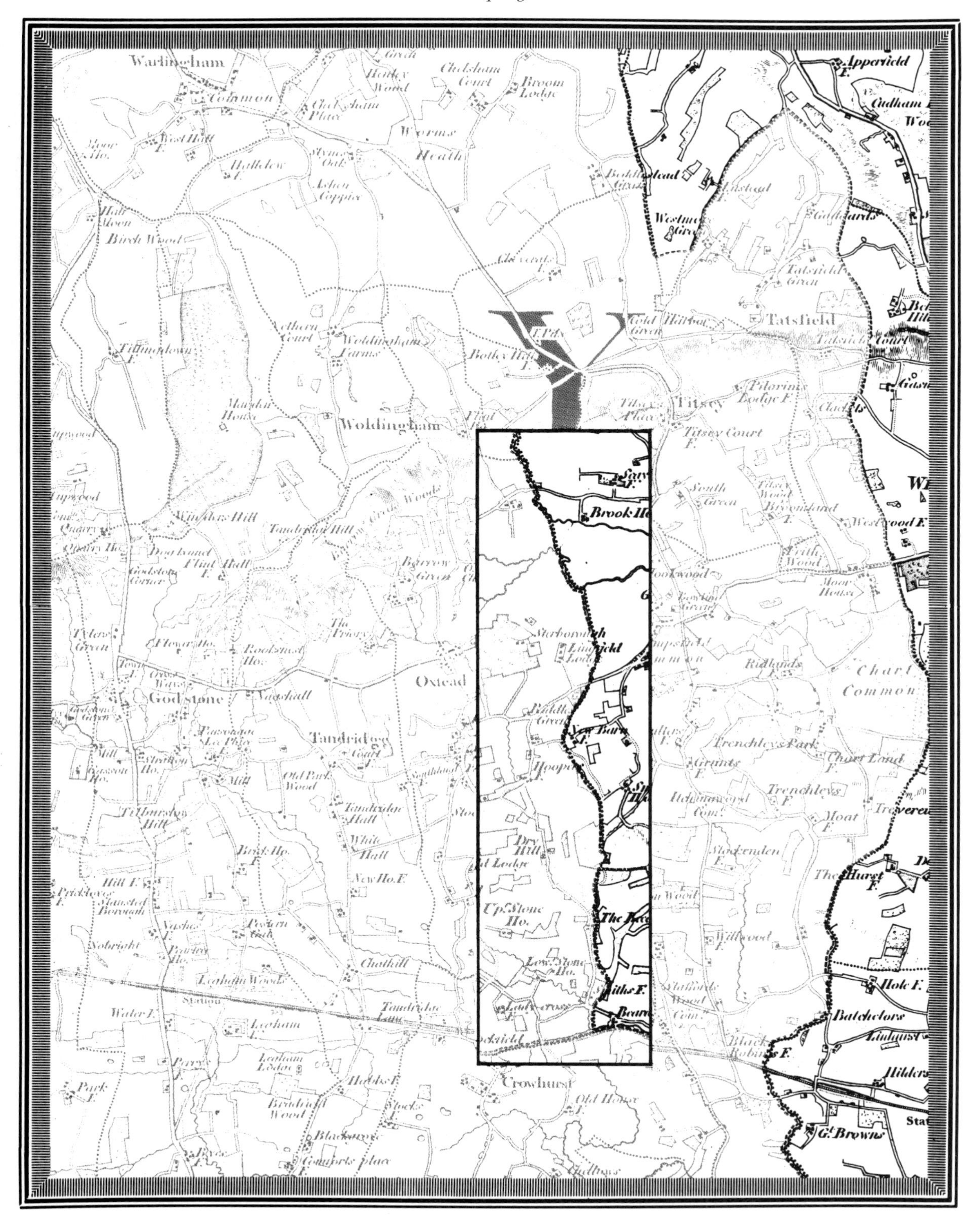
Warlingham
Common
Chelsham Court
Broom Lodge
Chelsham Place
Worms Heath
West Hall
Halliloo F.
Slynes Oak
Ashen Coppice
Birch Wood
Apperfield F.
Cudham
Tatsfield Green
Tatsfield
Titsey
Titsey Place
Titsey Court F.
Pilgrims Lodge F.
Woldingham Farms
Woldingham
Botley Hill F.
Marden House
Brook Ho.
South Green
Westwood F.
Moor House
Oxted
Godstone
Tandridge
Tandridge Court
Tandridge Hall
Old Park Wood
White Hall
New Ho. F.
Starborough
Limpsfield Lodge
New Barn F.
Chart Common
Trenchleys Park
Trenchleys F.
Chart Land F.
Moat F.
The Hurst F.
Dry Hill
Up. Stone Ho.
Low. Stone Ho.
The Hurst
Batchelors
Hole F.
Gt. Browns
Crowhurst
Old House F.
Tilburstow Hill
Chathill
Leaham Wood
Station
Water F.
Park F.
Nobright
Comforts place
Hill F.

followed a similar course of development to Margate and in recent years has become a significant port for cross-channel services. Broadstairs had a mere 1600 souls in 1801, but developed rapidly after the coming of the railway and had a population of more than 7000 by 1901. This pattern of growth has continued and the whole area from Margate round the North Foreland to Pegwell Bay has become a single conurbation.

Map 19 (previous page) The narrow strip of land forming the boundary between Kent and Surrey from the Kent Water at Cowden in the south to Tatsfield and Chelsham in Surrey in the north includes the North Downs where Biggin Hill airfield is now situated. The boundary lies for much of the way along a former Roman road from London to Lewes which can also be seen in the straight stretch of road at Edenbridge (see map on page 89).

Map 20 This map shows the western extremity of Kent from the downland through Holmesdale to Brasted Chart and Four Elms. It includes the small town of Westerham, home of General James Wolfe, the village of Brasted where Wolfe's Commander-in-Chief, General Amherst, was born, and, on the hills to the south, Chartwell which was the home of Sir Winston Churchill. Brasted Chart is the highest point in Kent, reaching a height of 771 feet (235 metres), and is still largely covered by woodland belonging to the National Trust. In the north centre of the map lies Chevening, the former home of the Earls Stanhope and now the official residence of the Foreign Secretary. Altogether this is an area of great houses and of magnificent views, especially southwards over the Weald from vantage points such as Ide Hill.

Map 21 (overleaf) Although only part of the town of Sevenoaks is on this map, the rest appearing on page 69, its distinctive V-shaped road pattern is apparent and has survived to this day. This also is an area of great houses with the most famous, Knole, still dominating the town to which it is adjacent. Others like Montreal, the home of Earl Amherst after the taking of Canada in 1758–60, have given way to housing estates. To the north is the village of Otford with its ruins of an archiepiscopal palace, while to the south lie more hills and woodland with views over the Weald.

Map 22 (page 71) shows two distinct areas which were separated at the beginning of the nineteenth century by the woods and heaths of the ragstone ridge from Great Comp to East Malling. Northwards lies the well peopled Holmesdale with the market town of West Malling as the principal centre of population, an area now crossed by the railway and the motorway; southwards of the ridge is the heavy clay of the Weald and the valley of the Medway. Mereworth Place or Castle was the home of the Earls of Westmoreland and at Hadlow a mock Gothic castle was built at the beginning of the last century, now represented by the tower, a folly visible over much of the Wealden area.

Map 23 and modern map 23 (pages 72–3) This map includes the Medway valley from Barming through the heart of Maidstone to Aylesford, the beautiful downland beyond Boxley and Detling, and the great open area of Cox Heath between the villages of Loose and Langley, Linton and Boughton Monchelsea. At the southern extremity the map reaches the banks of the Beult, the slow winding river of the low Weald. Aylesford was a very ancient crossing place of the Medway and may have been the site of the battle of Aeglesford in 455.

Map 20

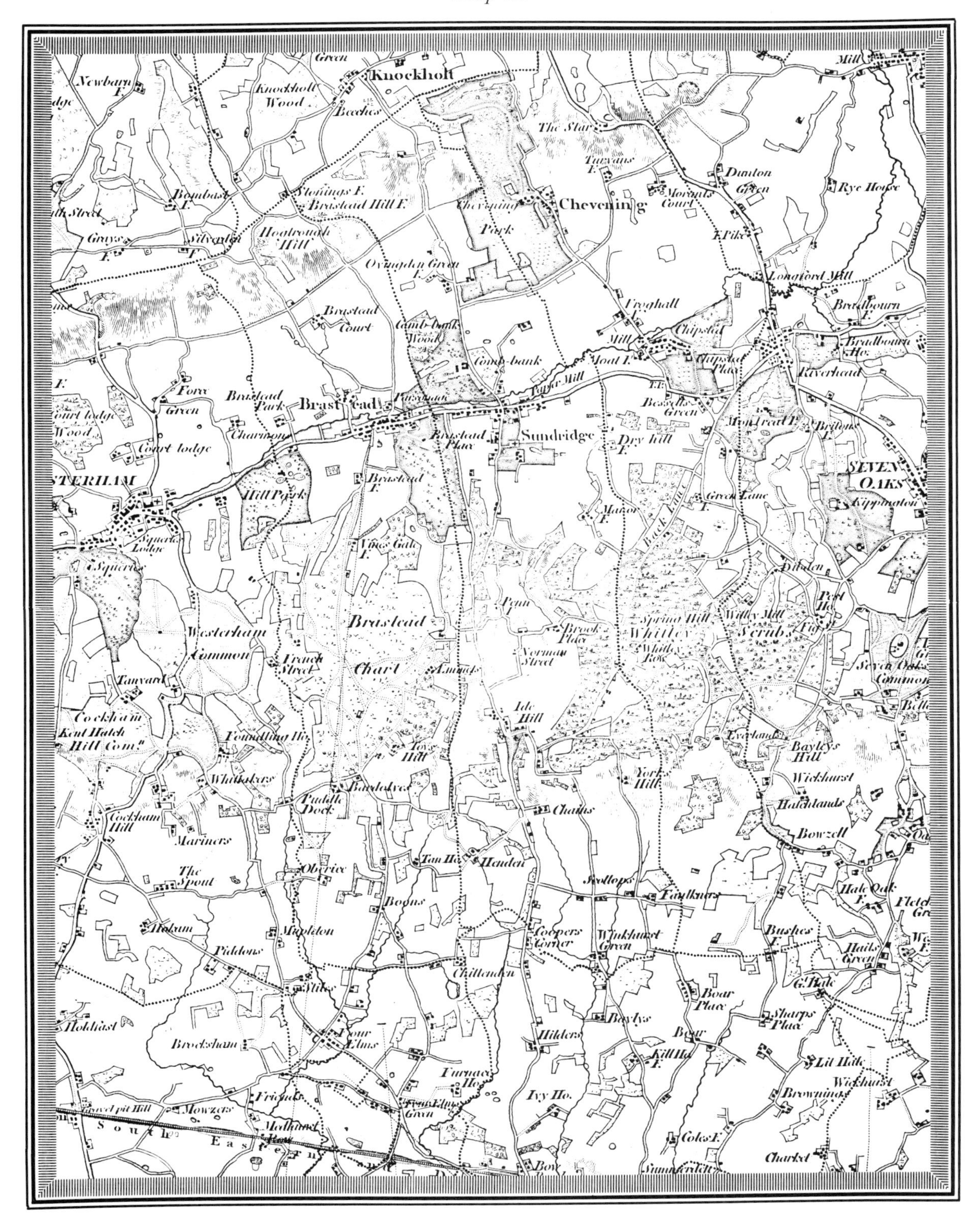
Knockholt
Knockholt Wood
Beeches
Newbarn F.
The Star
Turvans F.
Dunton Green
Morants Court
Rye House
Chevening
Chevening Park
Bombast F.
Stonings F.
Brastead Hill F.
Grays F.
Hogtrough Hill
Oyngdon Green
F. Pike
Longford Mill
Bradbourn F.
Froghall
Chipstead
Brastead Court
Comb-bank Wood
Comb-bank
Mill
Moat F.
Chipstead Place
Bradbourn Ho.
Riverhead
Force Green
Brastead Park
Brastead
Paper Mill
Bessels Green
Montreal P.
Court lodge Wood
Charmons
Court lodge
Brastead Place
Sundridge
Dry hill F.
STERHAM
Hill Park
Brastead F.
Green Lane
SEVEN OAKS
Kippington
Squerries Lodge
Squerries
Manor F.
Back Lane
Vines Gate F.
Dibden
Penn
Spring Hill
Whitley Mill
Brook Place
Whitley
Scrubs
Westerham Common
French Street
Brastead Chart
Norman Street
Whitley Row
Seven Oaks Common
Tanyard
Ide Hill
Cockham
Kent Hatch
Hill Com.
Foundling Ho.
Toys Hill
Everlands
Bayleys Hill
York Hill
Whitakers
Puddle Dock
Wickhurst
Cockham Hill
Mariners
Chains
Hatchlands
Bowzell
Tan Ho.
Henden
The Spout
Obries
Scollops
Faulkners
Boons
Hale Oak F.
Mapleton
Coopers Corner
Winkhurst Green
Bushes F.
Piddons
Hails Green
Chittenden
Stiles
G. Hale
Boar Place
Sharps Place
Holdhurst
Brocksham
Four Elms
Hilders
Baylys
Boar
Kill Ho. F.
Lit Hale
Furnace Ho.
Ivy Ho.
Wickhurst
Browning
Gravel pit Hill
Mowzers
Friends
Four Elms Green
Coles F.
Charket
South Eastern
Summerhill

Map 21

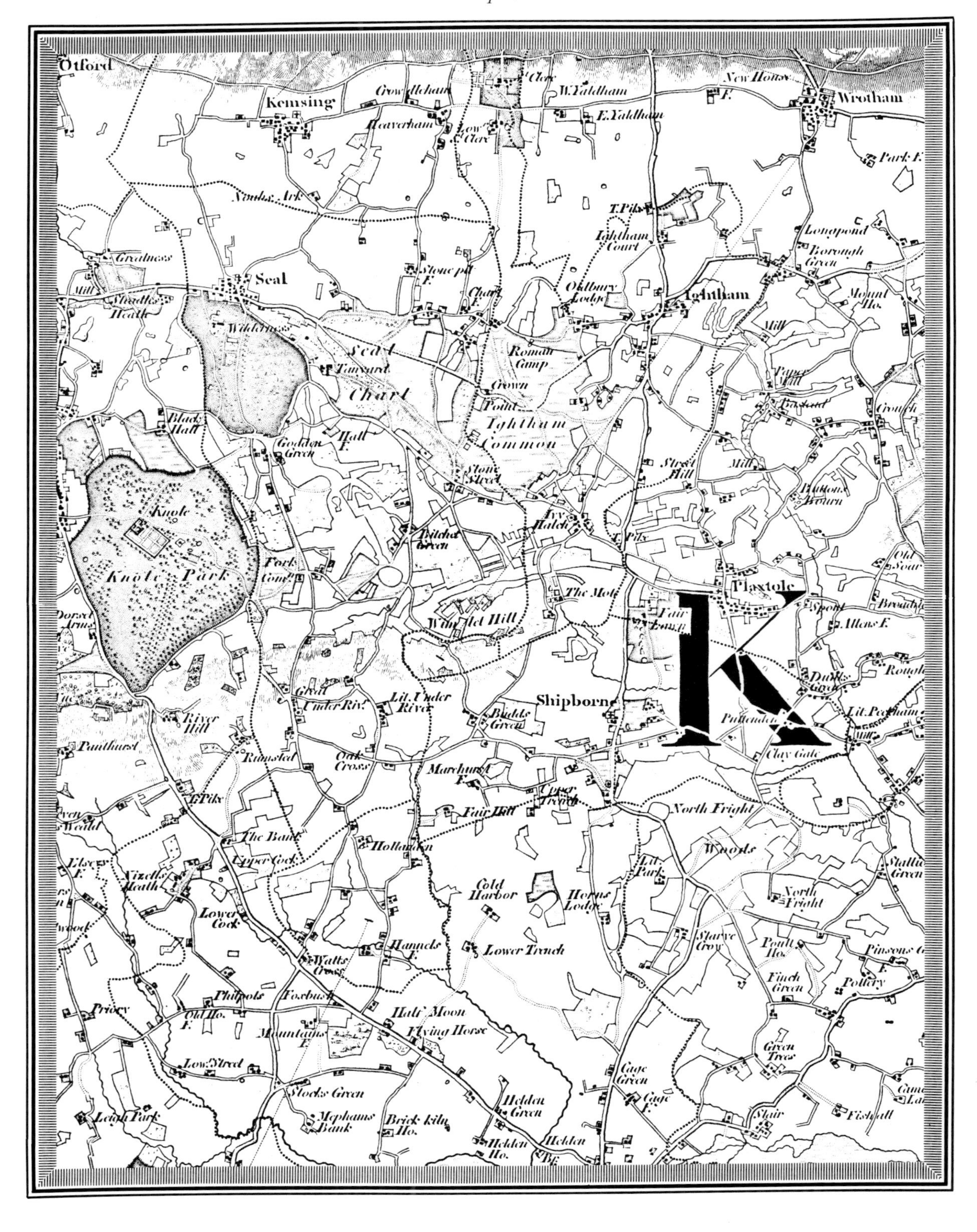
Otford
Kensing
Heaverham
W. Yaldham
E. Yaldham
Wrotham
New House
Park F.
Noahs Ark
T. Pike
Ightham Court
Longpond
Borough Green
Seal
Ightham
Stone pit F.
Chart F.
Oldbury Lodge
Mount Ho.
Wilderness
Seal Chart
Tanyard
Roman Camp
Crown Point
Paper Mill
Basted
Black Hall
Godden Green
Hall F.
Ightham Common
Stone Street
Street Hill
Mill
Buttons Brown
Knole
Knole Park
Ivy Hatch
Bitchet Green
Fork Court
Plaxtole
Old Soar
The Mote
Fair Lawn
Allens F.
Dorset Arms
K
Shipborne
Great Under River
Lit. Under River
Budds Green
Puttenden
Lit. Peckham
River Hill
Panthurst
Rumsted
Oak Cross
Clay Gate
Marchurst F.
Upper Trench
T. Pike
Fair Hill
North Fright
Woods
The Bank
Hollanden
Upper Cock
Nizells Heath
Lit. Park
Cold Harbor
Herns Lodge
North Fright
Lower Cock
Starve Crow
Poult Ho.
Hannels F.
Lower Trench
Watts Cross
Finch Green
Pottery
Philpots
Foxbush
Priory
Old Ho. F.
Half Moon
Flying Horse
Mountains F.
Green Trees
Low Street
Cage Green
Cage F.
Stocks Green
Helden Green
Leigh Park
Mephams Bank
Brick kiln Ho.
Fishall
Helden Ho.
Helden

Map 22

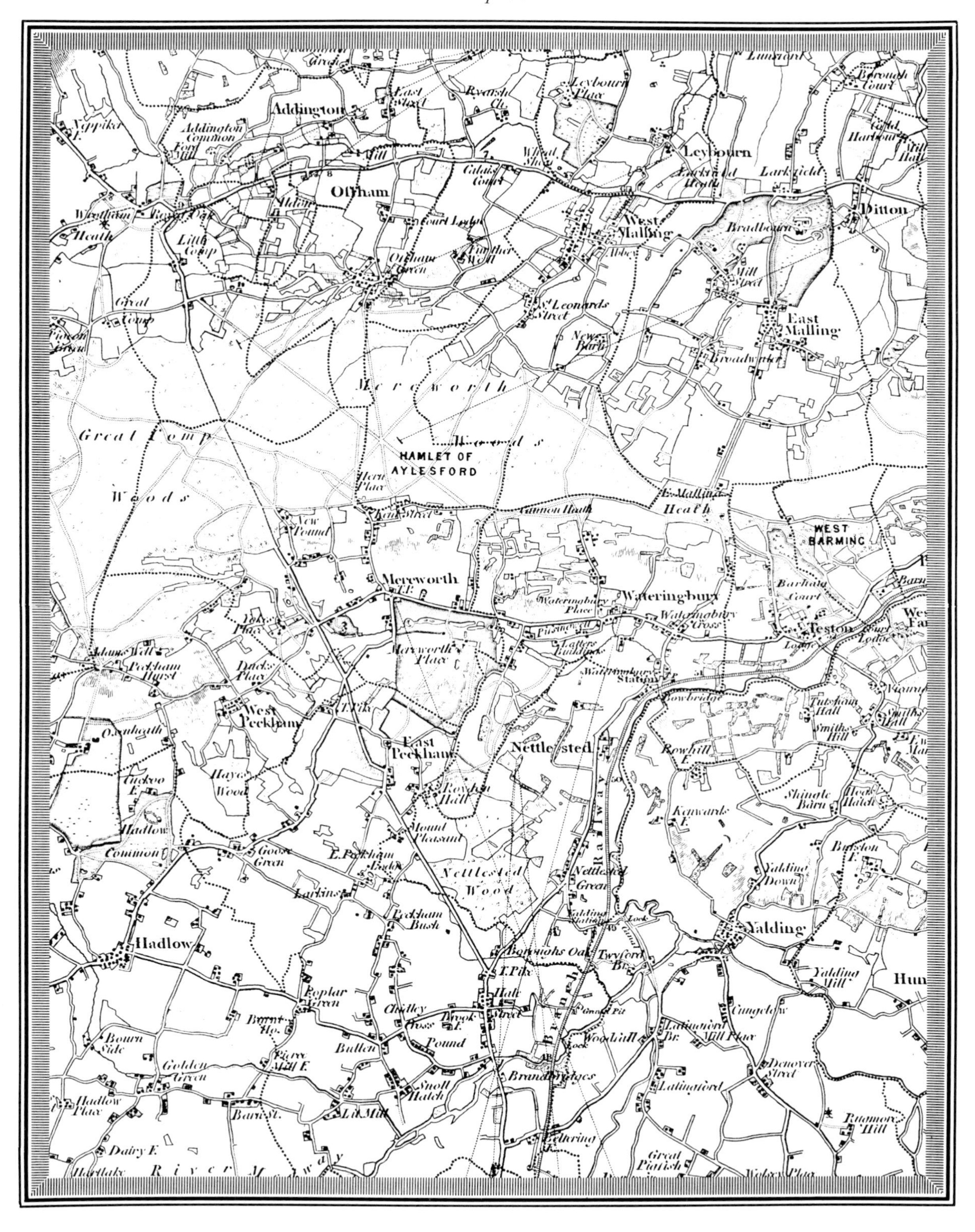
Addington
Addington Common
Leybourn
Larkfield
Offham
Ditton
West Malling
Bradbourn
Wrotham Heath
Little Comp
Offham Green
St. Leonards Street
East Malling
Broadwater
Great Comp
Mereworth Woods
Great Comp Woods
HAMLET OF AYLESFORD
E. Malling Heath
WEST BARMING
Mereworth
Wateringbury
Teston
Mereworth Place
Wateringbury Station
West Peckham
East Peckham
Nettlested
Roydon Hall
Hayes Wood
Hadlow Common
Goose Green
Mount Pleasant
Nettlested Wood
Nettlested Green
Yalding Down
Yalding
Peckham Bush
Hadlow
Twyford Br.
Yalding Mill
Poplar Green
Brook F.
Pound
Bullen
Woodhill
Latingford
Golden Green
Snoll Hatch
Brandbridges
Denover Street
Hadlow Place
Barn St.
Dairy F.
Great Pattish
Railway
River Medway

Aylesford
Aylesford Place
Preston Hall
Little Preston
Boarley
Boxley
Boxley Abbey
Grange
Harpole F.
Detling
Thurnham
Allington
Quarries
Sandlin
The Grange
Penenden Heath
Newnham Court
Little Buckland
Gt. Buckland
Summerfield House
MAIDSTONE
Barracks
New Gd.
T.P.
Vinters
Grove Green
Weavering Street
Bearsted
Otterden
Thurnham Wood
Binbury Wood
East Malling
Woods
Hermitage
Barming Heath
Station
Mote
Mangravet
Low Tovil
Up. Tovil
Fant
EAST
Barming
Shepherds Street
Otham
Green Hill
Willington Street
East Farleigh
Dane Street
Hall Place
Cold Harbour
Gore Court
Otham Street
Prospect Place
Farleigh Court
Paper Mill
Loose Court
Gold Court
Boughton Mount
Cripple Street
Bell Wood
Rumwood Green
Fright Wood
Well Street
Loose
Boughton Quarry
Gt. Park Wood
Lt. Park W.
Langley Park
Langley
Coxheath
Clock Ho.
Star Inn
Cock Street
Four Wents
Parsonage
Linton
Loddington Farm
Hamber Green
Chart Corner
Norton Pond
Linton Place
Boughton Monchelsea
Wierton Place
Hunton Street
Loddington Street
Chart Hill
Chart Sutton
Hunton
Borough Boundary
River Beult
Chainhurst
Crabb Tree
Gt. Tilden

W
N
MAIDSTONE
MAIDSTONE DISTRICT
Mote Park
Monkdown Wood
Newlands Wood
Lower Cox Street
Rose Cottage (ruin)
Eccles
Rowe Place Fm
Grange Fm
Pollyfield
Stockings Wood
Harp Fm
Boarley Fm
North Downs Way
Pilgrims Way
Trackway
Pratling Street
Aylesford
Millhall
Industrial Estate
Tyland Fm
Boxley Ho
Boxley
Mount Ho
Kent County Agricultural Showground
Abbey Gate
Boxley Abbey (rems of)
Park Ho
Friningham
Forstal
Little Preston
Cemy
Sandling
Motel
Mus
East Court
Harbourland
Harpole
Detling
Castle (rems of)
Civiley Wood
Thurnham
Allington
Allington Castle
Park Wood
Royal British Legion Village
Industrial Estate
Holt Hill
Ringlestone
Bks
Penenden Heath
Horish Wood
Court Fm
Thurnham Keep Fm
Cobham Manor
Newnham Court Fm
Honeyhills Wood
BARMING STA
A 20
A 229
A 249
A 26
A 274
B 2010
B 2163
B 2163
Earthwork
Crem
Birling Ho
Ware Street
Longham Wood
Moat
H.M.Prison
County Hall
Vinters
Grove Green
Hermitage Fm
Weavering Street
Hospls
Ditton Common
Oakwood Park
Roseacre
Coll
Hospl
Barming Heath
Wood
Wr Twr
Bearsted
Woodcut Fm
Mote Ho
The Tudor Ho
Milgate
Hall Place
Fant
Weir
East Barming
Tovil
Fulling Mill Fm
Green Hill
Hayle Place
The Priory
Abbey Gate Place
Willington
Caring
Court Lodge
Kettle Corner
Shepway
Merriams Fm
Otham
Stoneacre
Gore Court
Cemy
Brogden
East Farleigh
West Farleigh
Dean Street
Loose Valley
Holly Fm
Gallants Fm
Arnold Fm
West Farleigh Hall
Farleigh Green
Pimp's Court
Otham Hole
Rumwood Court
Ewell Manor
Loose Hill
Boughton Mount
Loose
Quarry Wood
Hospital Barn Fm
The Quarries
Park Wood
Langley Park Fm
Langley
Langley Heath
Fox Pitt
Forstal Fm
Boughton Green
Brishing Court
Coxheath
Mount Pleasant Fm
Rectory Fm
Abbey Wood
Barn Hill
Boughton Monchelsea
Cock Street
Five Wents
Pleasant Fm
Fir Tree Fm
Gennings Fm
Reason Hill
Clock Ho
Hill House Fm
Langley Lodge
Chart Corner
Old Savage
Westerhill Fm
Court Lodge
Loddington Fm
Amberfield
Boughton Monchelsea Place
Deer Park
Wierton Place
Chart Sutton
Warmlake
Chart Hill
Hunton
Linton
Linton Park
East Hall
Tower Ho
Hunton Court
Burford Fm
Rankins Fm
Bishop's Fm
Sutton Valence
Stallance
Lamb's Cross
Spark's Hall
The Harbour
Boughton Bottom
Reed Court Fm
Charlton Fm
Chart Bottom Fm
Moat Fm
Brook Ho
Great Tilden
Stile Bridge
Old Hertsfield
Holbrook
Dairy Ho
Chainhurst
Lake Fm
Den Fm
Chain Dene Fm
Little Tilden Fm
Hurst Green
Rabbit's Cross
Elderden Fm
Devil's Den
Lake Fm
New Lodge Ho
ROMAN ROAD

It is now the centre of the paper industry in the lower Medway valley. Maidstone, the county town, had some sea-borne traffic in earlier days and was an important cloth-producing town. Little of medieval Maidstone survives apart from the buildings around the parish church of All Saints, but just north of the town in the river valley is Allington Castle, home of Sir Thomas Wyatt, the poet and lover of Anne Boleyn. The ancient road from London crossed the Medway at Aylesford and ran across Penenden Heath to the north of Maidstone where the ancient shire court was held and criminals were executed. The present gaol was not built until 1819 and appears as New Gaol on the map. Cox Heath was enclosed in 1817 and has subsequently been developed, with the new parish of Coxheath created after the Second World War.

Map 24 This area shows part of the heartland of Kent with the London to Hythe road (now the A20) running across the centre of the map. To the south of this road lies the village of Leeds, and nearby the beautifully situated Leeds Castle nestling in the lake created from the waters of the river Len. Lenham was a small market town which has a fine square, but much of this region is still unspoilt and above the chalk hills are remote villages such as Hucking, Bicknor and Wormshill. The last named means 'hill of Woden', one of the few

Maidstone c *1830. A print of the High Street, taken from a drawing by G. Shepherd, looking westward from 'Top of the Town' towards the bridge. The dominant Town Hall divides the broad High Street from narrow Bank Street.*

Map 24

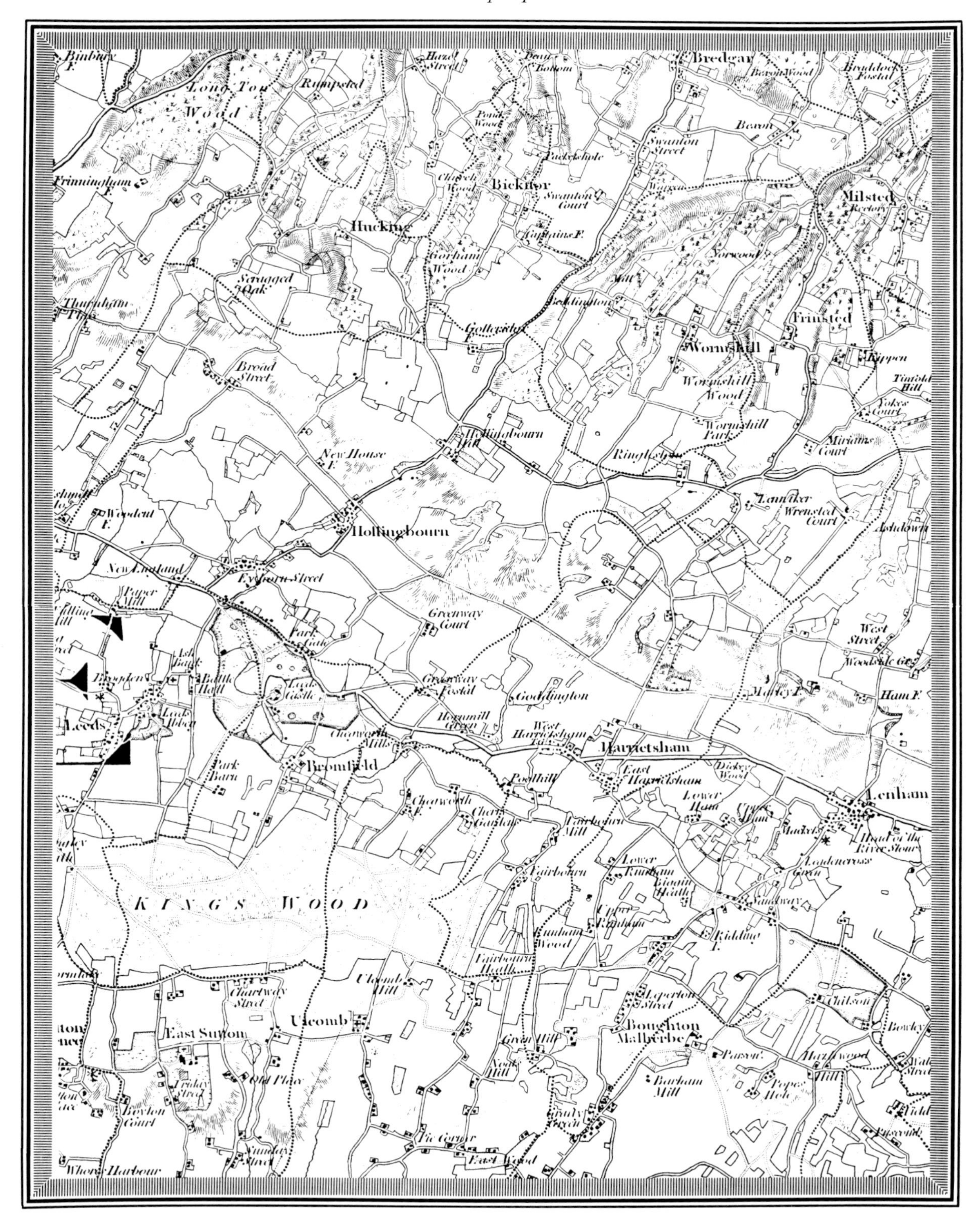

Binbury F.
Long Ton Wood
Rumpsted
Hazel Street
Dean Bottom
Bredgar
Bexon Wood
Braddock Fostal
Pond Wood
Beven
Swanton Street
Frinningham F.
Church Wood
Bicknor
Swanton Court
Milsted
Hucking
Gorham Wood
Norwood
Scragged Oak
Frinsted
Wormshill
Broad Street
Wormshill Wood
Yokes Court
Wormshill Park
Hollingbourn Hill
New House F.
Ringlestone
Miriams Court
Woodcut F.
Hollingbourn
Wrensted Court
Ashdown
New England
Eyhorn Street
Paper Mill
Greenway Court
West Street
Park Gate
Broomden
Ash Bank
Battle Hall
Leeds Castle
Greenway Fostal
Goddington
Ham F.
Leeds
Leeds Abbey
West Harrietsham
Harrietsham
Park Barn
Bromfield
East Harrietsham
Dickey Wood
Lenham
Poolhill
Chegworth F.
Lower Ham
Upper Ham
Fairbourn Mill
Head of the River Stour
Lower Runham
Fairbourn
Biggin Heath
Sandway
K I N G S W O O D
Upper Runham
Kidding F.
Runham Wood
Fairbourn Heath
Ulcomb Hill
Chartway Street
Leperton Street
Chilson
East Sutton
Ulcomb
Boughton Malherbe
Bowley
Green Hill
Parson
Noaks Hill
Old Place
Barham Mill
Popes Hall
Friday Street
Boyton Court
Grafty Green
Pie Corner
East Wood
Sunday Street
Where Harbour

Map 25

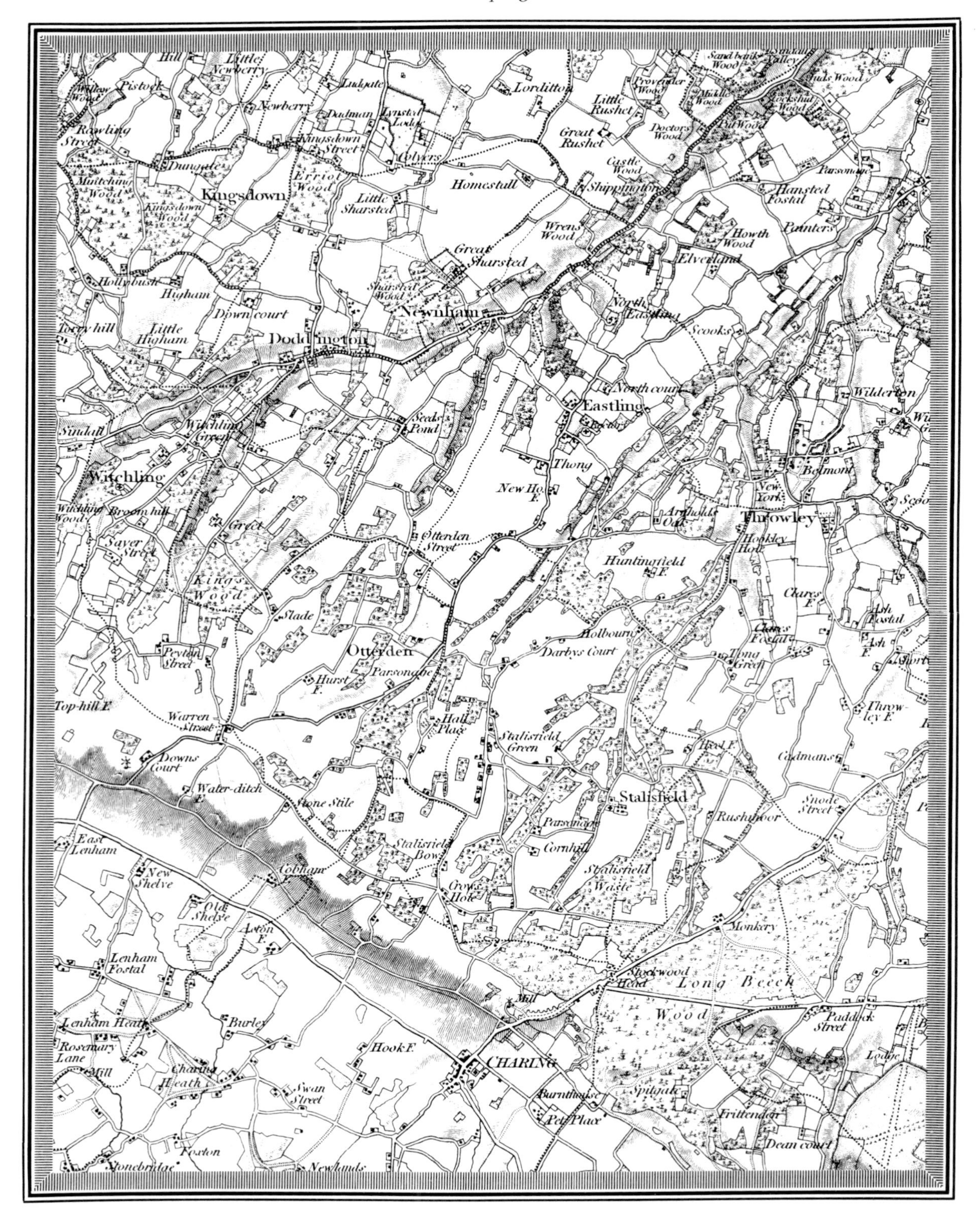

Hill
Little Newberry
Pistock
Rawling Street
Newberry
Ludgate
Dadman
Lynsted Lodge
Kingsdown Street
Colyers
Lorditton
Little Rushet
Great Rushet
Doctors Wood
Provender Wood
Middle Wood
Sand bank Wood
Syndale Valley
Judds Wood
Pel Wood
Castle Wood
Shippington
Parsonage
Hansted Fostal
Dungate
Muntching Wood
Kingsdown Wood
Kingsdown
Erriot Wood
Little Sharsted
Homestall
Wrens Wood
Howth Wood
Painters
Elverland
Great Sharsted
Sharsted Wood
Hollybush
Higham
Down court
Newnham
North Eastling
Scooks
Torry hill
Little Higham
Doddington
North court
Eastling
Rectory
Wilderton
Sindall
Witchling Green
Seeds Pond
Witchling
Belmont
Thong
New Ho. F.
New York
Witchling Wood
Broom hill
Great
Arnolds Oak
Throwley
Sayer Street
Otterden Street
Hockley Hole
Huntingfield F.
Kings Wood
Clares F.
Ash Fostal
Slade
Holbourn
Clares Fostal
Peyton Street
Otterden
Darbys Court
Tong Green
Ash F.
Hurst F.
Parsonage
Top-hill F.
Warren Street
Hall Place
Throw-ley F.
Stalisfield Green
Reed F.
Codmans
Downs Court
Water-ditch F.
Stone Stile
Stalisfield
Snode Street
Parsonage
Rushmoor
East Lenham
Stalisfield Bow
Cornhill
New Shelve
Cobham F.
Crow Hole
Stalisfield Waste
Old Shelve
Monkery
Lenham Fostal
Stockwood Head
Long Beech Wood
Paddock Street
Mill
Lenham Heath
Burley
Rosemary Lane
Mill
Hook F.
CHARING
Charing Heath
Lodge
Swan Street
Burnthouse
Spitgate
Pett Place
Frittenden
Dean court
Foxton
Stonebridge
Newlands

pagan place-names in Kent. On the crest of the Downs is Thurnham castle, while southwards on the ragstone is another small castle at Sutton Valence.

Map 25 The region between Charing and Faversham is a land of hills and deep valleys, notably that running from Wichling through Doddington and Newnham towards Ospringe on Walting Street. At Charing there was an archbishop's palace and an Eleanor Cross. Part of the former survives near the church but the latter was removed to London. Near Throwley lies Belmont, the fine home of Baron Harris of Seringapatam, whose ancestor conquered Mysore. Little has changed since 1801 and this remains a beautiful and undeveloped part of the county.

Map 26 (overleaf) This is another area of largely unspoilt villages including Godmersham, with its Jane Austen associations, and Chilham, a heritage village with a Norman keep and Jacobean mansion. This well preserved village surrounds a fine square lying between the church and the gates of the big house. Northwards the map includes much of the forest of Blean, where the Courtenay riots took place in 1838, and also touches the outskirts of Faversham and the suburb of Ospringe with its Maison Dieu. To the south is

Chilham square facing east towards the church in 1903. Careful preservation has ensured that this beautiful square has remained essentially unspoilt (see page 83).

Map 26

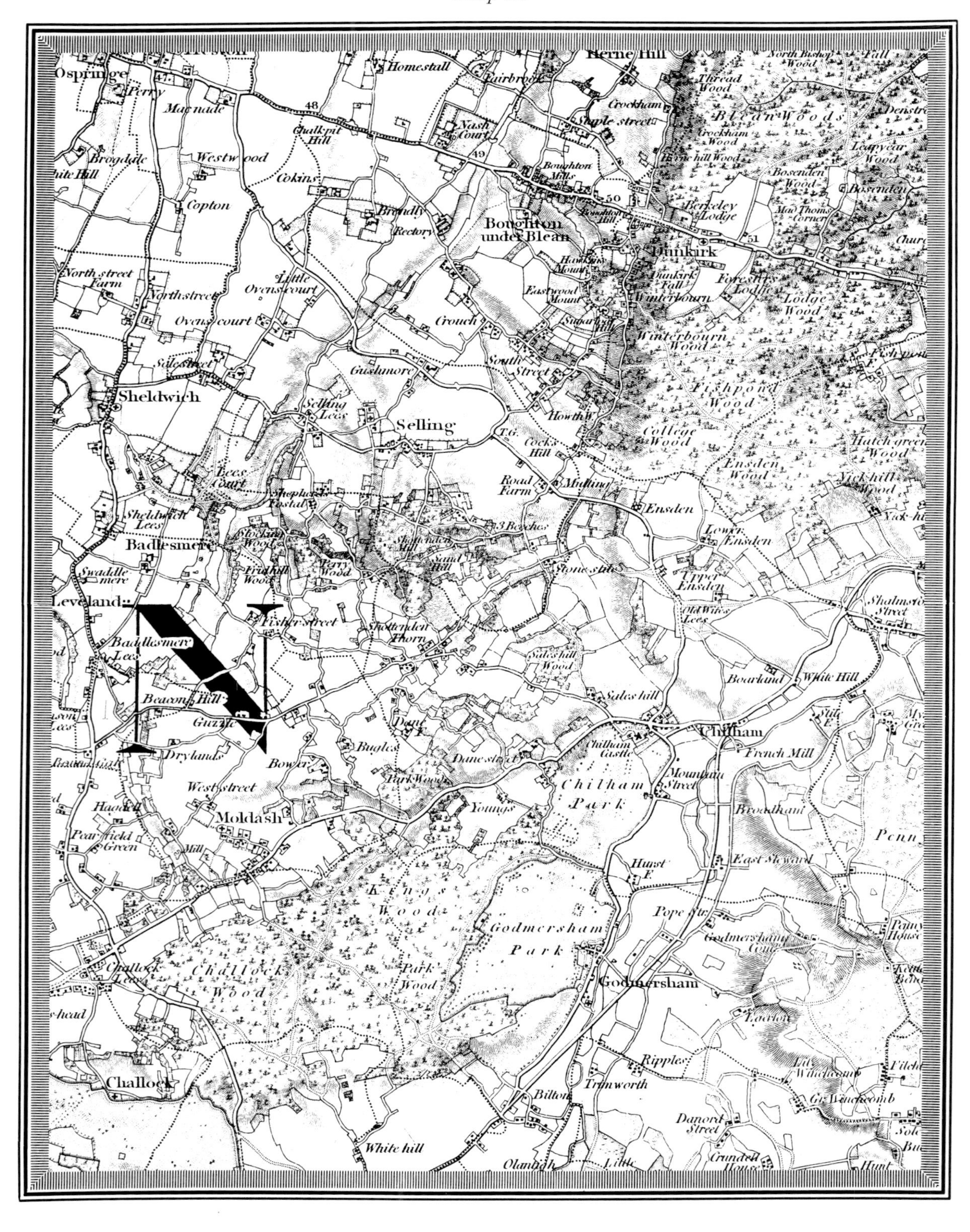

Ospringe
Perry
Homestall
Fairbrook
Herne Hill
Thread Wood
Crockham
Blean Woods
Marnade
Chalkpit Hill
Nash Court
Staple street
Crockham Wood
Leapyear Wood
Brogdale
Westwood
Cokins
Boughton Mills
Bosenden Wood
Copton
Brendly
Rectory
Boughton under Blean
Berkeley Lodge
Dunkirk
North street Farm
Little Ovens court
Northstreet
Ovens court
Crouch
Eastwood Mount
Winterbourn
Lodge Wood
Winterbourn Wood
Sales street
Gushmore
South Street
Sheldwich
Selling Lees
Selling
Fishpond Wood
College Wood
Cocks Hill
Ensden Wood
Lees Court
Road Farm
Ensden
Sheldwich Lees
Badlesmere
Lower Ensden
Upper Ensden
Perry Wood
Stone stile
Swaddle mere
Leveland
Fisher street
Shottenden Thorn
Old Wife's Lees
Badlesmere Lees
Sales hill Wood
Boarland
White Hill
Beacon Hill
Sales hill
Chilham
Chilham Castle
French Mill
Dryland
Bugles
Dane street
Bower
Park Wood
Chilham Park
Mountain Street
West street
Moldash
Youngs
Broadham
Penn
Pearfield Green
Mill
Hurst F.
East Stoward
Kings Wood
Pope str.
Godmersham Park
Godmersham Court
Challock Lees
Challock Wood
Park Wood
Godmersham
Ripples
Challock
Billton
Trimworth
Gr. Winchcomb
Danord Street
Crundell House
White hill
Olantigh

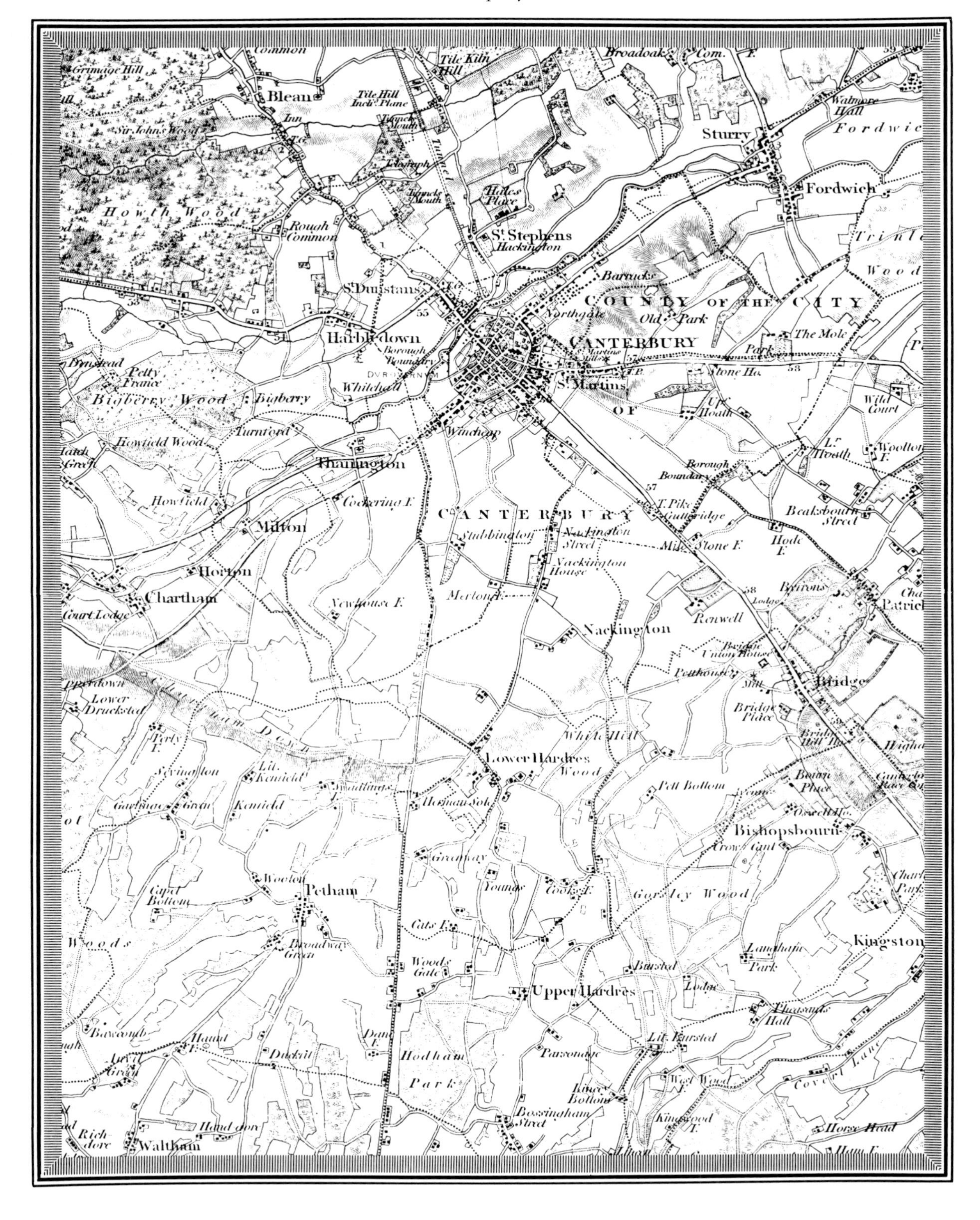
Common
Grimage Hill
Sir John's Wood
Howth Wood
Blean
Tile Kiln Hill
Tile Hill Incl. Plane
Broadoak Com.
Walmore Hall
Sturry
Fordwich
Fordwich
Hales Place
Rough Common
St. Stephens
Hackington
St. Dunstans
Barracks
COUNTY OF THE CITY
Northgate
Old Park
The Mole
Harbledown
Borough Boundary
CANTERBURY
St. Martins
Stone Ho.
Petty France
Bigberry Wood
Bigbury
Whitehall
OF
Upr. Howth
Wild Court
Turnford
Howfield Wood
Wincheap
Lr. Howth
Thannington
Borough Boundary
Howfield
Cockering F.
T. Pike
Gutteridge
Beaksbourn Street
CANTERBURY
Milton
Stubbington
Nackington Street
Mile Stone F.
Hode F.
Nackington House
Horton
Chartham
Court Lodge
Merton
Newhouse F.
Byrons
Lodge
Patrick
Nackington
Renwell
Bridge Union House
Petthouse
Mill
Bridge
Lower Druckstead
STONE STREET
Bridge Place
Perty F.
White Hill
Bridge Hill Ho.
Lower Hardres
Wood
Lit. Kenfield
Pett Bottom
Bourn Place
Kenfield
Oswell Ho.
Bishopsbourn
Crow's Camp
Wootton
Petham
Capel Bottom
Youngs
Cooks F.
Gardley Wood
Cats F.
Woods
Broadway Green
Kingston
Woods Gate
Bursted
Langham Park
Upper Hardres
Lodge
Pheasants Hall
Bawcomb
Dane F.
Duckitt
Hodham Park
Parsonage
Lit. Bursted
West Wood
Covert Lane
Bossingham Street
Kingwood
Horse Head
Richdore
Waltham

Map 26 cont

the ancient forest of King's Wood and the valley of the Great Stour, across which from Chilham there is a distinctive clump of trees on the hillside, a barrow known as Julliberrie's Grave.

Map 27 (previous page) This map shows the city of Canterbury with its environs. Although in recent years the city itself has expanded, the pattern of the medieval town is still apparent. The magnificent cathedral dominates the city, and there are extensive sections of the town walls extant, with the remains of St Augustine's Abbey without the city centre. The bombing of Canterbury in 1942 severely damaged the southern end of the medieval town and also half of the nearby village of Sturry. The tiny town of Fordwich was a chartered borough, a limb of Sandwich and the port for Canterbury on the Great Stour. The south-eastern part of the map is crossed by the Little Stour or Nailbourne, which gives its name to a series of villages.

Detail map 27 (overleaf) The city of Canterbury at the end of the last century, including the cathedral of Christchurch, Burgate and the High Street. The area to the south of Christchurch Gate (i.e. the bottom right hand quarter of the map), was almost wholly destroyed in the raid of 1942 and has since been redeveloped in a modern style.

Canterbury High Street, looking north towards Westgate at the turn of the century (opposite). This part of the town escaped the worst of the destruction in 1942 and many of these old buildings survive (below).

GAYWOOD'S
CANTERBURY
RESTAURANT
DINING ROOMS
The New
MACKESON'S
HYTHE
ALES
OLD CHINA
WORKS OF ART
KILMARNOCK
WHISKY
PHILPOT'S
CYCLE
DEPOT

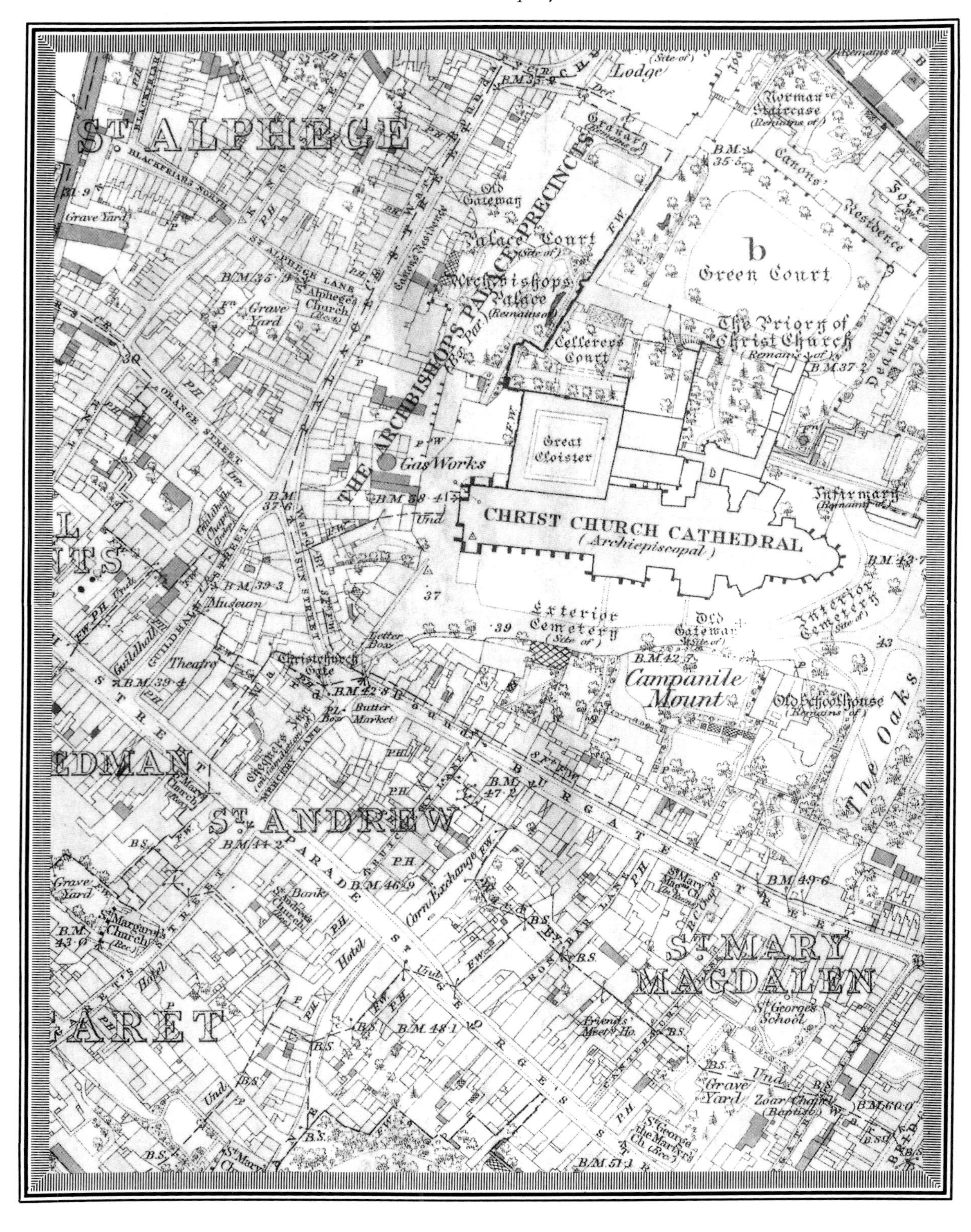
St. ALPHEGE
BLACKFRIARS NORTH
Grave Yard
St. ALPHEGE LANE
St. Alphege Church (Rec.)
Grave Yard
ORANGE STREET
Lodge
Granary
Norman Staircase (Remains of)
Canons' Residence
Old Gateway
THE ARCHBISHOP'S PALACE PRECINCTS
Palace Court (Site of)
Archbishop's Palace (Remains of)
Cellerer's Court
b
Green Court
The Priory of Christ Church (Remains of)
Deanery
Great Cloister
Gas Works
Infirmary (Remains of)
CHRIST CHURCH CATHEDRAL
(Archiepiscopal)
SUN STREET
Museum
Guildhall
GUILDHALL
Theatre
Christchurch Gate
Butter Market
MERCERY LANE
Letter Box
Exterior Cemetery (Site of)
Old Gateway (Site of)
Interior Cemetery (Site of)
Campanile Mount
Old Schoolhouse (Remains of)
The Oaks
BURGATE STREET
St. ANDREW
PARADE
Corn Exchange
St. Andrew's Church (Rec.)
Bank
Hotel
Grave Yard
St. Margaret's Church (Rec.)
St. MARY MAGDALEN
St. Mary Mag. Ch.
St. George's School
Friends' Meet. Ho.
Grave Yard
Zoar Chapel (Baptist)
St. George the Martyr's Ch. (Rec.)
ST. GEORGE'S STREET
ARET
EDMAN
ITS
B.M. 35·9
B.M. 38·4
B.M. 39·3
B.M. 39·4
B.M. 42·8
B.M. 42·7
B.M. 43·7
B.M. 44·2
B.M. 46·9
B.M. 47·2
B.M. 48·1
B.M. 49·6
B.M. 51·1
B.M. 60·0
B.M. 37·2
B.M. 35·5
B.M. 43·6
31·9

Chilham in 1987 appears little changed since 1903 except for the increase in traffic (see map 77).

The view of the sea front at Deal from the pier today (see overleaf).

Apart from the addition of a clock in the church tower, this view of Sandwich is little changed (see page 88).

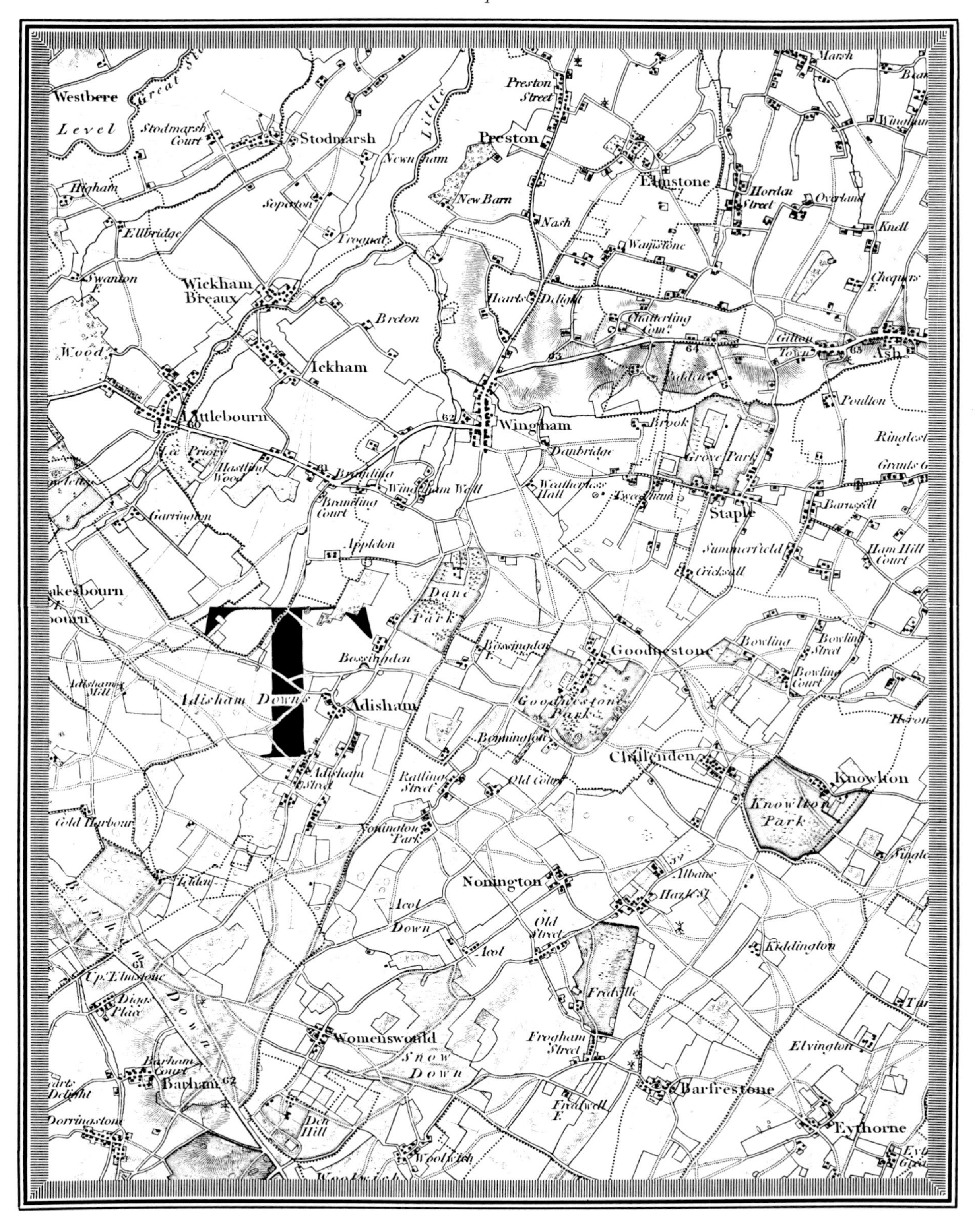
Westbere
Stodmarsh Court
Stodmarsh
Preston Street
Preston
Elmstone
Horden Street
Overland
Newnham
New Barn
Nash
Wickham Breaux
Ickham
Littlebourn
Wingham
Staple
Goodnestone
Goodnestone Park
Adisham
Adisham Downs
Adisham Street
Chillenden
Knowlton
Knowlton Park
Nonington
Womenswould
Snow Down
Barham Court
Barham
Barfrestone
Eythorne
Elvington
Fredville
Frogham Street
Kiddington
Acol
Ash
Dane Park
Bossingden
Appleton
Grove Park
Brook
Weatherless Hall
Tweedham
Summerfield
Ham Hill Court
Ringlest
Poulton
Knell
Chequers F.
Gilton Town
Chatterling Court
Hearts Delight
Breton
Ellbridge
Swanton F.
Higham
Soperton
Trognal
Wamstone
Lee Priory
Hastling Wood
Garrington
Bramling
Bramling Court
Wingham Well
Danbridge
Barnsall
Bowling Street
Bowling Court
Rattling Street
Old Court
Bonnington
Nonington Park
Acol Down
Old Street
Up. Elmstone
Diggs Place
Gold Harbour
Dorrinaston
Den Hill
Woolwich
Fredwell F.
Bossingden F.
Cricksall
Adisham Mill
Level
Wood

Map 28 (previous page) This is still an unspoilt area of east Kent, even though there is a coal mine at Snowdon in Nonington, and since the first Ordnance Survey map the new mining village of Aylesham has been developed on Acol Down. Even so it is a well populated area with numerous settlements of considerable antiquity. Wingham has a tree-lined main street and a fine church, and the Norman church at Barfreston is also of note. Below Littlebourne on the Little Stour lies Wickhambreaux, a name which gave rise to a rare mistake on the 1801 map for it also appears at West Wickham near Beckenham.

Map 29 This region marks the centre of early Saxon settlement in the county. In the north is Richborough, the Roman fort and depot, with its vast walls still standing. Nearby is the town of Sandwich with its three fine churches and other evidence of medieval wealth. In the centre of the map lies Eastry—the eastern region—and also Woodnesborough—the 'hill of Woden'. The hamlet of Finglesham means the 'place of the prince'. This is also an area of more recent industrial growth with the Kent coalfield, although the mine at Tilmanstone has now been closed, but traditionally it was an area of arable farming and until recent

Deal sea front from the pier in 1902. This view is virtually unchanged and the conglomeration of seventeenth- and eighteenth-century houses still presents a unique vista (see page 84).

Map 29

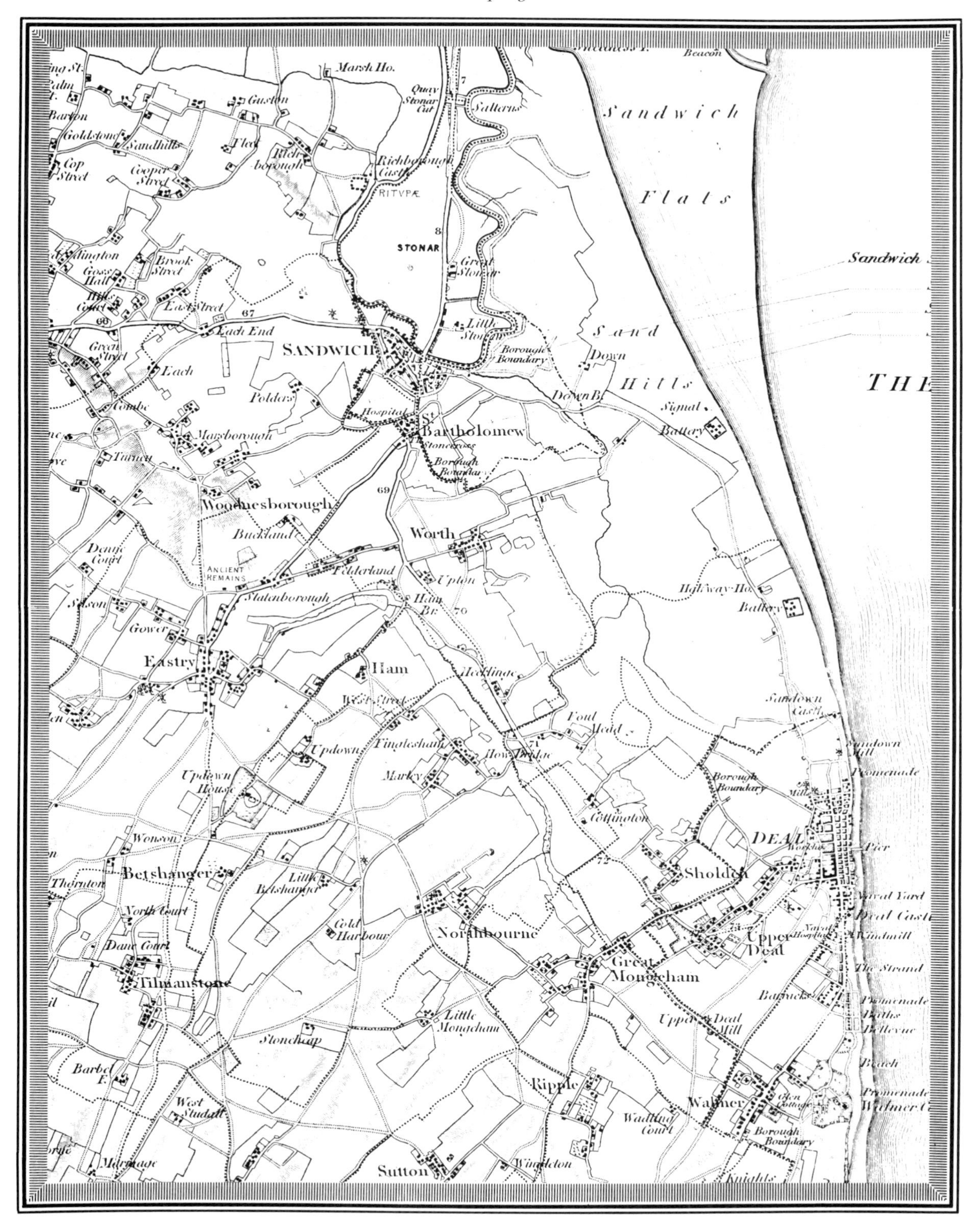

Marsh Ho.
Quay
Stonar Cut
Salterns
Sandwich Flats
Beacon
Guston
Goldstone
Sandhills
Fleet
Rich-borough
Richborough Castle
RITVPÆ
Cop Street
Cooper Street
STONAR
Great Stonar
Sandwich
Brook Street
Goss Hall
Hills Court
East Street
Each End
SANDWICH
Little Stonar
Borough Boundary
Sand Down Hills
Green Street
Each
Polders
Down B.
Signal Battery
THE
Combe
Hospital
St. Bartholomew
Stonecross
Marsborough
Borough Boundary
Woodnesborough
Buckland
Worth
Dene Court
ANCIENT REMAINS
Felderland
Upton
Statenborough
Ham Br.
Halfway Ho.
Battery
Gower
Eastry
Ham
West Street
Hacklinge
Sandown Castle
Foul Mead
Sandown Hill
Promenade
Updown
Tinglesham
How Bridge
Marley
Updown House
Borough Boundary
Mill
Cottington
DEAL
Pier
Betshanger
Little Betshanger
Sholden
Thornton
North Court
Cold Harbour
Northbourne
Naval Yard
Deal Castle
Windmill
Upper Deal
Naval Hospital
Dane Court
Great Mongeham
The Strand
Tilmanstone
Barracks
Promenade
Baths
Bellevue
Upper Deal Mill
Little Mongeham
Barbel F.
Beach
Ripple
Promenade
Walmer
Glen Cottage
West Studdal
Borough Boundary
Sutton
Knights
7
8
67
68
69
70
71
72

The corner of Market Street and King Street, Sandwich, with the tower of St Clement's Church behind in about 1880. Although the shops have been modernized and dress has changed, this is still a recognizable view of Sandwich with its narrow streets and dominating churches (see page 83).

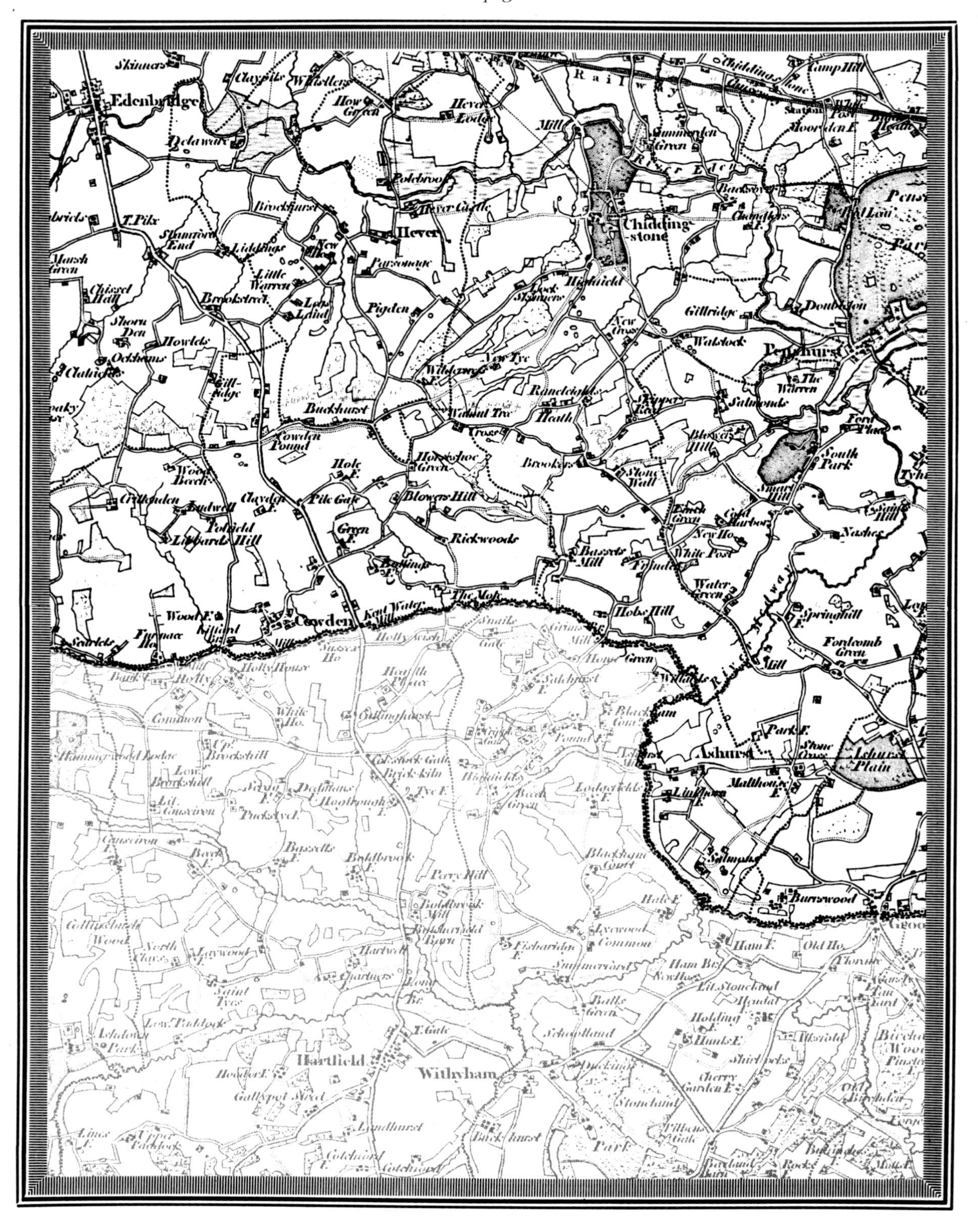
Skinners
Claypits
Edenbridge
Delaware
How Green
Hever Lodge
Railway
Mill
Summerden Green
Camp Hill
Station
River Eden
Poolbrook
Hever Castle
Hever
Brockhurst
T. Pike
Chiddingstone
Parsonage
Liddings
Little Warren
Brookstreet
Marsh Green
Chissel Hill
Shorn Den
Howlets
Ockhams
Pigden
Highfield
Gillridge
Doubleton
Walstock
Penshurst
The Warren
Buckhurst
Cowden Pound
Walnut Tree
Cross
Heath
Salmonds
South Park
Ford Place
Horseshoe Green
Blowers Hill
Hole F.
Pile Gate
Green F.
Brookers
Stone Wall
Smart Hill
Cold Harbor
New Ho.
White Post
Rickwoods
Bassetts Mill
Water Green
Hobs Hill
Crittenden
Ludwell
Wood Beech
Wood F.
Furnace Ho
Cowden
Kent Water Mill
The Moat
River Medway
Springhill
Fordcomb Green
Nashes
Mill
Ashurst
Park F.
Stone Cross
Malthouse F.
Burnswood
Perry Hill
Hale F.
Ham F.
Old Ho.
Holding F.
Hunts F.
Ashdown Park
Hartfield
Withyham
Gallypot Street
Stoneland
Park

Map 29 cont

years had rare survivals of open-field husbandry. The coast from the mouth of the Stour to Kingsdown south of Walmer Castle is protected by the Goodwin Sands and was a safe anchorage for sailing vessels in bad weather; three of Henry VIII's castles – Sandown, Deal and Walmer – were built here. Deal was an important port for colliers from the north-east and now relies in part upon Betteshanger colliery, just west of the town, for its prosperity.

Map 30 (previous page) This south-west corner of the county includes Hever with its castellated mansion, home of Anne Boleyn; Edenbridge, a small market town on the headwaters of the Medway where there has been some growth of commuter traffic; and Cowden with its furnace pond, a memory of the former Wealden iron industry. It is a largely unspoilt area merging imperceptibly into Surrey and Sussex, the actual boundary being a stream called the Kent Water, a tributary of the Medway. The area also includes the National Trust village of Chiddingstone, although the pattern of the nineteenth-century village was altered when High Street House was demolished and the mock Gothic castle was built somewhat further from the church. Penshurst, the home of the Sidney family, is another unspoilt village with the fourteenth-century Place nestling in a loop of the Medway.

Map 31 The ancient town of Tonbridge with its crossing of the Medway and its Norman castle controlled entry to the Weald, but southwards was forest and heathland. In 1606 a chalybeate spring was discovered by accident in this forested area and the spa, Tunbridge Wells, was born. The district round the spring, with the famous Pantiles, was built up during that century, but the real growth came in the nineteenth century. The coming of the railway to Tonbridge, and later to the Wells, signalled a rapid growth through Southborough to the Sussex border. Pembury, Bidborough and Leigh have also grown since the beginning of the nineteenth century, but this is still a region of woodland and heath and of outcrops of sandstone, of which High Rocks on the county boundary is the most famous.

Detail map 31 (overleaf) The heart of Tunbridge Wells, including the Pantiles, as it had developed by the end of the last century. The centre of population has now moved northwards beyond the station and towards Southborough.

Map 32 (overleaf) This map shows the heart of the Weald from Paddock Wood, in the north, to the Sussex border at Lamberhurst. It comprises both the heavy clays of the Medway valley and the hills of the high weald from Brenchley to Horsmonden and Goudhurst. It is a rich agricultural region and a major hop-producing district. A railway called 'the Hop Pickers' Line' was built from Paddock Wood on the main Tonbridge to Ashford line, to Goudhurst and beyond, but was closed after the mechanization of hop-picking. On the southern border lies Scotney Castle, the medieval ruin on the River Teise, and the nineteenth-century mansion on higher ground. A similar development took place at Bayham, west of Lamberhurst, where the low-lying abbey and original mansion were abandoned for a site on the ridge during the last century. The abbey is now in the care of the Department of the Environment.

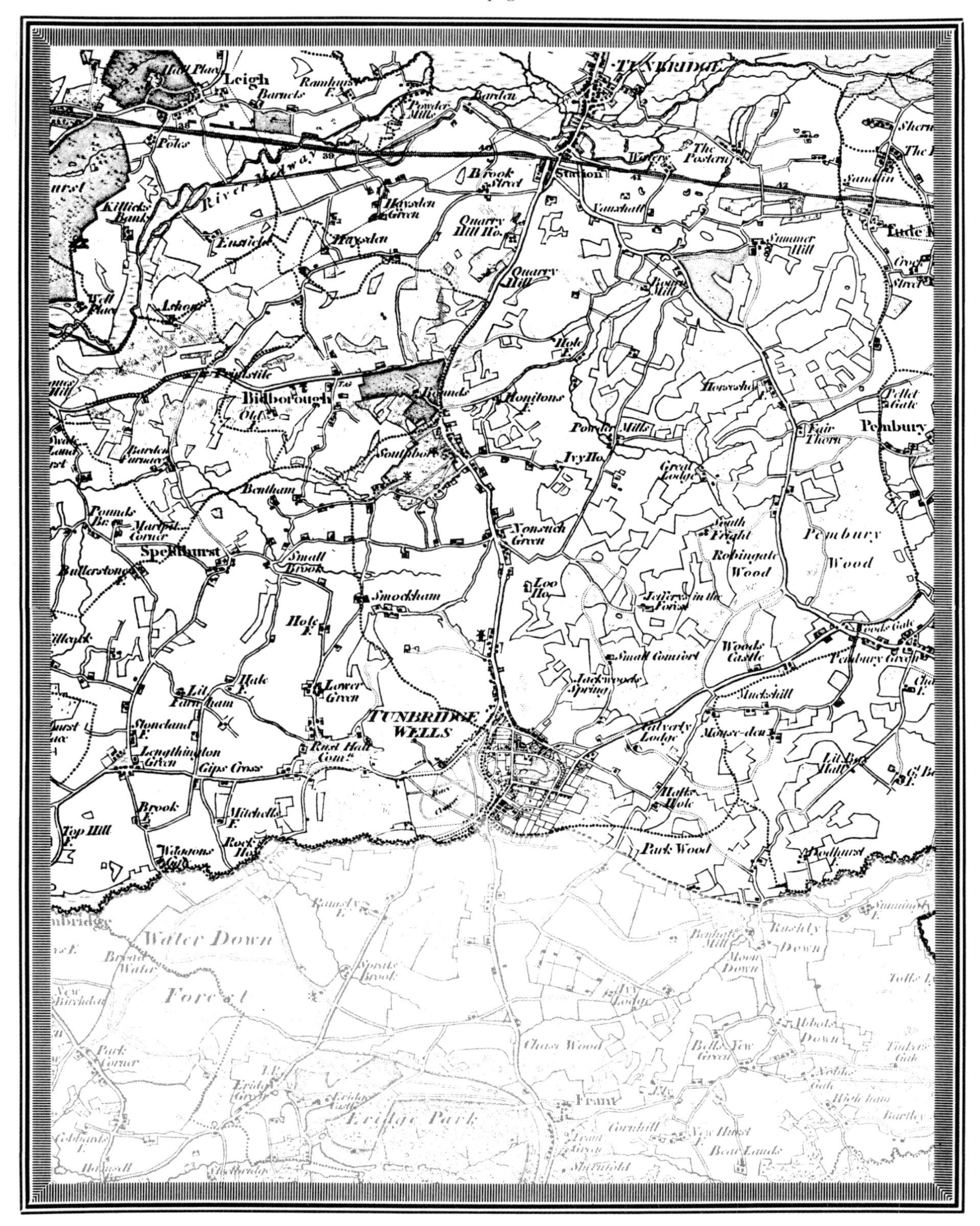
Leigh
Hall Place
Barnets
Powder Mills
Barden
Poles
River Medway
Brook Street
Station
The Postern
Vauxhall
Haysden Green
Haysden
Quarry Hill Ho.
Killicks Bank
Summer Hill
Quarry Hill
Well Place
Hole F.
Pellet Gate
Pembury
Fair Thorn
Bidborough
Bounds
Honitons F.
Powder Mills
Southborough
Ivy Ho.
Great Lodge
Bentham
Nonsuch Green
South Fright
Pembury Wood
Robingate Wood
Pounds Br.
Speldhurst
Small Brook
Loo Ho.
Smockham
Jefferys in the Forest
Hole F.
Woods Castle
Pembury Green
Small Comfort
Jackwoods Spring
Muckshill
Hale F.
Lower Green
Lit. Farnham
TUNBRIDGE WELLS
Stoneland F.
Calverly Lodge
Mouse-den
Lengthington Green
Gips Cross
Rust Hall Com.
Brook F.
Mitchells F.
Top Hill
Rock Hall
Park Wood
Water Down
Forest
Rushly Down
Moon Down
Ivy Lodge
Abbots Down
Chase Wood
Bells Yew Green
Park Corner
Eridge Park
Frant
Cornhill
Beau Lands

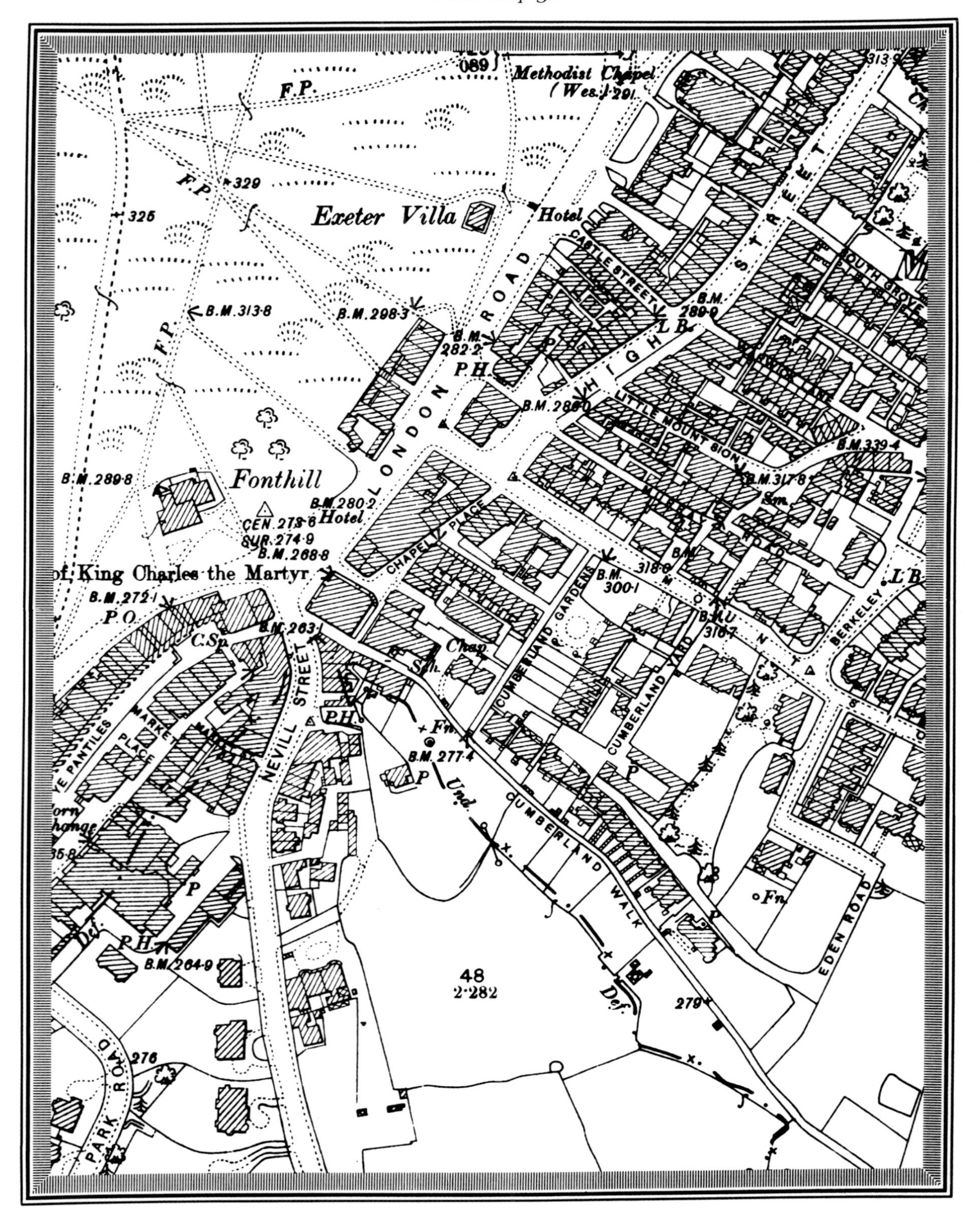
Methodist Chapel (Wes.) 291
F.P.
Exeter Villa
Hotel
CASTLE STREET
HIGH STREET
LONDON ROAD
SOUTH GROVE
LITTLE MOUNT SION
Fonthill
Hotel
of King Charles the Martyr
CHAPEL PLACE
CUMBERLAND GARDENS
CUMBERLAND YARD
BERKELEY
P.O.
NEVILL STREET
MARKET PLACE
PANTILES
CUMBERLAND WALK
EDEN ROAD
PARK ROAD
48
2·282
B.M. 313·8
B.M. 298·3
B.M. 289·8
B.M. 280·2
B.M. 268·8
B.M. 272·1
B.M. 263·1
B.M. 277·4
B.M. 264·9
B.M. 339·4
B.M. 317·8
B.M. 300·1
CEN. 273·6
SUR. 274·9

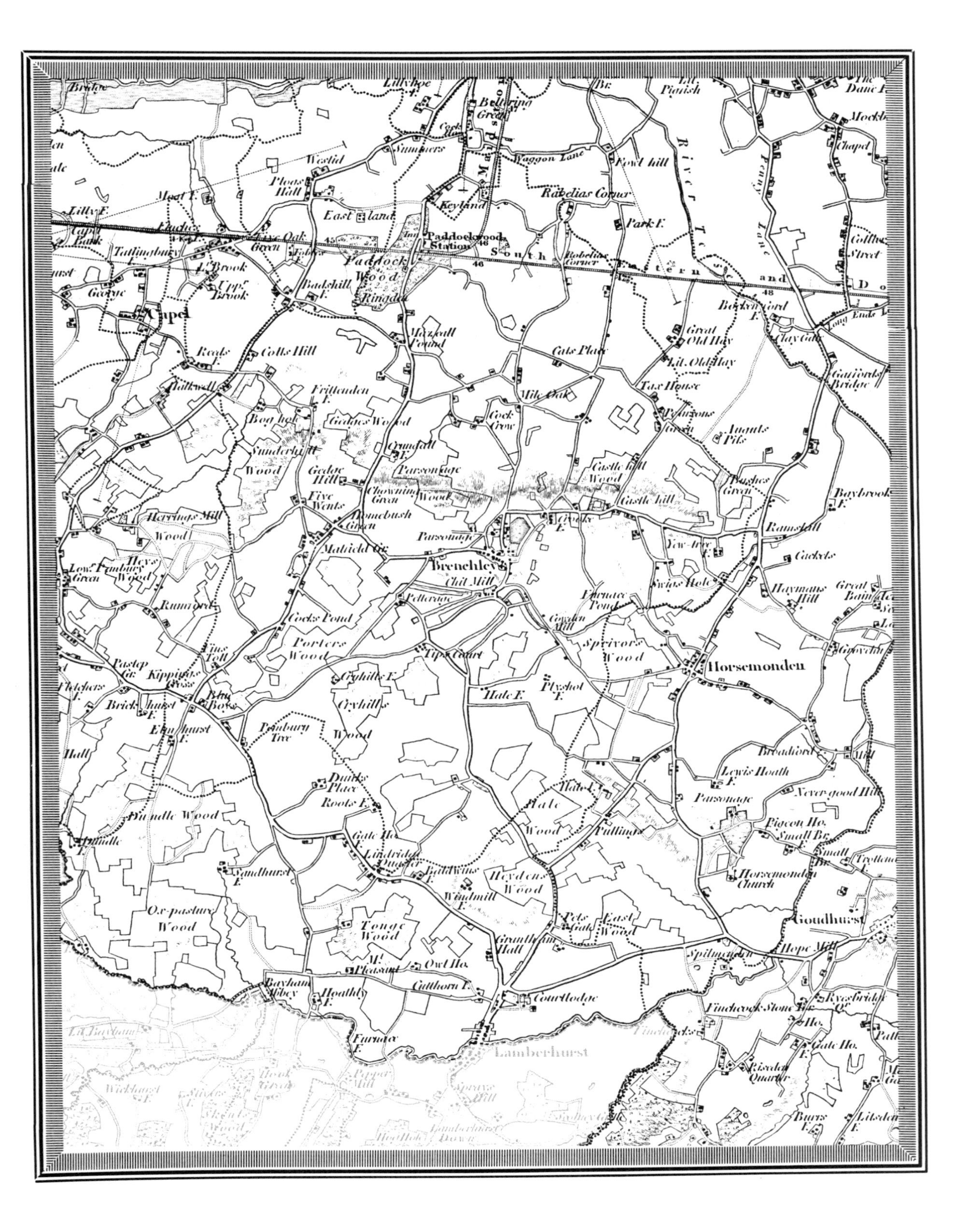

Lillyhoe
Beltring Green
Summers
Westid
Ploas Hall
Moat F.
Lilly F.
Waggon Lane
Fowl hill
Rabelias Corner
Keyland
East land
Park F.
Paddockwood Station
Paddock Wood
Ringden
Tatlingbury
Five Oak Green
Badshill F.
George
Capel
Mazeall Pound
Colts Hill
Reads
Cats Place
Great Old Hay
Lit. Old Hay
Tax House
Mile Oak
Frittenden F.
Gedges Wood
Cock Crow
Crundall F.
Parsonage
Castle hill Wood
Castle hill
Gedge Hill
Five Wents
Chowning Wood
Homebush Green
Herrings Mill
Wood
Bushes Green
Baybrook F.
Ramstill
Cackets
Yew-tree F.
Swiss Hole
Mathield Gr.
Brenchley
Chit Mill
Furnace Pond
Haymans Hill
Heys Wood
Rumford
Cocks Pond
Porters Wood
Tips Court
Spririors Wood
Horsemonden
Pastep Gr.
Kippings Cross
Blue Boys
Cryhills F.
Cryhills Wood
Hale F.
Plyshot F.
Brick hurst F.
Elmhurst F.
Pembury Tree
Broadford
Lewis Heath
Parsonage
Never good Hill
Dundle Wood
Ducks Place
Roots F.
Hale Wood
Pullings
Pigeon Ho.
Small Br.
Horsemonden Church
Gate Ho.
Lindridge Quarter
Baldwins
Heydens Wood
Windmill F.
Sandhurst F.
Ox-pasture Wood
Tonge Wood
Pets Gate
East Wood
Goudhurst
Grantham Hall
Spilmonden
Hope Mill
Mt. Pleasant
Owl Ho.
Bayham Abbey
Heathly F.
Catthorn F.
Courtlodge
Finchcock Stone Ho.
Ryesbridge Gr.
Furnace F.
Lamberhurst
Gate Ho.
Risden Quarter
Burrs F.
Lisden F.
South Eastern and Dover
River Teise
Penny Lane
Bockingford F.
Clay Gate
Long Ends
Gatfords Bridge
Augets Pits
Great Bain
Goudhurst
Chapel
Mockbeggar
Colliers Street
Lit. Pixtish
The Dane

SOLD
Parsons

The old clothworkers' hall at Biddenden now converted into homes (see page 99).

Collier Street
Rankins Fm
Bishop's Fm
Sutton Valence
Boyton Court
Stallance
The Harbour
Lamb's Cross
Spark's Hall
Boughton Bottom
Charlton Fm
Roman Road
Chart Bottom
Moat Fm
Brook Ho
Reed Court Fm
River Beult
Great Tilden
Stile Bridge
Old Hertsfield
Holbrook
Lake Fm
Dairy Ho
Chainhurst
Den Fm
Chain Dene Fm
Little Tilden Fm
Hurst Green
Rabbit's Cross
Elderden Fm
Devil's Den
Lake Fm
New Lodge Ho
Ashurst Court
Lower Fm
Hearnden Green
Spitzbrook
Underling Green
Bogden Fm
Brandenbury
Broad Forstal Fm
Home Fm
Cross-at-Hand
Parkenden Fm
Dunbury Fm
Murzie Fm
Haviker Street
Blue House Fm
Moatenden Fm
Farthing Green
Gatehouse Fm
Milebush
The Grange
Babylon Fm
New Barn Fm
Plumtree Green
Little Pattenden
Clapper Fm
Sweetlands
Couchman Green
Bardingley
Stone Stile
Brook Fm
Church Fm
Newstead Fm
Hawkenbury
Leighbridge Fm
Longend Fm
Great Pattenden
Cemy
Wanshurst Green
Boarden Fm
Overbridge Fm
Duckhurst Fm
Summerhill Fm
Black Mill Fm
Claygate
Turkey Farmhouse
Fisher's Fm
Kelsham Fm
Gravelpit Farm Cotts
Marden
Mountain Fm
Lindridge
Limekiln Fm
Inn
Slaney Place
Waterlane Fm
Westfield Ho
Little Cheveney Fm
Cannon Fm
Park Ho
Spills Hill Fm
Place Fm
Staplehurst
Aydhurst Fm
The Plain
Pagehurst
Spilsill Court
Marden Beech
Widehurst
Exhurst Manor
Beale Fm
Marden Thorn
Appleton Fm
Springfield
Brattle Fm
Hennhurst Fm
The Old Manor
Sinkhurst Green
Baybrooks
Great Cheveney
Saynden Fm
Ely Court
Broadlake
Maplehurst
Little Brookwood
Northiam Fm
Plain Fm
Chapmans Fm
Convent
Loves Fm
Tanner Ho
Bletchingley Fm
Iden Grange
Cherry Tree Fm
School House Fm
Snoad Wood
Lovehurst Manor
Bromley Barn
Peasridge Fm
Ash Fm
Harts Heath Fm
Little Wadd Fm
Frittenden
Hushheath Manor
Mathurst Fm
Earthwork
Ponds Fm
Grovehurst
Winchet Hill
Curtisden Green
Great Horden Fm
Knox Bridge
Great Wadd Fm
Tanyard
Bounds End Fm
Paley Fm
Rock Fm
Catherine Wheel
Finchurst
Blantyre Ho
(HM Detention Centre)
Tolehurst Fm
Whitsunden
Worms Hill
Hartridge Manor Fm
Brissenden Fm
Gore Court
Combourne Fm
Folly Hill Fm
Lowland Fm
Swan Fm
Round Green
Park Fm
Brewers Wood
Moats
Bockingfold Fm
Hartridge Ho
Comenden Manor
Little Brandfold
Blue Barn Fm
Colliers Green
Hocker Edge
Camden Hill
Bettenham Manor
Lidwells Ho
Ladham Ho
Hazelden Fm
Cranbrook Common
Sissinghurst Castle
Old Park Wood
Friezley
Trowswell
Frog's Hole
Whitewell Oasts
Roundshill Park Wood
Hammer Mill Fm
Hammer Wood
Four Wents
Wilsley Pound
Goudhurst
Iden Green
Flishinghurst
Kennel Holt Hotel
Sissinghurst
Lime Tree Fm
Trigg's Fm
Branden
Roger's
Cook's Wood
Spratsbourne Fm
Buckhurst Fm
Wilsley Green
Old Wilsley
Great Swifts
Smugley Fm
Glassenbury
High Tilt
Glassenbury Ho
Angley Ho
Causton Wood
Stream Fm
Golford
Middleton Fm
Angley Wood
Cranbrook
Cemy
Forge Fm
Angley Fm
Goddard's Green
Coursehorn
Chittenden Wood
Baker's Cross
Old Cloth Hall
Blackbush Wood
Hancock's Fm
Hemsted Forest
Dockenden
Mount Ephraim
Tilsden
dismantled railway
Twyssenden Manor
Hartley Ho
Little Coursehorne
Three Chimneys
Furnace Fm
Chittenden Fm
Goddard's Green
Bedgebury Cross
Pricklegate
Dove's Fm
Crabtree Fm
Bedgebury Park School
Hartley
Sch
Chequertree Fm
Robin's

Map 33

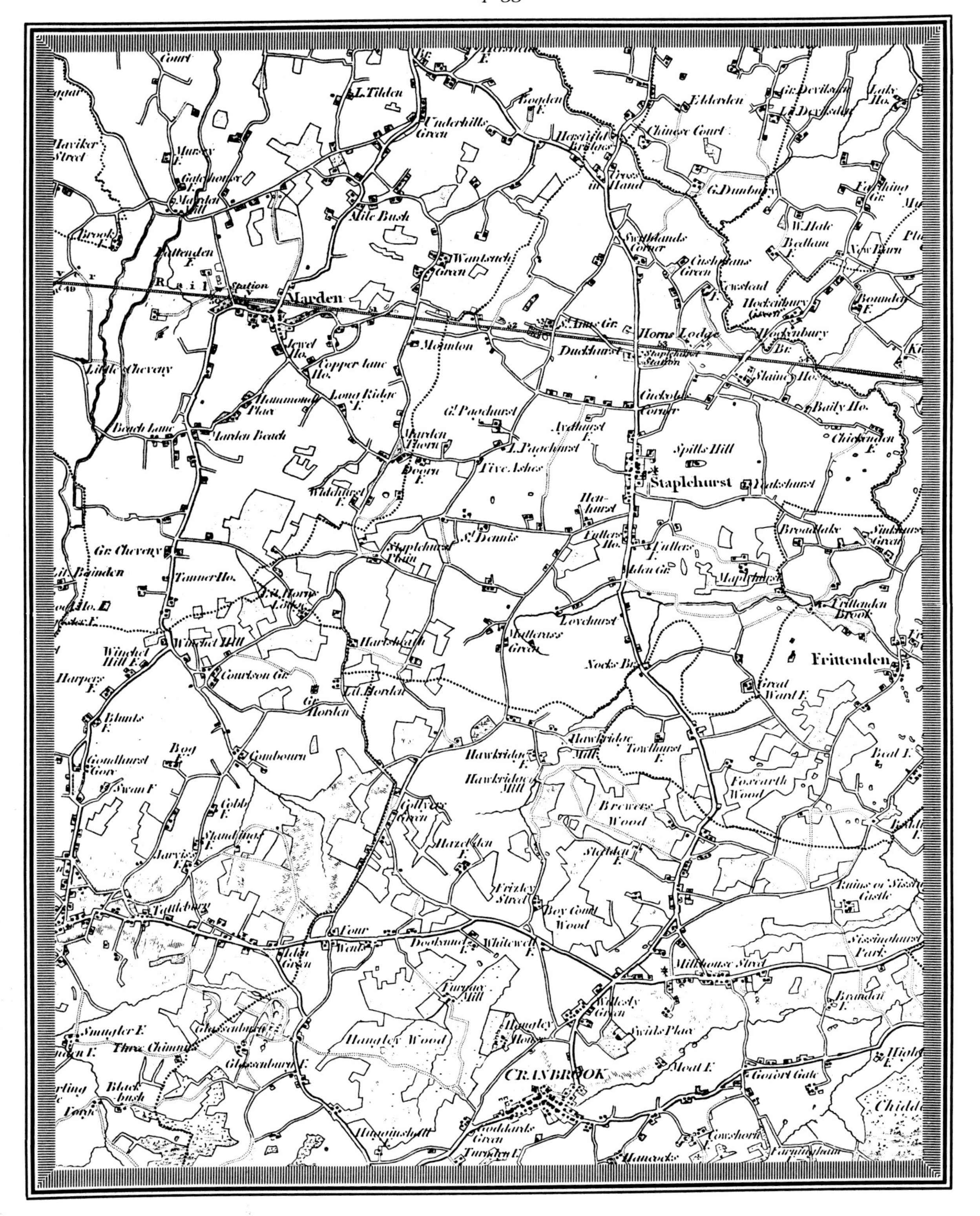

Court
L. Tilden
Underhills Green
Boogden F.
Elderden
Gr. Devilsden
Lt. Devilsden
Lake Ho.
Haviker Street
Mumsey F.
Gatehouse F.
Marden Hill
Hawkhurst Bridges
Chinese Court
Cross in Hand
G. Dunbury
Farthing Gr.
Mile Bush
W. Hale
Bedlam
New Barn
Brook F.
Pattenden F.
Wantsuch Green
Swithlands Corner
Cushmans Green
Newstead
Hockenbury Green
Bounder F.
Station
Marden
St. Anns Gr.
Horns Lodge
Hockenbury Br.
Little Cheveny
Jewel Ho.
Copper lane Ho.
Mounton
Duckhurst
Staplehurst Station
Slaney Ho.
Long Ridge F.
Hammond Place
Cuckold Corner
Baily Ho.
Beach Lane
Marden Beach
Gt. Pagehurst
Aydhurst F.
Chickenden F.
Marden Thorn
L. Pagehurst
Spills Hill
Doorn F.
Five Ashes
Staplehurst
Yokehurst
Wildhurst F.
Hen-hurst
Broadlake
Sinkhurst Green
Gr. Cheveny
Staplehurst Place
St. Dennis
Fullers Ho.
Fullers F.
Lit. Bainden
Tanner Ho.
Iden Gr.
Maplehurst
Lit. Horne Lodge
Frittenden Brook
Lovehurst
Winchet Hill F.
Winchet Hill
Hartshuth
Mattenss Green
Harpers F.
Courtson Gr.
Nocks Br.
Frittenden
Lit. Horden
Great Ward F.
Gr. Horden
Blunts F.
Hawkridge Mill
Towlhurst F.
Bog F.
Combourn
Hawkridge F.
Beal F.
Goudhurst Gore
Swan F.
Hawkridge Mill
Foxearth Wood
Cobb F.
Gillyers Green
Brewers Wood
Standings F.
Jarvis F.
Hazelden F.
Stylden F.
Ruins of Sissinghurst Castle
Frizley Street
Tattlebury
Boy Court Wood
Four Wents
Dooksnade F.
Whitewell F.
Iden Green
Sissinghurst Park
Milkhouse Street
Furnace Mill
Brandon F.
Wilsely Green
Smugler F.
Three Chimneys
Glassenbury
Hangler Ho.
Hangler Wood
Swifts Place
Glassenbury F.
Meat F.
Black-bush
CRANBROOK
Goford Gate
Hammonshill F.
Goddards Green
Turnden F.
Cowshorn
Hancocks
Farningham
Child

Map 33 and modern map 33 (previous page) This area of heavy clay is crossed by bands of Bethersden marble between Marden and Frittenden, but rises by low hills to Cranbrook in the south, the principal centre of population and a former cloth town. This was an undeveloped district before the coming of the railway from Tonbridge to Ashford but in the last forty years both Marden and Staplehurst have grown as commuter towns, although the area round Frittenden remains remote and undeveloped.

Map 34 (overleaf) This is another area of Wealden Kent where little has changed despite the fact that the main line to Ashford

runs through it. Villages such as Headcorn, Smarden and Biddenden are rich with fine medieval hall houses and dwellings formerly used by clothiers and their workers. Headcorn has become a commuter town, but otherwise little has changed in this area of clay and the streams of the Beult valley.

The clothworkers' hall at Biddenden in 1901. These houses have now been renovated and are a major attraction of the main street of this former centre of the clothmaking industry (see page 94).

Map 34

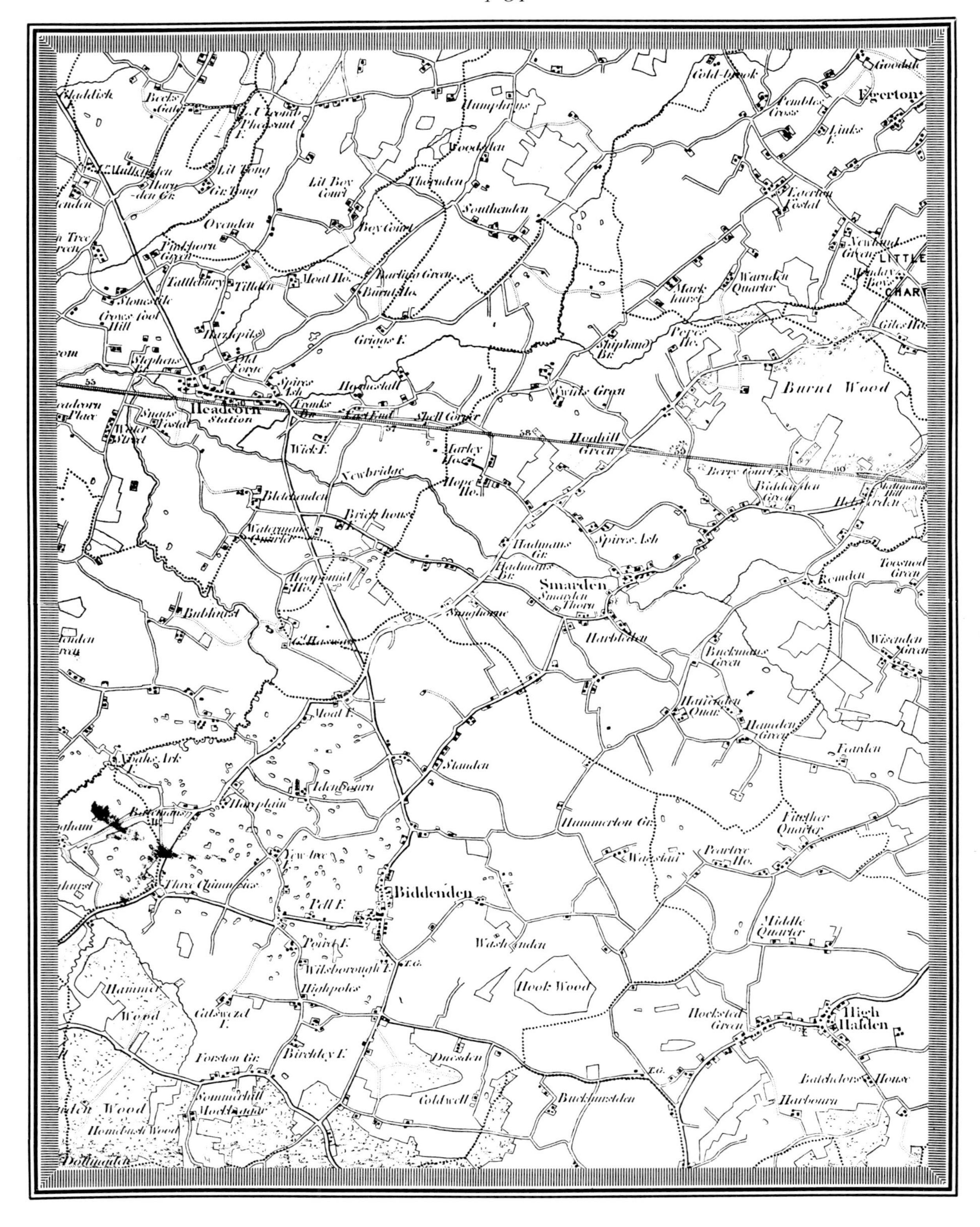
Egerton
Humphreys
Woodsden
Thornden
Southenden
Lit Boy Court
Boy Court
Ovenden
Pinkhorn Green
Tattlebury
Tillden
Moat Ho.
Burnt Ho.
Griggs F.
Stonestile
Crows foot Hill
Hazlepits
Old Forge
Spires Ash
Headcorn
Station
Shell Corner
Wick F.
Newbridge
Harley Ho.
Hope Ho.
Bletchenden
Brick house
Watermans Quarter
Hadmans Gr.
Spires Ash
Smarden
Harbleden
Mark hurst
Warnden Quarter
Shipland Br.
Burnt Wood
Hoathill Green
Berry Court
Biddenden Green
LITTLE
CHART
Giles Ho.
Bubhurst
Moat F.
Standen
Idenbourn
Hawplain
Hummerton Gr.
Peartree Ho.
Further Quarter
Yew tree F.
Three Chimnies
Pell F.
Biddenden
Washenden
Hook Wood
Wilsborough F.
Highpoles
Catswezel F.
Middle Quarter
Hockstead Green
High Halden
Forston Gr.
Birchley F.
Duesden
Coldwell
Buckhurstden
Batchelors House
Harbourn
Hammer Wood
Sommerhill
Homebush Wood
Dollingden

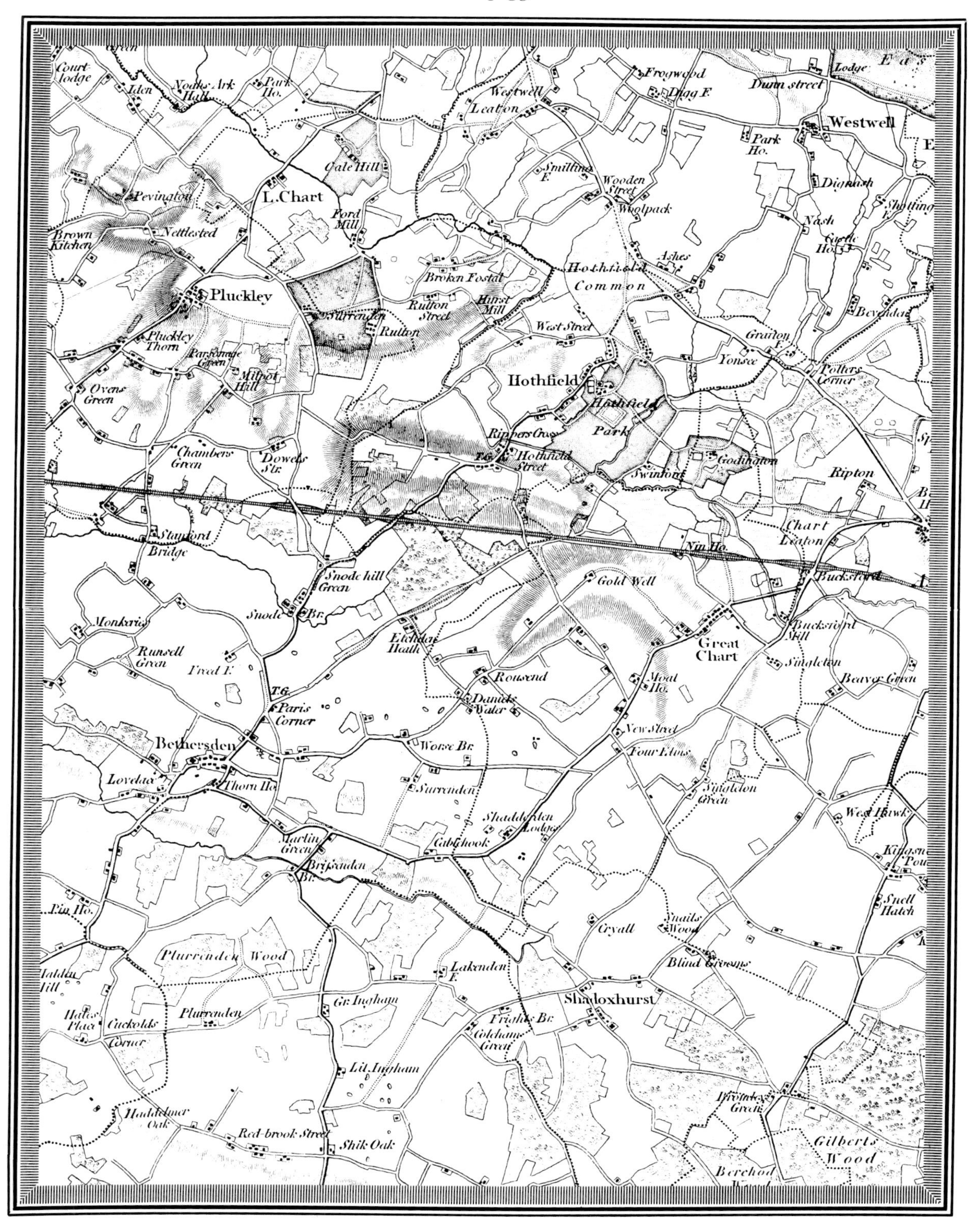
Court-lodge
Iden
Noahs Ark Hall
Park Ho.
Westwell Leaton
Frogwood
Digg F.
Dunn street
Lodge
Westwell
Park Ho.
Cale Hill
Pevington
L. Chart
Smilling F.
Wooden Street
Woolpack
Dignash
Shilling F.
Ford Mill
Brown Kitchen
Nettlested
Nash
Castle Ho.
Ashes
Broken Fostal
Hothfield Common
Pluckley
Surrenden
Rulton
Rulton Street
Hurst Mill
West Street
Grafton F.
Yonsee
Pluckley Thorn
Parsonage Green
Milpot Hill
Potters Corner
Hothfield
Ovens Green
Hothfield Park
Rippers Cross
Chambers Green
Dowels Str.
Hothfield Street
Godinton
Swinford
Ripton
Stanford Bridge
Chart Leaton
Nin Ho.
Bucksford
Snode hill Green
Gold Well
Snode
Br.
Monkaries
Etchden Heath
Bucksford Mill
Great Chart
Runsell Green
Freed F.
Singleton
Rousend
Moat Ho.
Beaver Green
Daniels Water
Paris Corner
Bethersden
Yew Street
Worse Br.
Four Elms
Lovelace
Thorn Ho.
Surrenden
Singleton Green
West Hawk
Shadoxhurst Lodge
Marlin Green
Gablehook
Brissenden Br.
Snell Hatch
Pin Ho.
Cryall
Snails Wood
Plurrenden Wood
Blind Grooms
Lakenden F.
Shadoxhurst
Gr. Ingham
Hales Place
Cuckolds Corner
Plurrenden
Frights Br.
Colcham Green
Lit. Ingham
Haddelmer Oak
Red-brook Street
Shik Oak
Gilberts Wood
Berchod

Map 35 (previous page) This district south of Charing reaches to the marshes and includes the villages of Pluckley, Hothfield and Bethersden. The last gives its name to veins of marble building-stone which cross the Weald. It remains an agricultural area although threatened in the south by the growth of Ashford. Pluckley and Little Chart have lost the former mansions of Surrenden and Calehill, and Hothfield Place also has been demolished. Little Chart church was destroyed in the Second World War, but the tower is preserved as an ancient monument.

Map 36 and modern map 36 (overleaf) Ashford, a small market town in 1801, developed rapidly after the coming of the railway in 1842 and more especially after the South-Eastern Railway works were opened seven years later. It has remained an important route centre and also an important market for livestock. In recent years Kennington to the north and the area southwards towards Kingsnorth have been extensively developed in connection with London overspill, and Ashford promises to be the principal rail centre should the Channel Tunnel be built. Wye to the north nestles below a beautiful stretch of downland which includes the spectacular Devil's Kneading Trough above Brook, where there is now an agricultural museum. These Downs are in part a nature reserve. Wye is a very ancient settlement on the Great Stour and the present agricultural college uses in part the remains of a medieval college of priests adjacent to the

Ashford High Street looking west towards the junction with North Street in 1905. While shop fronts have been altered, the upper parts of buildings still show their early origins. The middle row with the clock remains (see page 106).

Map 36

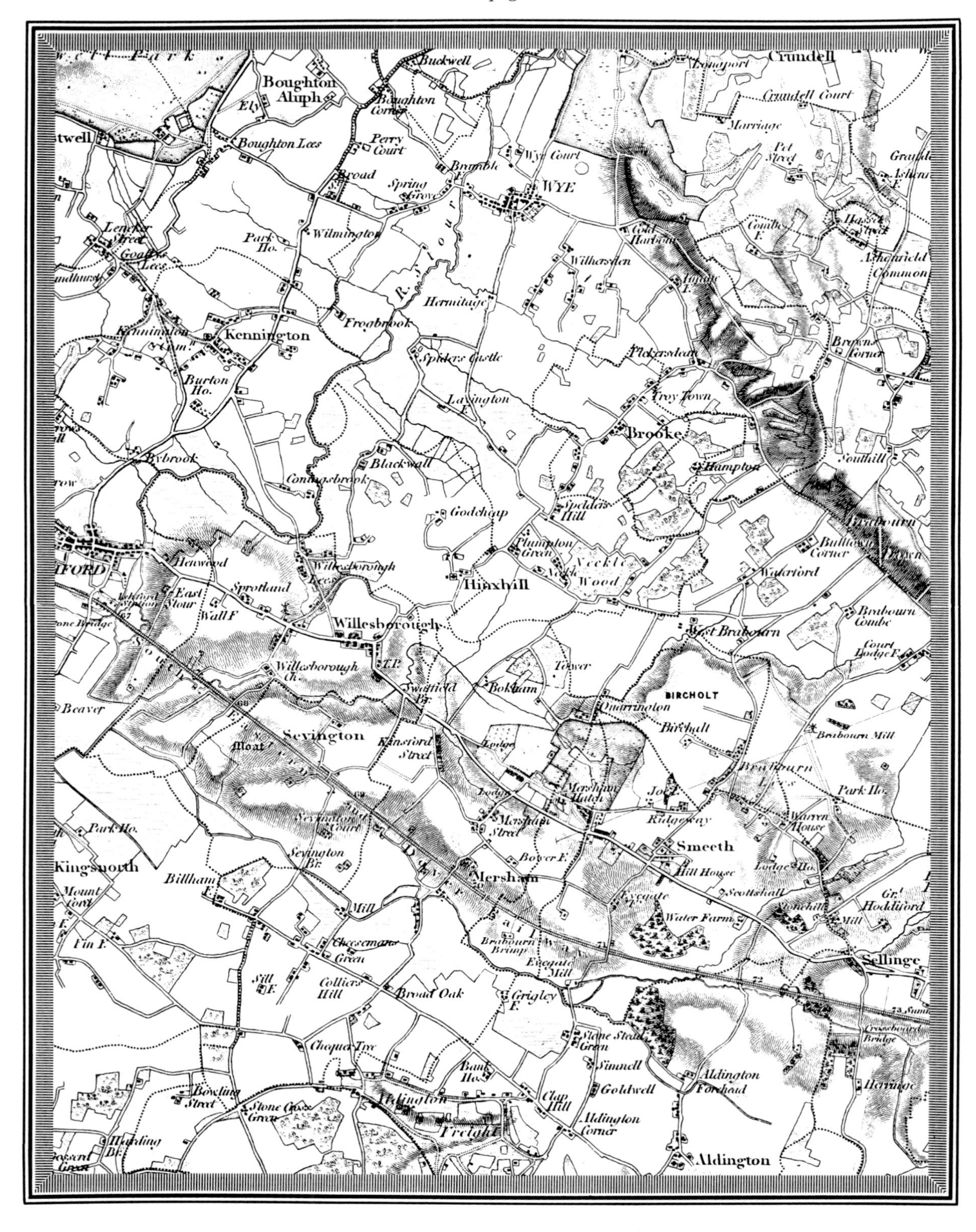

Buckwell
Boughton Aluph
Ely
Boughton Corner
Crundell
Crundell Court
Marriage
Boughton Lees
Perry Court
Wye Court
Bramble
WYE
Broad
Spring Grove
Pet Street
Lenacre Street
Goathes Lees
Park Ho.
Wilmington
Cold Harbour
Combe F.
Hassel Street
Ashenfield Common
Wilhersden
Hermitage
Frogbrook
Kennington
Spiders Castle
Pickersdean
Browns Corner
Burton Ho.
Lavington F.
Troy Town
Brooke
Bybrook
Blackwall
Hampton
Southill
Cunningsbrook
Godcheap
Spelders Hill
Plumpton Green
Neckle Wood
Henwood
Sprotland
East Stour
Wall F.
Willesborough Lees
Hinxhill
Bullford Corner
Walerford
Willesborough
East Brabourn
Brabourn Combe
Court Lodge F.
Willesborough Ch.
T.P.
Swatfield Br.
Tower
Bokham
BIRCHOLT
Beaver
Quarrington
Birchall
Sevington
Moat
Kinsford Street
Lodge
Brabourn Mill
Brabourn Lees
Park Ho.
Mersham Hatch
Ridgeway
Sevington Court
Mersham Street
Warren House
Smeeth
Park Ho.
Kingsnorth
Sevington Br.
Bower F.
Mersham
Billham
Hill House
Lodge Ho.
Scottshall
Evegate
Gr.t Hoddiford
Mill
Water Farm
Stonehill
Mill
Cheeseman Green
Brabourn Bump
Evegate Mill
Sellinge
Fin F.
Sill F.
Colliers Hill
Broad Oak
Grigley F.
Cheque Tree
Stone Stead Green
Crossbourne Bridge
Simnell
Bank Ho.
Aldington Forehead
Goldwell
Bowling Street
Stone Cross Green
Clap Hill
Aldington Corner
Harding Br.
Aldington

Davies&Tate
BROTHERS

EK
GIZZI
GIZZI
Pickford
Travel
BUS
STOP

Map 36 and modern map 36 cont

splendid church. On the same map is the mansion of Mersham-le-Hatch, home of the Knatchbull-Hugessen family, the representative of which takes his title from the nearby village of Brabourne.

Present-day Ashford High Street (see page 102).

(Below) A horse-drawn bus in Ashford High Street in 1902 and (opposite, below) its modern counterpart.

Map 37 (overleaf) The Elham Valley is another of the principal beauty spots of the county. It is watered by the Nailbourne or Little Stour, which is a chalk stream flowing intermittently. Along its course are the ancient settlements of Elham and Lyminge, the latter an early regional centre of Saxon Kent. A railway, built in 1887–8 from Canterbury to Folkestone, ran along this valley, but it never proved profitable and was abandoned in this century. This area is liable to be severely affected by the Channel Tunnel, especially in the vicinity of Newington. The western part of the map around Elmstead is one of the most remote areas still to be found in Kent.

Map 38 (overleaf) This hilly and largely undeveloped area of land lying north of Folkstone includes the villages of Hawkinge

Map 37

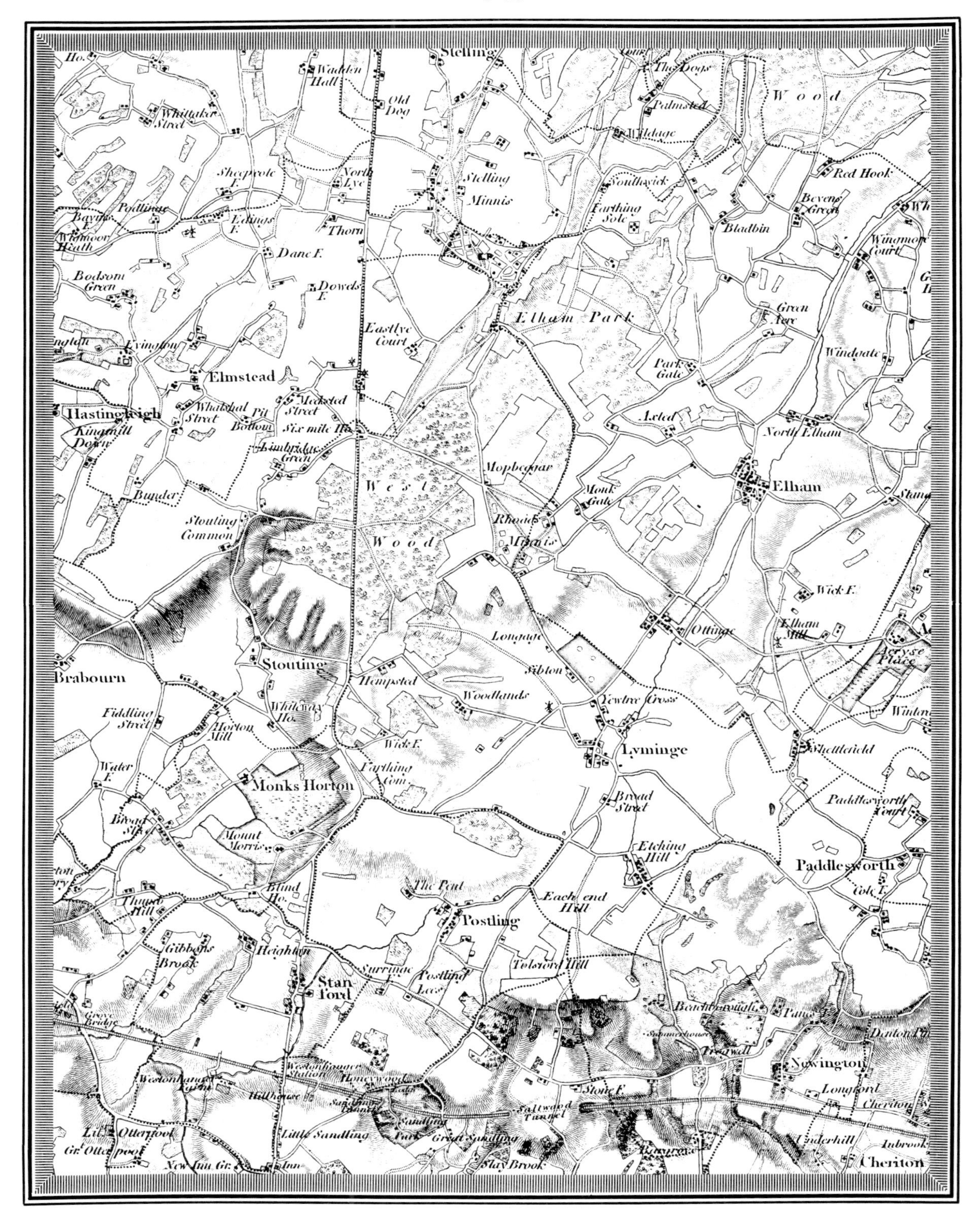
Stelling
Wadden Hall
Old Dog
The Dogs
Palmsted
Wood
Whittaker Street
Wildage
Red Hook
Sheepcote F.
North Lye
Stelling Minnis
Southwick
Bevens Green
Podlinge
Bavins F.
Edings F.
Thorn
Farthing Sole
Bladbin
Wingmore Court
Dane F.
Bodsom Green
Dowels F.
Elham Park
Green Acre
Eastlye Court
Evington
Elmstead
Windgate
Park Gate
Hastingleigh
Whatsal Street
Pit Bottom
Hedsted Street
Six mile Ho.
Kingmill Down
Limbridge Green
Axted
North Elham
Mopbeggar
Elham
Bunder
West Wood
Monk Gate
Stouting Common
Rhodes Minnis
Wick F.
Ottinge
Elham Mill
Acryse Place
Longage
Brabourn
Stouting
Hempsted
Sibton
Woodlands
Yewtree Cross
Fiddling Street
Horton Mill
Whiteway Ho.
Wick F.
Lyminge
Shuttlefield
Water F.
Farthing Com.
Monks Horton
Broad Street
Paddlesworth Court
Broad St.
Mount Morris
Etching Hill
Paddlesworth
Blind Ho.
The Peal
Third Hill
Each end Hill
Cole F.
Postling
Gibbons Brook
Heighton
Stanford
Surrinden
Postling Lees
Tolsford Hill
Grove Bridge
Beachborough
Summerhouse
Frogwell
Newington
Westenhanger Station
Honeywood
Westenhanger
Hillhouse
Stone F.
Longford
Cheriton
Saltwood Tunnel
Sandling
Lit. Otterpool
Gr. Otterpool
Little Sandling
Park
Great Sandling
Underhill
Inbrook
New Inn Gr.
Slay Brook
Cheriton

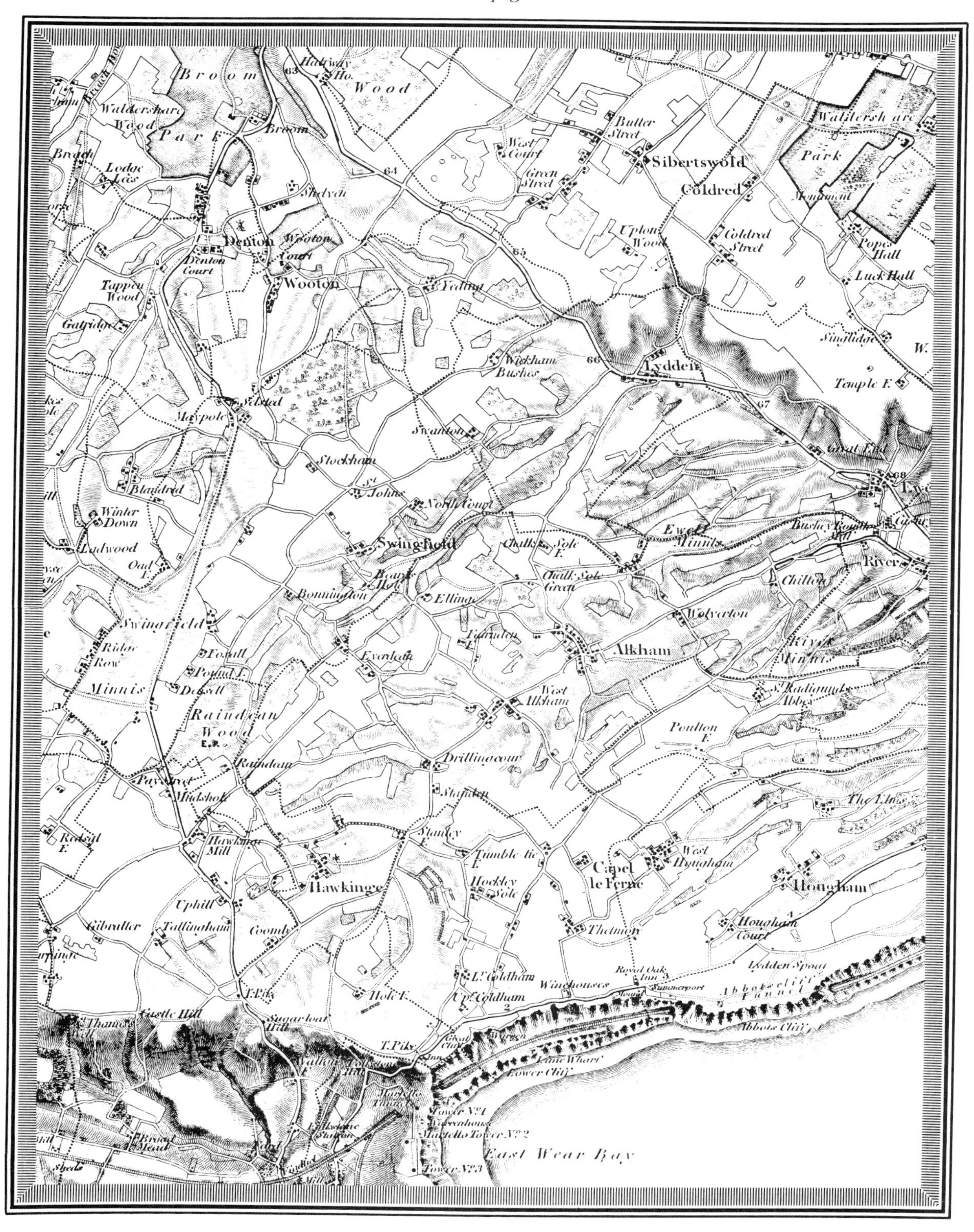
Broom
Halfway Ho.
Wood
Waldershare Wood
Park
Broom
Brach
Lodge Lees
Shelvin
Denton
Wooton Court
Denton Court
Wooton
Tappen Wood
Gatridge
Butter Street
West Court
Sibertswold
Green Street
Coldred
Walters hare Park
Monument
Upton Wood
Coldred Street
Popes Hall
Luck Hall
Yeding
Singlidge
W.
Wickham Bushes
Lydden
Temple F.
Maypole
Swanton
Stockham
St. Johns
North Court
Great End
Blandred
Winter Down
Ladwood
Oad F.
Swingfield
Ewell Minnis
Bushey Ruff
Chalk Sole F.
Chalk Sole Green
River
Chilton
Bonnington
Elling
Wolverton
Swingfield
Ridge Row
Minnis
Everden
Alkham
Pound F.
Raindean Wood
West Alkham
St. Radigunds Abbey
Poulton F.
Drellingcour
Raindam
Paystreet
Standen
The Lines
Redsil F.
Hawkinge Mill
Stanley F.
Tumble-tie F.
West Hougham
Capel le Ferne
Hougham
Hawkinge
Hockley Sole
Uphill
Gibralter
Tallingham
Coomb
Hougham Court
Royal Oak Inn
Lydden Spout
Lr. Coldham
Winehouses
Abbots cliff Tunnel
Up. Coldham
Holt F.
T. Pike
Castle Hill
Sugarloaf Hill
T. Pike
Abbots Cliff
Lime Wharf
Lower Cliff
Broad Mead
Tower No. 1
Martello Tower No. 2
Tower No. 3
East Wear Bay
63
64
65
66
67
68

Map 38 cont

and Alkham, Swingfield and Lydden. It is threatened by road improvements and the Channel Tunnel plans. Broom Park in the north-western corner was the home of Lord Kitchener of First World War fame. The southern part of the map below the line of the hills is now all part of the town of Folkestone, in the early nineteenth century little more than a fishing village.

Map 39 (overleaf) Dover lies at the mouth of the deep-cut valley of the River Dour, between high chalk cliffs ending in the South Foreland and Shakespeare's Cliff. Despite its importance for travel and defence this situation has much restricted Dover's growth, and the country round about is still largely unspoilt. The great castle overlooking the town and harbour includes the Roman pharos

or lighthouse, the medieval church of St Mary in Castro, as well as extensive defence works and Churchill's bunker. The present harbour is largely a nineteenth-century development, with only the inner harbour by Snargate Street representing the old port of Dover as shown on the map. The ancient parish of St Margaret's-at-Cliffe has developed the precipitous but attractive resort of St Margaret's

A view of Dover from 1894 looking westward towards the docks with the fine Regency parade of houses which were largely destroyed during the Second World War and replaced with blocks of flats (see overleaf).

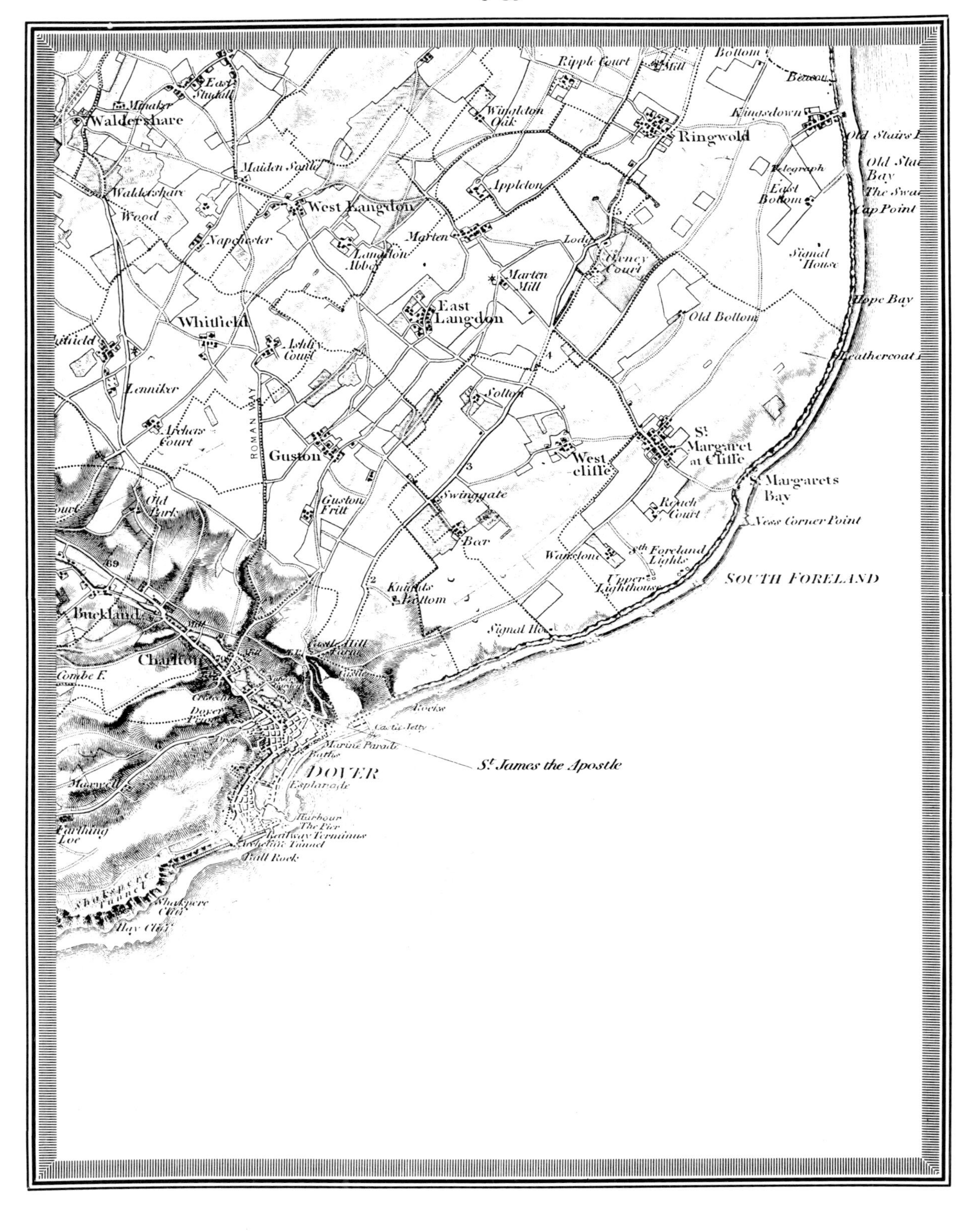

Ripple Court
Mill
Bottom
Beacon
East Studdal
Waldershare
Wingleton Oak
Kingsdown
Ringwold
Old Stairs Bay
The Swan
Maiden Sole
Telegraph
East Bottom
Cap Point
Appleton
Waldershare Wood
West Langdon
Marten
Napchester
Langdon Abbey
Lodge
Oxney Court
Signal House
Marten Mill
East Langdon
Hope Bay
Old Bottom
Whitfield
Ashley Court
Leathercoat Point
Lenniker
Solton
Archers Court
ROMAN WAY
Guston
St. Margaret at Cliffe
West cliffe
St. Margarets Bay
Old Park
Swingate
Guston Fritt
Rough Court
Ness Corner Point
Bear
Wanstone
Sth. Foreland Lights
Upper Lighthouse
SOUTH FORELAND
Knights Bottom
Buckland
Mill
Signal Ho.
Castle Hill Farm
Charlton
Combe F.
Castle
Rocks
Dover Priory
Castle Jetty
Marine Parade
Baths
St. James the Apostle
DOVER
Esplanade
Maxwell
Harbour
The Pier
Railway Terminus
Farthing Loe
Archcliff Tunnel
Bull Rock
Shakspere Tunnel
Shakspere Cliff
Hay Cliff

Map 39 cont

Bay, and there has been some housing growth on the cliff top. The land northwards drops towards Deal and the Stour marshes. Close to the signal house marked near the South Foreland is the spot where Bleriot landed after his flight from France in 1909, now commemorated by a monument.

Map 40 (page 116) This area on the Sussex border consists of part of Bedgbury Forest and a region south of the main road, which is now flooded and part of Bewl Bridge Reservoir, also called Bewl Lake. This was created by damming the headwaters of the Teise and affects the area from Stone Crouch to Wiskets Wood on the early map.

The present-day sea front at Dover (see page 111).

Map 41 (page 117) This map shows the Kent and Sussex border around Hawkhurst, which is the one considerable settlement, a widely scattered village with centres at Highgate and at the Moor. The area has changed little since 1801 and from Hartley in the north to the Kent Ditch on the border is still a land of forest. Hemsted Mansion, now Benenden School, lies close to the attractive village of that name, and on the border is Sandhurst, not far from the Sussex castle of Bodiam on the other side of the Rother.

Tenterden High Street looking west with the front of the Town Hall just visible on the right. The fine timber-framed house on the left is now the Tudor Rose Tea Rooms. Some idea of the splendid width of this road can be gained from this photograph of 1901 by considering the foreground on the right which is today filled with parked cars (see page 123).

TADDY & Co
TOBACCO & CIGARETTES.
TADDY'S
CIGARETTES
TOBACCO
and
CIGARS

Map 40

Bewl Bridge
Chingley Wood
Chingley Farm
Combwell
Stone Crouch
Pillory Fm
Lady Meads
Great Wiskets
Halls Wood
Beaumans
Hazlehurst
Coppings
Welches
New Barn
Wishtown Farm
Greenwood Farm
Brick Kiln
Bigseys
Bolsters Gate
Bricklehurst
Bardown
Limden
Little Limden
Wards Brook
Church Settle
Stone Gate
Coopers
St Peters Ch.
Parsonage
Cottenden Street
Miskens
Little Hammerden
Hammerden
Ticehurst Road Station
Barchurst
Clay Hall
Battenhurst
Turzeys
Cinder Bank
Short Ridge
Kitchenham
Withernden's Bridge
Hastings Branch
Kickly Br.
Brookmarle
Frenches
Brownings
Thatchers
Woodknowl
Winters
Swing Gate
Burwash
Tots F.
Hutchinns F.
Willards Hill
Hackwood
Brick Ho.
Fishers
Dudwell Mill
Batemans
Park Mill
Green Hill
Plots Fm
Burwash Wheel
Park Wood
Bowmans
Pookhill
New Ho.
Brown

Map 41

Furnace
Bishops Farm
Hurtley
Freight
Lit. Huncockes
Folly F.
Swattenden
Doddlesden
Doves Fm
Ghillenden
Godards Green
Whitelime F.
Tubslake F.
Gitthole
Hemsted Park
Osborne
Waterlands
Mount F.
Roses F.
Four Wents
Bennenden
Gills Green
Scullsgate
Tilden F.
Beals Green
Sarnden F.
Chatham Dock F.
Woodsden
Pauls Farm
Iden Green
Hockeley
Furnace Mill
Eaglesden
High Street
Tongs
Mill Street Mill
Standing Street
Hawkhurst
Field Green
Foxhole
Hoath Mill
Sandhurst Green
Silverden F.
Conghurst F.
Parsonage
Boxhurst F.
Sandhurst
Eppingham F.
Marsh Quarter
Mill
River Ro
Kent Ditch
Cold Harbour
Merriments Farm
Bodyham
Courtlodge
Bodyham Castle
Bodyham Br.
Park F.
Higham
Moat F.
Salehurst
Abbey Farm
Robertsbridge
Ewhurst

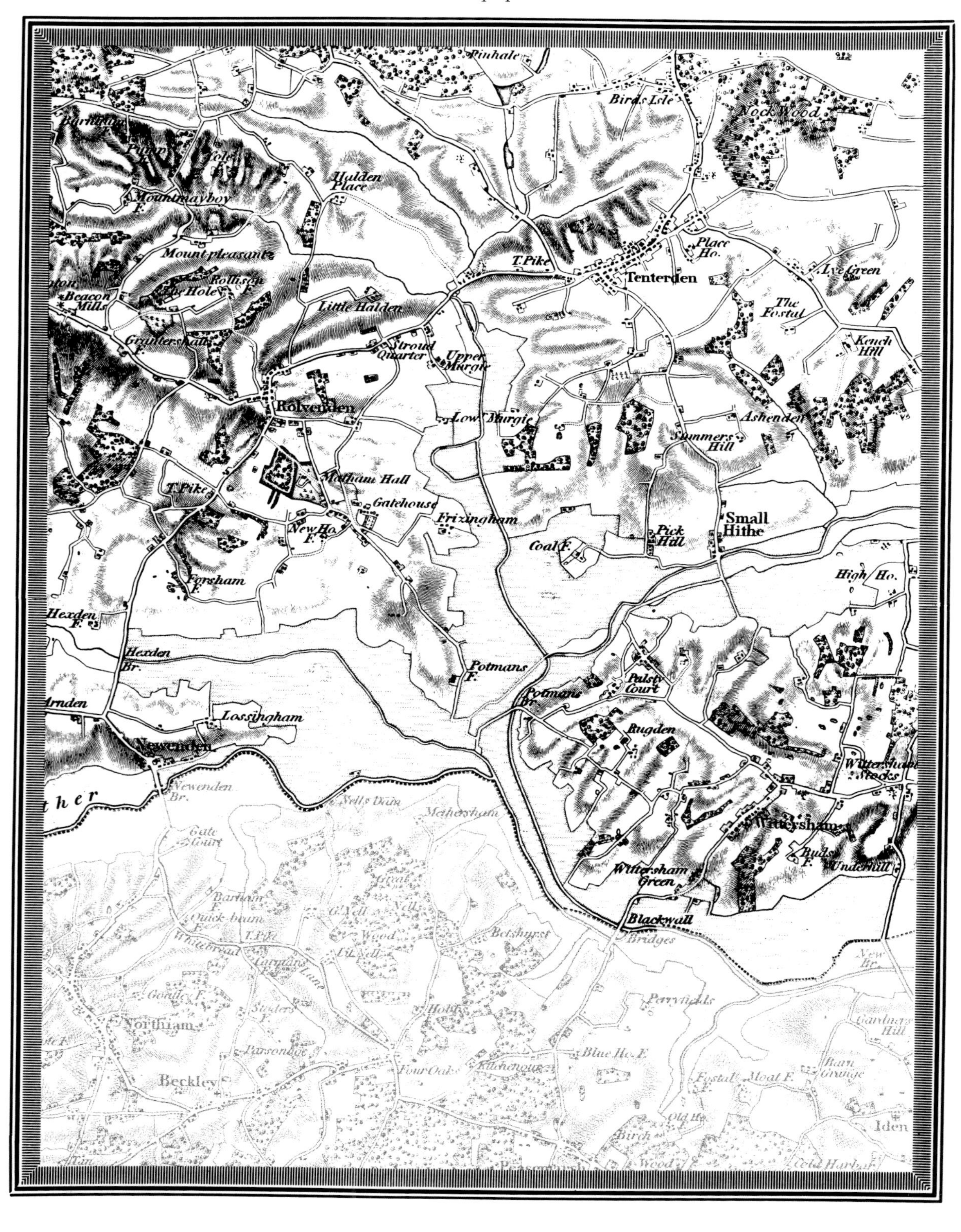
Pinhale
Birds Isle
Nock Wood
Halden Place
Mountmayboy F.
Mount pleasant
Rollison
Beacon Mills
Little Halden
T. Pike
Place Ho.
Tenterden
Lye Green
The Fostal
Kench Hill
Stroud Quarter
Upper Murgie
Rolvenden
Low Murgie
Ashenden
Summers Hill
Motham Hall
Gatehouse
Frizingham
New Ho. F.
Small Hithe
Pick Hill
Coal F.
Forsham F.
High Ho.
Hexden F.
Hexden Br.
Potmans F.
Potmans Br.
Palsty Court
Lossingham
Newenden
Rugden
Wittersham Stocks
Newenden Br.
Wittersham
Buds F.
Underhill
Wittersham Green
Blackwall
Bridges
Betshurst
Northiam
Parsonage
Beckley
Four Oaks
Blue Ho. F.
Fostal
Moat F.
Iden

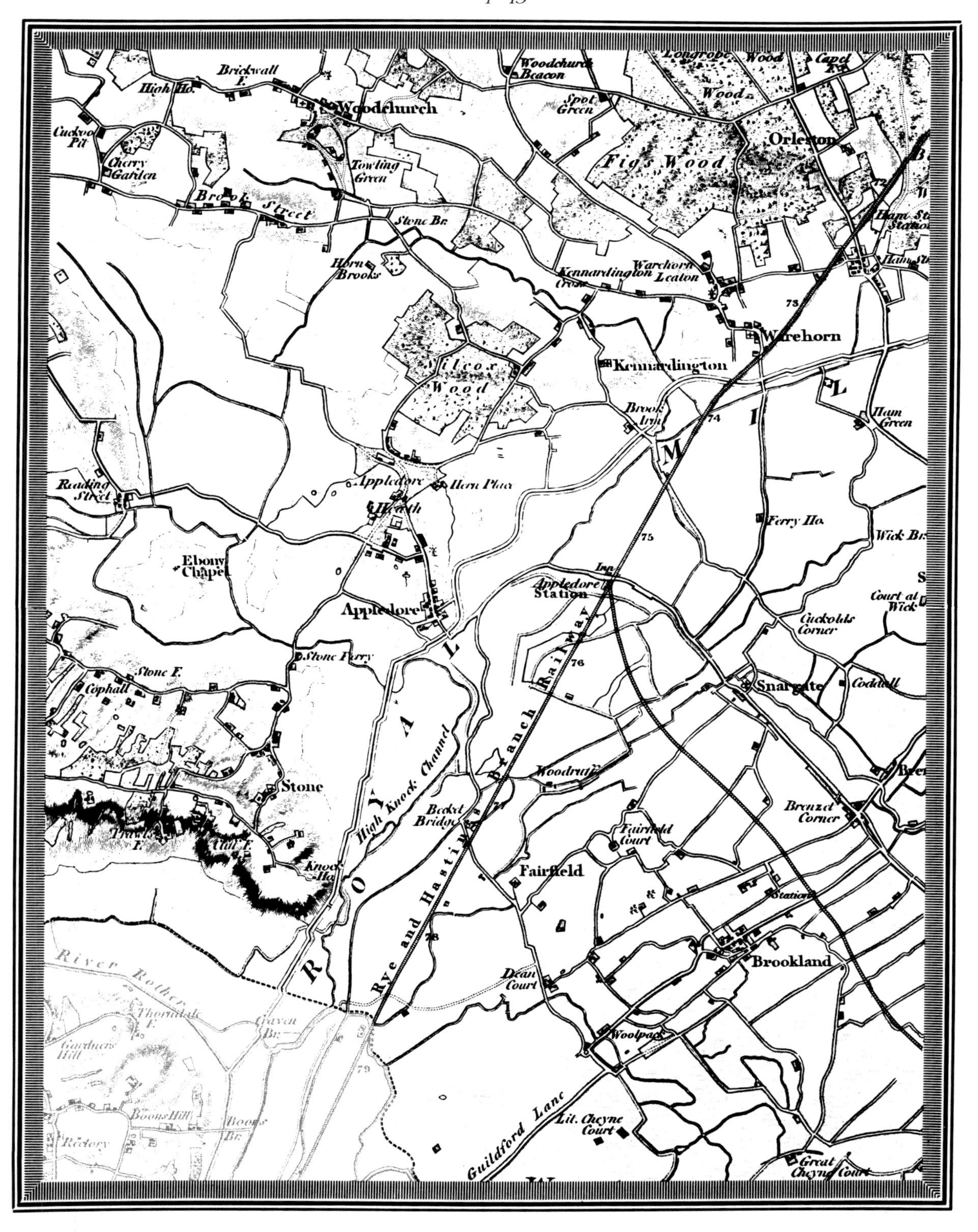
Woodchurch
Woodchurch Beacon
Brickwall F.
High Ho.
Cuckoo Pit
Cherry Garden
Towling Green
Brook Street
Stone Br.
Spot Green
Figs Wood
Orleston
Horn Brooks
Kennardington Cross
Warehorn Leaton
Warehorn
Kennardington
Silcox Wood
Brook Inn
Ham Green
Reading Street
Appledore Heath
Horn Place
Ferry Ho.
Ebony Chapel
Appledore Station
Appledore
Court at Wick
Cuckolds Corner
Stone Ferry
Stone F.
Cophall
Snargate
Coddull
Rye and Hastings Branch Railway
High Knock Channel
Woodruff
Stone
Becket Bridge
Brenzet Corner
Fairfield Court
Fairfield
Station
Brookland
Dean Court
River Rother
Woolpack
Guildford Lane
Lit. Cheyne Court
Great Cheyne Court
Boons Hill
Rectory

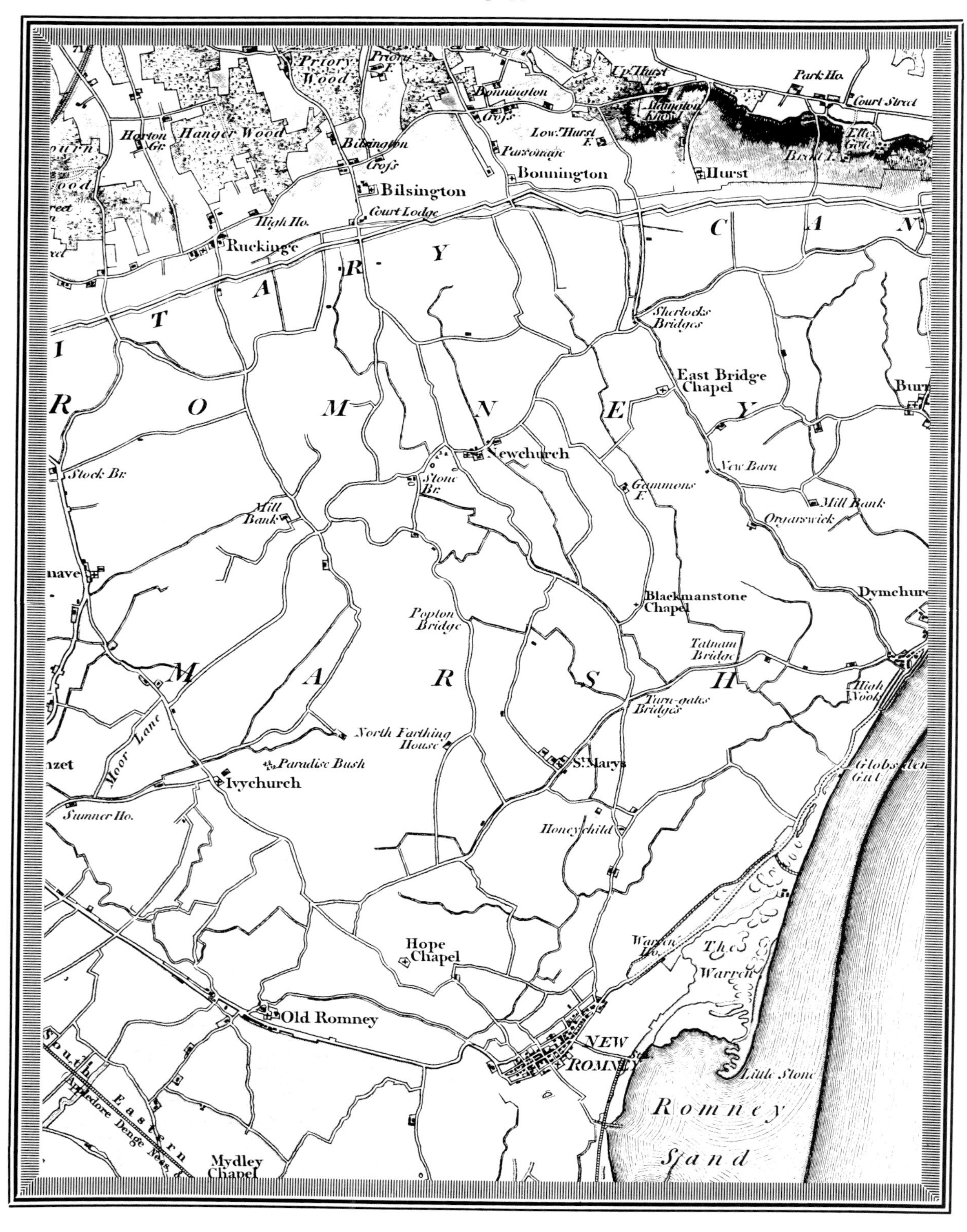
Priory Wood
Priory F.
Up. Hurst F.
Park Ho.
Court Street
Bonnington
Bilsington Cross
Horton Gr.
Hanger Wood
Low. Hurst F.
Parsonage
Bonnington
Hurst
Bilsington
High Ho.
Court Lodge
Ruckinge
C A N
R Y
T A
I
R O M N E Y
Sherlocks Bridges
East Bridge Chapel
Newchurch
Stock Br.
Stone Br.
New Barn
Gammons F.
Mill Bank
Mill Bank
Orgarswick
Blackmanstone Chapel
Dymchurch
Popton Bridge
Talnam Bridge
M A R S H
Turn-gates Bridges
High Nook
North Farthing House
Paradise Bush
St. Marys
Moor Lane
Ivychurch
Sumner Ho.
Honeychild
Warren Ho.
The Warren
Hope Chapel
Old Romney
NEW ROMNEY
Little Stone
Romney Stand
South Eastern
Appledore Denge Ness
Mydley Chapel

Map 42 (previous page) Tenterden is a limb of Rye in the Cinque Ports Confederation and became a borough in 1449. It is noted for its wide High Street, the great church of St Mildred and the hamlet of Small Hythe, the former lading place on the Rother where there is still a fine timber-framed house, now the Ellen Terry museum. Southwards lies the Isle of Oxney, still surrounded by dikes but formerly separated by the sea at high tide. To the north of Tenterden lies Bird's Isle, now the modern suburb of St Michaels, and the only part lost to recent development, while westward is the fine village of Rolvenden and on the Sussex border the ancient head of navigation and lading place of Newenden.

Map 43 (previous page) Here the western marshes include part of the Isle of Oxney and that of Ebony. The chapel shown at Ebony in 1801 was moved to Reading Street half a mile away late in the last century. Appledore, one of the beauty spots of this area, was at one time threatened by the tides which swept in across the Rother marshes. The division between upland and marsh was effectively drawn when the Royal Military Canal was built during the first decade of the last century as a defence work against Napoleon.

Map 44 This map shows much of the marshland areas of Romney and Walland, lying on either side of the Rhee Wall, probably a medieval canal built to help keep open the harbour of New Romney. The town of New Romney was a flourishing port before storms at the end of the thirteenth century led to the removal of the mouth of the Rother across the marsh to Rye. This left a large and shallow lagoon between Littlestone-on-Sea and Greatstone-on-Sea, which was only drained at the beginning of the present century. Romney Marsh, 'the fifth quarter of the globe', is a region of wide open spaces, of magnificent churches of which Newchurch is the chief, and of the lost villages of Blackmanstone, Orgarswick, Eastbridge and Hope. This was a prime area for smuggling in the last century but now has holiday camps served by the Romney, Hythe and Dymchurch Light Railway.

Map 45 (overleaf) This narrow strip of coastline includes the ancient head port of Hythe and the newer flourishing resort and cross-channel port of Folkestone. The latter was a small fishing town and limb of Dover which began to grow when soldiers were encamped nearby during the Napoleonic wars. Real growth came after 1843 with the arrival of the railway, and by the end of the last century it was a town with a population of 30,000. Its Victorian layout and architecture are still a feature of Folkestone. Hythe haven closed in the seventeenth century, and the town with its outstanding church of St Leonard is now a mile from the sea. The Royal Military Canal enters the ocean at Seabrook east of Hythe and not far from Sandgate where there is one of Henry VIII's castles. The coast also boasts a number of Martello towers, defence works against Bonaparte, while behind Hythe lies Saltwood Castle where the plot to kill archbishop Thomas à Becket was hatched. Dymchurch, at the eastern edge of the map, is still the principal marshland village and New Hall, near the church, is the meeting place of both the Lords, Bailiff and Jurats of Romney Marsh (the former custodians of land drainage) and the Bailiff, Jurats and Commonalty (former administrators of the Liberty of Romney Marsh). These ancient corporations still survive but are stripped of their former powers.

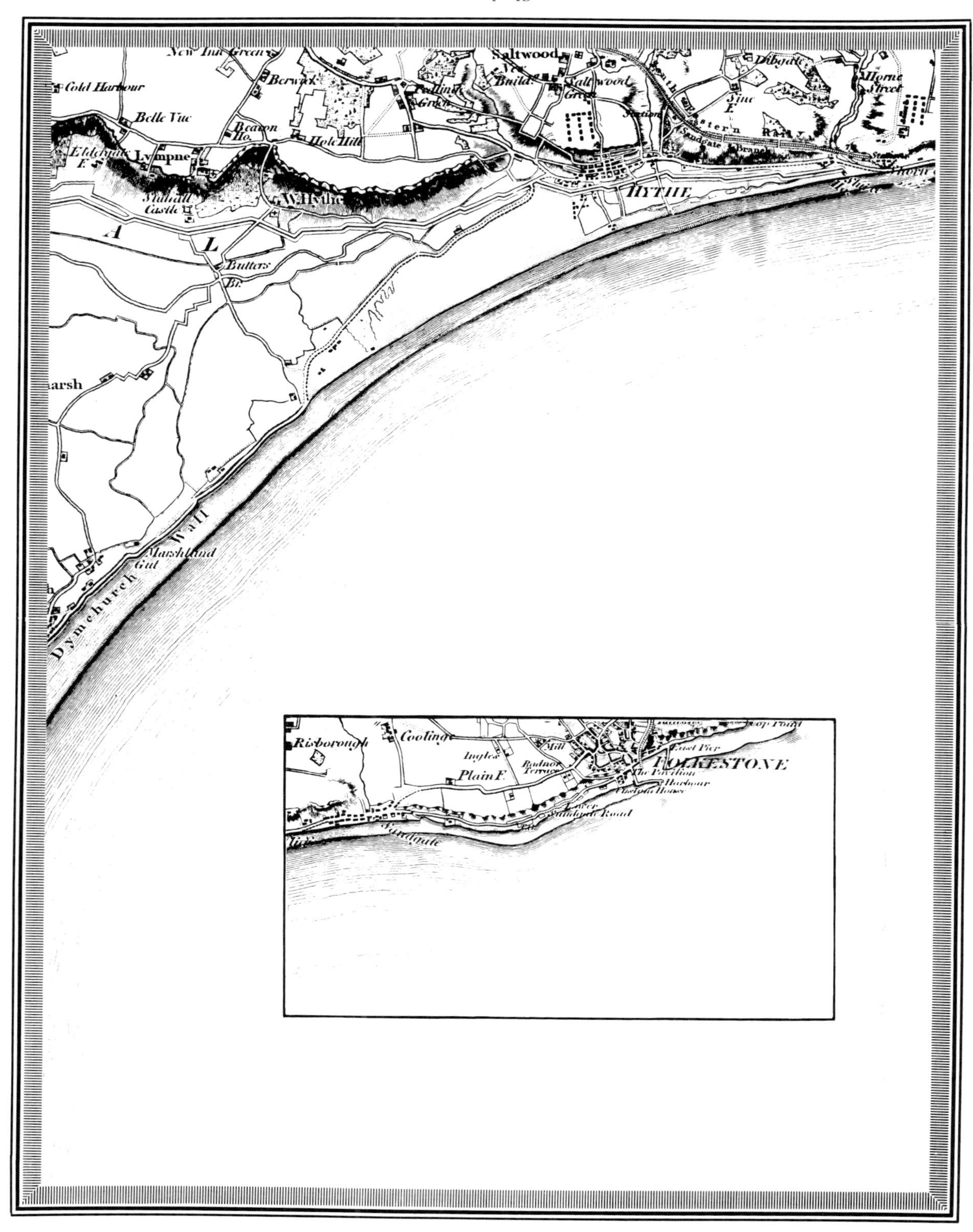
New Inn Green
Cold Harbour
Berwick
Saltwood
Belle Vue
Beacon Ho.
Hole Hill
Lympne
W. Hythe
HYTHE
A
L
Butters Br.
arsh
Marshland Gut
Dymchurch Wall
Dibgate
Horne Street
Sandgate Branch
Risborough
Cooling
Ingles
Plain F.
Mill
Radnor Terrace
FOLKESTONE
East Pier
The Pavilion
Harbour
Custom House
Lower Sandgate Road
Sandgate

Present-day Tenterden (see page 115).

(Opposite) A view of Folkestone town and harbour with a paddle ferry in the foreground from 1895. The buildings on Grace Hill dominate the centre of the town, and the parish church of the original fishing village can be seen to the far left although it is now obscured by an office block (above).

Map 46 (overleaf) This small part of Walland Marsh forms the boundary with Sussex, and is the site of the lost parish of Broomhill which was sometimes regarded as being within Kent, and at other times as within Sussex. It is now represented by Camber Sands, the popular holiday spot just over the border.

Map 47 (overleaf) Denge Marsh, shown here, is the semi-barren district between New Romney, Lydd and Dungeness. The Romney, Hythe and Dymchurch Light Railway now follows the coast and has, in part, led to the growth of Greatstone-on-Sea and Lydd-on-Sea, with their holiday camps, places unknown at the time of the map. The whole area, from being the isolated home of a few hardy fishermen, is now dominated by the nuclear power station which dwarfs the tower of the former lighthouse. Lydd is the site of a large army camp and much of the western half of this area is now used for firing ranges.

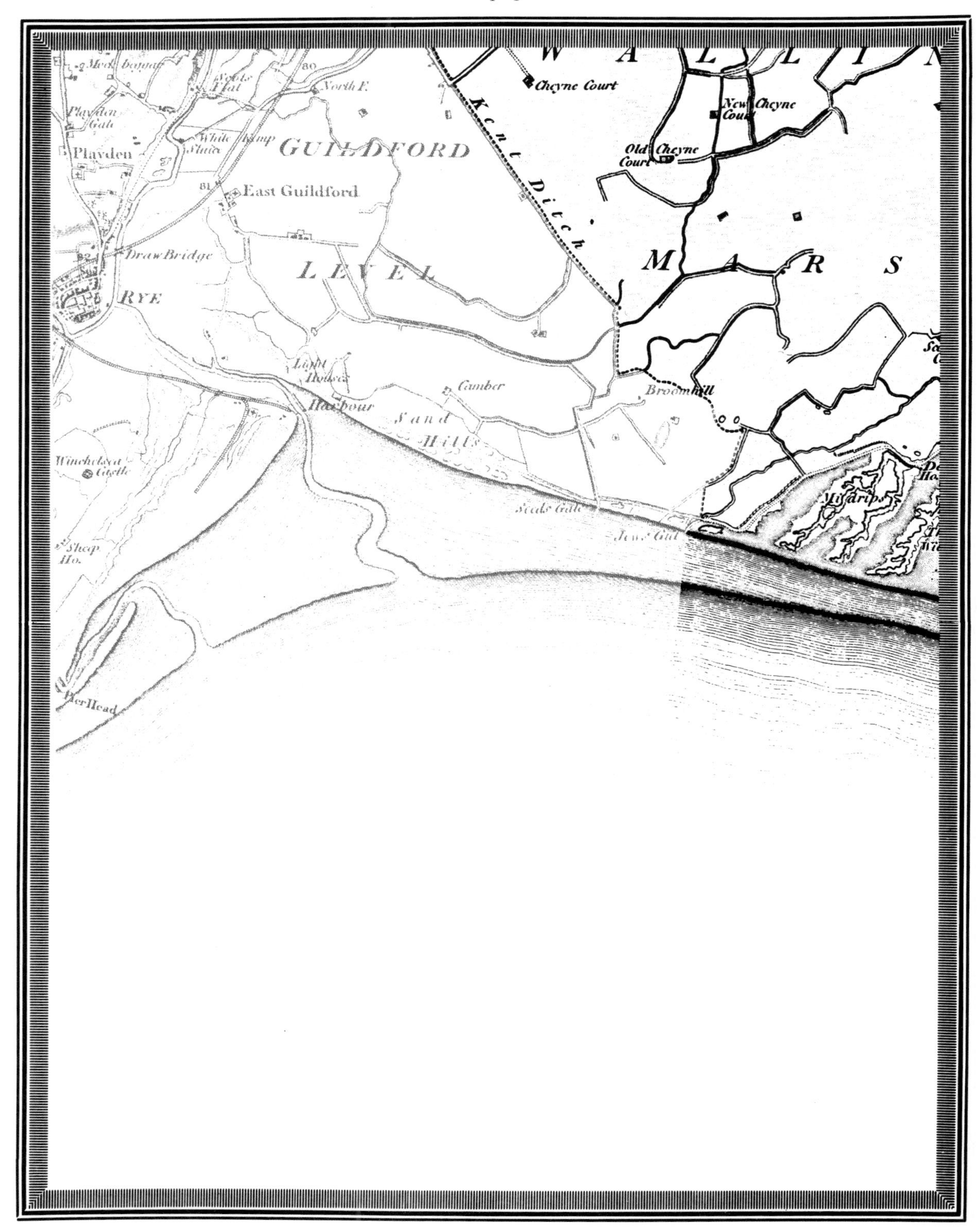
Cheyne Court
New Cheyne Court
Old Cheyne Court
GUILDFORD
Kent Ditch
Playden
East Guildford
Draw Bridge
LEVEL
RYE
MARS
Light House
Camber
Broomhill
Harbour
Sand Hills
Winchelsea Castle
Jews Gut
Sheep Ho.
Pier Head
North F.
White Sluice

Map 47

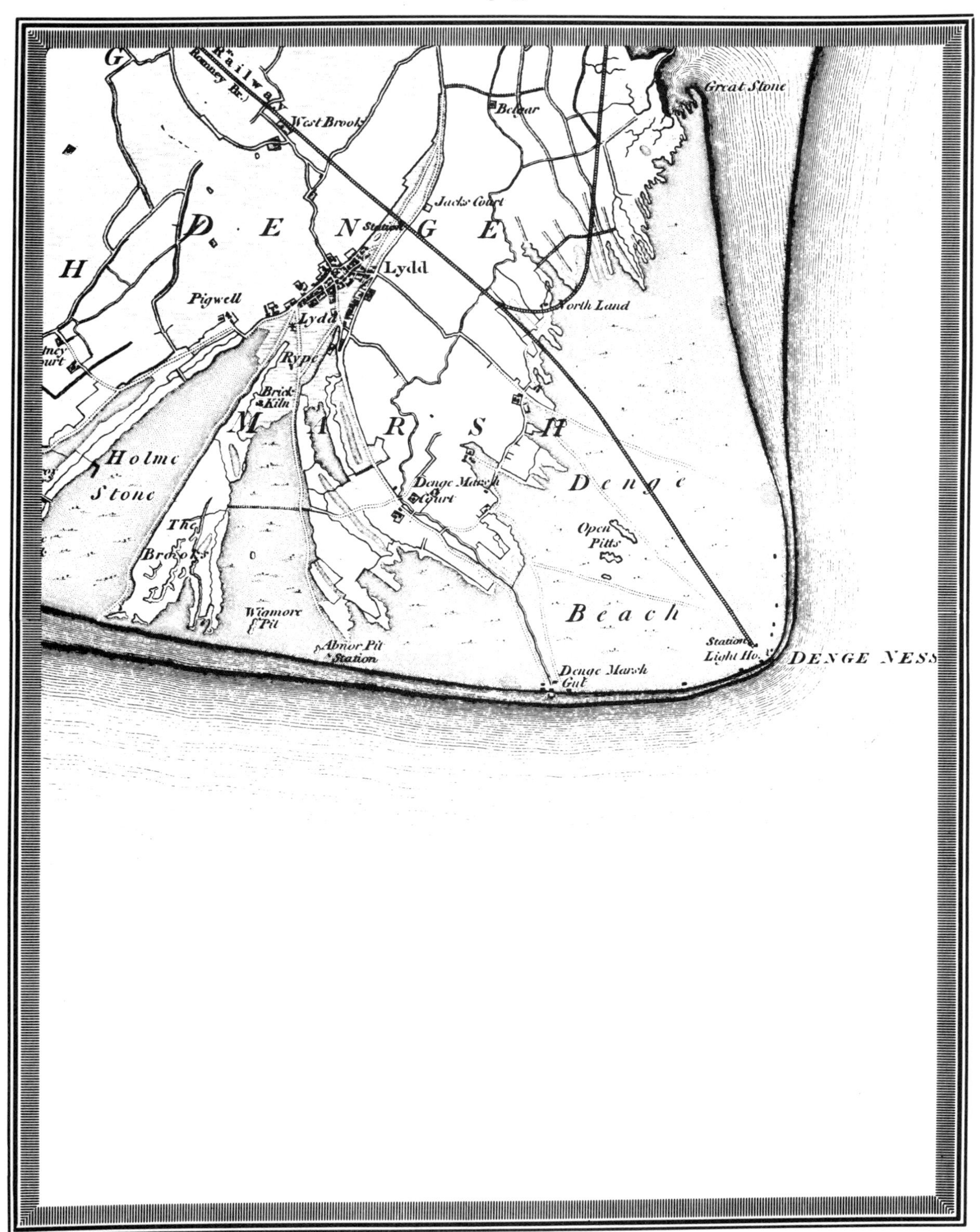
Railway
Romney Br.
West Brook
Belgar
Great Stone
Jacks Court
D E N G E
Station
Lydd
Pigwell
Lydd
North Land
Rype
Brick Kiln
M A R S H
Holme Stone
Denge Marsh Court
Denge
Open Pitts
The Brooks
Beach
Wigmore Pit
Abnor Pit Station
Station
Light Ho.
DENGE NESS
Denge Marsh Gut

Bibliography

Archaeologia Cantiana (Volumes I–CIII Transactions of the Kent Archaeological Society)
Brentnall, M., *The Cinque Ports and Romney Marsh* (1972)
Crouch, M., *Kent* (1976)
Everitt, A. M., *The Community of Kent and the Great Rebellion* (1966)
Gardiner, D., *Companion into Kent* (3rd edition, 1949)
Hasted, E., *History and Topographical Survey of the County of Kent* (1797–1801)
Jessup, F. W., *A History of Kent* (1958)
Kentish Sources (Series of source books published by Kent Archives Office)
Victoria County History of Kent (Volumes 1–3, 1908–32)
Winstanley, M., *Life in Kent at the turn of the Century* (1978)

Useful Addresses

Kent County

Canterbury City and Cathedral Archives, Cathedral Library, The Precincts, Canterbury, CT1 2EG (access by appointment)

Kent Archaeological Society, c/o Hon. Secretary, Pring's Cottage, Upper Halling, Rochester, ME2 1HR

Kent County Archives Office, County Hall, Maidstone, ME14 1XQ

Branches: South East Kent, c/o Folkestone Library, Grace Hill, Folkestone
Thanet, c/o County Library, Guildford Lawn, Ramsgate
Sevenoaks, c/o County Library, The Drive, Sevenoaks
Rochester on Medway, c/o Civic Centre, High Street, Strood (officially open from 1989)

Kent County Library Headquarters and Local Studies Room, Springfield, Maidstone, ME14 2LH

Kent County Local History Committee, c/o County Archivist, County Hall, Maidstone, ME14 1XQ. (This is the coordinating body for the very large number of local history societies in Kent.)

Maidstone Museum, Faith Street, Maidstone

There are Town Centre Libraries in Ashford, Broadstairs, Canterbury, Chatham, Dartford, Deal, Dover, Faversham, Folkestone, Gillingham, Gravesham, Herne Bay, Hythe, Maidstone, Margate, Ramsgate, Rochester, Sevenoaks, Sheerness, Sittingbourne, Strood, Swanley, Tenterden, Tonbridge, Tunbridge Wells and Whitstable.

Metropolitan Kent

Bromley Public Library and Archives, High Street, Bromley, BR1 1EX

Greenwich Local History Library, Woodlands, 90 Mycenae Road, Blackheath, London SE7 7SE

Lewisham Archives and Local History Department, The Manor House, Old Road, Lee, London SE13 5SY

GAZETTEER INDEX DIAGRAM

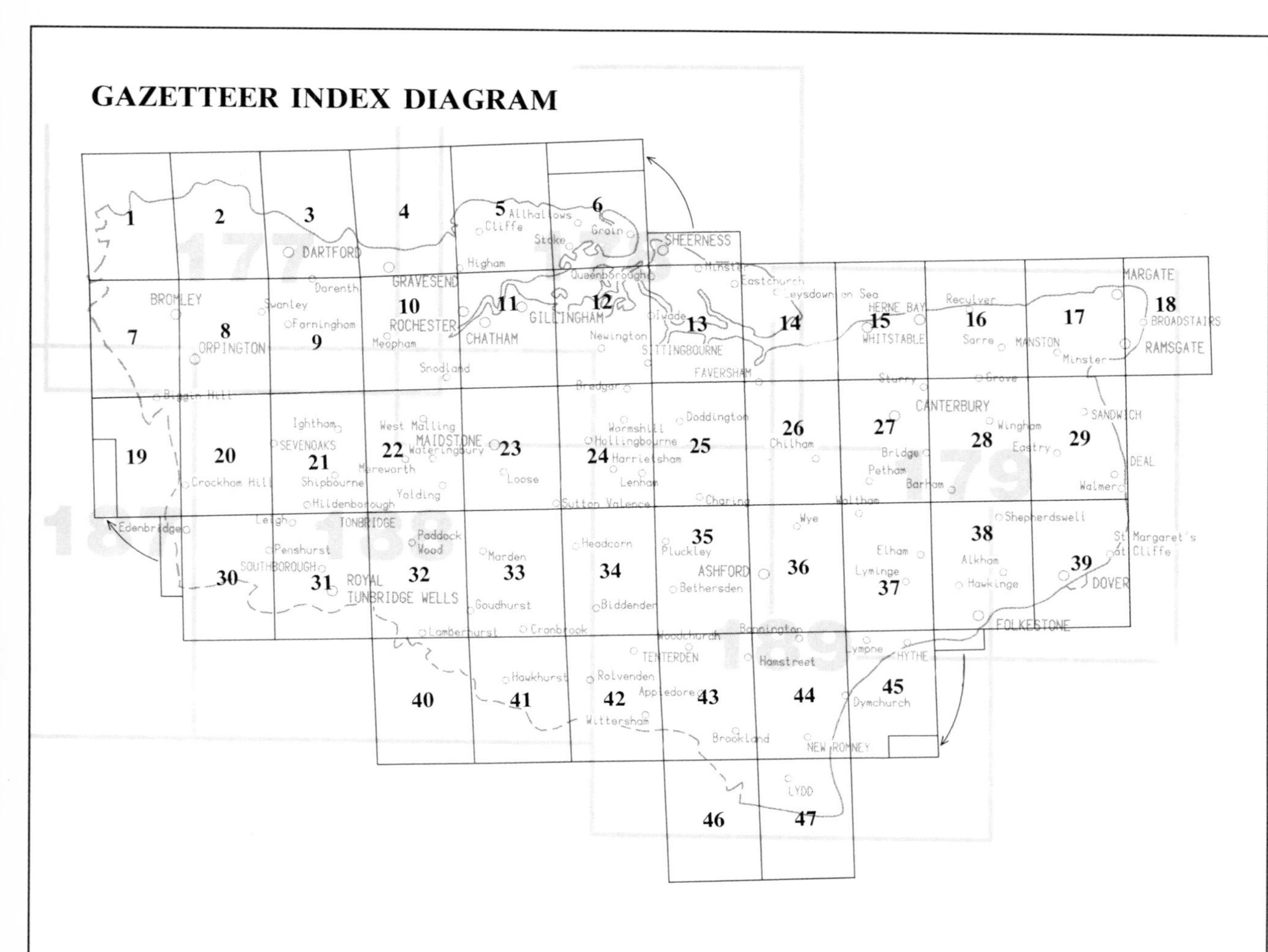

KEY

ONE INCH EDITION MAPS

1:50 000 LANDRANGER SHEET LINES

GAZETTEER

This Gazetteer contains the modern names of cities, towns and villages in the county of Kent as shown on Ordnance Survey 1:50,000 scale Landranger maps. Each Gazetteer entry gives the place name, the Landranger map number(s) on which it appears and its National Grid reference number. Having identified the place name and the Landranger map number that includes it, references to the diagram on the left will show the page numbers of early Ordnance Survey mapping in this book where the name can be located. By purchasing the relevant Landranger map, the National Grid reference number also included in the Gazetteer will enable you to pinpoint the name and its position in the modern landscape precisely. Ordnance Survey Landranger maps are available from most booksellers, stationers and newsagents.

Ordnance Survey can also supply monochrome copies of a selection of early OS maps held in its Record Map Library. Enquiries on this service should be addressed to Fixed Price Services, Ordnance Survey, Romsey Road, Maybush, Southampton, SO9 4DH. Telephone Southampton (0703) 792338.

Kent

A

Abbey Gate	178 188	TQ7558
Abbey Wood	177	TQ4678
Acol	179	TR3067
Addington	178 188	TQ6559
Adisham	179 189	TR2253
Aldington	179 189	TR0636
Aldington Frith	179 189	TR0436
Alkham	179	TR2542
Allhallows	178	TQ8377
Allhallows-on-Sea	178	TQ8378
Allington	178 188	TQ7457
Anvil Green	179 189	TR1049
Aperfield	187	TQ4258
Appledore	189	TQ9529
Appledore Heath	189	TQ9530
Arpinge	179 189	TR1939
Ash	177 188	TQ6064
Ash	179	TR2958
Ashbank	188	TQ8353
Ashford	189	TR0042
Ashley	179	TR3048
Ashurst	188	TQ5138
Avery Hill	177	TQ4474
Aycliff	179	TR3040
Aylesford	178 188	TQ7258
Aylesham	179 189	TR2352

B

Badgers Mount	177 188	TQ4962
Badlesmere	189	TR0053
Badlesmere Court	178	TR0155
Bagham	179 189	TR0753
Baker's Cross	188	TQ7835
Bapchild	178	TQ9262
Barden Park	188	TQ5746
Barfrestone	179	TR2650
Barham	179 189	TR2050
Barming Heath	178 188	TQ7255
Barnehurst	177	TQ5075
Barnes Cray	177	TQ5275
Barnes Street	188	TQ6448
Barnfield	189	TQ9247
Barnsole	179	TR2756
Barrowhill	179 189	TR1037
Basted	188	TQ6055
Bayley's Hill	188	TQ5151
Beal's Green	188	TQ7631
Bean	177	TQ5872
Bearsted	178 188	TQ7955
Beckenham	177	TQ3769
Bedgebury Cross	188	TQ7134
Bekesbourne	179	TR1955
Bekesbourne Hill	179	TR1856
Bell Green	177	TQ3672
Bellingham	177	TQ3771
Beltinge	179	TR1968
Beltring	188	TQ6747
Belvedere	177	TQ4978
Benenden	188	TQ8032
Benover	188	TQ7048
Berryfield	178	TR0072
Berry's Green	187	TQ4359
Berwick	179 189	TR1235
Bessels Green	188	TQ5055
Bethersden	189	TQ9240
Betsham	177	TQ6071
Betteshanger	179	TR3152
Bexley	177	TQ4675
Bexleyheath	177	TQ4875
Bickley	177	TQ4269
Bicknor	178	TQ8658
Bidborough	188	TQ5643
Biddenden	188	TQ8438
Biddenden Green	189	TQ8843
Biggin Hill	187	TQ4159
Bilsington	179 189	TR0434
Bilting	179 189	TR0549
Birchington	179	TR3069
Bircholt Forstal	179 189	TR0841
Birling	177 178 188	TQ6860
Bishopsbourne	179 189	TR1852
Bishopstone	179	TR2068
Bitchet Green	188	TQ5754
Blacketts	178	TQ9465
Blackfen	177	TQ4574
Blackheath	177	TQ3876
Blackheath Park	177	TQ4075
Bladbean	179 189	TR1747
Blean	179	TR1260
Bliby	189	TR0237
Blue Bell Hill	178 188	TQ7462
Bobbing	178	TQ8865
Bockhanger	189	TR0144
Bodsham	179 189	TR1045
Bonnington	179 189	TR0535
Borden	178	TQ8862
Borough Green	188	TQ6057
Borstal	178	TQ7366
Bossingham	179 189	TR1548
Bossington	179	TR2355
Botolph's Bridge	179 189	TR1233
Bough Beech	188	TQ4946
Boughton Aluph	179 189	TR0348
Boughton Corner	179 189	TR0448
Boughton Green	188	TQ7651
Boughton Lees	189	TR0247
Boughton Malherbe	189	TQ8849
Boughton Monchelsea	188	TQ7651
Boughton Street	179	TR0659
Bowmans	177	TQ5273
Boxley	178 188	TQ7758
Boyden Gate	179	TR2265
Brabourne	179 189	TR1041
Brabourne Lees	179 189	TR0840
Brambledown	178	TQ9671
Bramling	179	TR2256
Branbridges	188	TQ6748
Brasted	188	TQ4755
Brasted Chart	188	TQ4653
Brattle	189	TQ9433
Breach	178	TQ8465
Breach	179 189	TR1947
Bredgar	178	TQ8860
Bredhurst	178 188	TQ7962
Brenchley	188	TQ6841
Brents, The	178	TR0161
Brenzett	189	TR0027
Brenzett Green	189	TR0128
Bridge	179 189	TR1854
Brissenden Green	189	TQ9339
Broad Ford	188	TQ7139
Broad Oak	179 189	TR0438
Broad Oak	179	TR1661
Broadstairs	179	TR3967
Broadstone	189	TQ8647
Broad Street	178 188	TQ8356
Broad Street	179 189	TR1140
Broad Tenterden	189	TQ8832
Broadwater Down	188	TQ5737
Brockley	177	TQ3674
Bromley	177	TQ4069
Bromley Common	177	TQ4167
Bromley Green	189	TQ9936
Bromley Park	177	TQ3969
Brompton	178	TQ7668
Bromstone	179	TR3867
Brook	179 189	TR0644
Brookland	189	TQ9825
Brooks End	179	TR2967
Brook Street	188	TQ5745
Brook Street	189	TQ9333
Broomfield	188	TQ8352
Broomfield	179	TR1966
Broom Hill	177	TQ4566
Broom Hill	178	TQ7369
Broomhill	179	TR2458
Broomhill Bank	188	TQ5640
Buckland	179	TR3042
Buckland Valley	179	TR3043
Bulleign	189	TQ8830
Burham	178 188	TQ7262
Burmarsh	189	TR1031
Burmarsh	179 189	TR1333
Buttsole	179	TR3054
Bybrook	189	TR0144

C

Cage Green	188	TQ5947
Calcott	179	TR1762
Camden Hill	188	TQ7938
Camer	177 178	TQ6567
Canterbury	179	TR1457
Capel	188	TQ6344
Capel-le-Ferne	179 189	TR2438
Capel-le-Ferne	179	TR2538
Castle Hill	188	TQ6942
Catford	177	TQ3873
Chainhurst	188	TQ7347
Chalk	177 178	TQ6773
Chalksole	179	TR2543
Chalkwell	178	TQ8964
Challock	189	TR0050
Chamber's Green	189	TQ9243
Charcott	188	TQ5247
Charing	189	TQ9549
Charing Heath	189	TQ9249
Charing Hill	189	TQ9650
Charlton	177	TQ4178
Chart Corner	188	TQ7950
Chartham	179 189	TR1054
Chartham	179	TR1055
Chartham Hatch	179	TR1056
Chart Sutton	188	TQ7950
Chatham	178 188	TQ7564
Chatham	178	TQ7665
Chattenden	178	TQ7571
Chegworth	188	TQ8452
Chelsfield	177 188	TQ4664
Cheriton	179 189	TR1936
Chesley	178	TQ8563
Chestfield	179	TR1365

Chestnut Street	178	TQ8763
Chevening	188	TQ4857
Chiddingstone	188	TQ4945
Chiddingstone Causeway	188	TQ5246
Chiddingstone Hoath	188	TQ4942
Childsbridge	188	TQ5557
Chilham	179 189	TR0653
Chillenden	179	TR2653
Chillmill	188	TQ6740
Chilmington Green	189	TQ9840
Chilton	179	TR3664
Chipstead	188	TQ5056
Chislehurst	177	TQ4470
Chislehurst West	177	TQ4371
Chislet	179	TR2264
Chitty	179	TR2264
Church Hougham	179	TR2740
Church Street	178	TQ7174
Church Whitfield	179	TR3145
Clapham Hill	179	TR1064
Clapper Hill	188	TQ8436
Claygate	188	TQ7144
Claygate Cross	188	TQ6155
Claypits	179	TR2555
Clement Street	177	TQ5370
Cliffe	178	TQ7376
Cliffe Woods	178	TQ7373
Cliffs End	179	TR3464
Cliftonville	179	TR3671
Cobham	177 178	TQ6768
Cock Street	188	TQ7750
Coldblow	177	TQ5073
Coldharbour	188	TQ5750
Coldred	179	TR2746
Collier Street	188	TQ7145
Colt's Hill	188	TQ6443
Coney Hall	177 187	TQ3964
Connaught Park	179	TR3142
Conyer	178	TQ9664
Cooling	178	TQ7576
Coolinge	179 189	TR2036
Cooling Street	178	TQ7474
Coombe	179	TR2957
Cooper's Corner	188	TQ4849
Cooper Street	179	TR3059
Coppins Corner	189	TQ9448
Copton	178	TR0159
Corner, The	188	TQ7041
Court-at-Street	179 189	TR0935
Cowden	188	TQ4640
Coxheath	188	TQ7451
Crabble	179	TR2943
Cranbrook	188	TQ7736
Crayford	177	TQ5174
Crit Hall	188	TQ7833
Crockenhill	177	TQ5067
Crockham Hill	187	TQ4450
Crockhurst Street	188	TQ6244
Crofton	177	TQ4466
Cross-at-Hand	188	TQ7846
Cross Keys	188	TQ5153
Crouch	188	TQ6155
Crowdleham	188	TQ5658
Crundale	179 189	TR0749
Culverstone Green	177 188	TQ6362
Curteis' Corner	189	TQ8539
Curtisden Green	188	TQ7440
Cuxton	178	TQ7066

D

Danaway	178	TQ8662
Dane Chantry	179 189	TR1349
Dane Park	179	TR3670
Dane Street	179 189	TR0553
Daniel's Water	189	TQ9541
Danton Pinch	179 189	TR1937
Darenth	177	TQ5671
Dargate	179	TR0761
Darland	178	TQ7865
Dartford	177	TQ5273
David Street	177 188	TQ6464
Davington	178	TR0061
Deal	179	TR3752
Deans Bottom	178	TQ8660
Deans Hill	178	TQ8660
Dean Street	188	TQ7452
Deerton Street	178	TQ9762
Denny Bottom	188	TQ5739
Densole	179 189	TR2141
Denstroude	179	TR1061
Denton	177 178	TQ6673
Denton	179 189	TR2147
Deptford	177	TQ3677
Derringstone	179 189	TR2049
Derry Downs	177	TQ4767
Detling	178 188	TQ7958
Dingleden	188	TQ8131
Ditton	178 188	TQ7157
Doddington	178	TQ9357
Donkey Street	189	TR1032
Dover	179	TR3141
Dover Hill	179 189	TR2337
Downe	177 187	TQ4361
Downham	177	TQ3971
Drellingore	179 189	TR2441
Dumpton	179	TR3866
Duncan Down	179	TR1065
Dungate	178	TQ9159
Dungeness	189	TR0916
Dunkirk	179	TR0759
Dunk's Green	188	TQ6152
Dunn Street	178 188	TQ7961
Dunn Street	189	TQ9948
Dunton Green	188	TQ5157
Durlock	179	TR2757
Durlock	179	TR3164
Durrant Green	189	TQ8836
Dymchurch	189	TR1029

E

Each End	179	TR3058
Easole Street	179	TR2652
East Barming	188	TQ7254
Eastchurch	178	TQ9871
East End	188	TQ8335
East End	178	TQ9673
East Farleigh	188	TQ7353
East Hill	177 188	TQ5562
East Langdon	179	TR3346
Eastling	178	TQ9656
East Malling	178 188	TQ7057
East Malling Heath	178 188	TQ6955
East Peckham	188	TQ6648
Eastry	179	TR3054
East Stourmouth	179	TR2662
East Street	179	TR3058
East Studdal	179	TR3249
East Wickham	177	TQ4677
Eccles	178 188	TQ7360
Eddington	179	TR1867
Edenbridge	187	TQ4446
Eden Park	177	TQ3668
Egerton	189	TQ9047
Egerton Forstal	189	TQ8946
Elham	179 189	TR1743
Elmers End	177	TQ3568
Elmstead	177	TQ4270
Elmstone	179	TR2560
Eltham	177	TQ4274
Elverton	178	TQ9862
Elvington	179	TR2750
Erith	177	TQ5077
Erriottwood	178	TQ9359
Etchinghill	179 189	TR1639
Evington	179 189	TR1045
Ewell Minnis	179	TR2643
Exted	179 189	TR1644
Eyhorne Street	188	TQ8354
Eynsford	177	TQ5365
Eythorne	179	TR2849

F

Fairbourne Heath	189	TQ8550
Fairseat	177 188	TQ6261
Falconwood	177	TQ4575
Fant	178 188	TQ7455
Farleigh Green	188	TQ7252
Farnborough	177 187	TQ4464
Farningham	177	TQ5466
Farthing Common	179 189	TR1340
Farthing Corner	178 188	TQ8163
Farthing Green	188	TQ8146
Farthingloe	179	TR2940
Faversham	178	TR0161
Fawkham Green	177	TQ5865
Felderland	179	TR3256
Finglesham	179	TR3353
Fir Toll	189	TQ9244
Five Oak Green	188	TQ6445
Five Wents	188	TQ8150
Fleet Downs	177	TQ5673
Flemings	179	TR2856
Fletcher's Green	188	TQ5350
Flishinghurst	188	TQ7537
Folkestone	179 189	TR2136
Foots Cray	177	TQ4770
Force Green	187	TQ4455
Fordcombe	188	TQ5240
Fordwich	179	TR1859
Forest Hill	177	TQ3573
Forstal, The	179 189	TR0439
Fostall	179	TR0661
Fosten Green	188	TQ8336
Four Elms	188	TQ4648
Four Throws	188 199	TQ7729
Four Wents	188	TQ7537
Four Wents	188	TQ7632
Foxbury	177	TQ4471
Foxendown	177 178	TQ6565
French Street	188	TQ4552
Frindsbury	178	TQ7469
Friningham	178 188	TQ8158
Frinsted	178	TQ8957
Frittenden	188	TQ8141
Frogham	179	TR2550
Froghole	187	TQ4451
Frogholt	179 189	TR1737
Frognal Corner	177	TQ4571
Frognall	179	TR2259
Further Quarter	189	TQ8939

G

Garlinge	179	TR3369
Garlinge Green	179 189	TR1152
Gibraltar	179 189	TR2039
Gillingham	178	TQ7767
Gillingham	178 188	TQ8064
Gill's Green	188	TQ7532
Glassenbury	188	TQ7436
Goathurst Common	188	TQ4952
Goddard's Green	188	TQ8134
Godden Green	188	TQ5555
Goddington	177	TQ4765
Godmersham	179 189	TR0650
Golden Green	188	TQ6348
Golford	188	TQ7936
Golgotha	179	TR2648
Goodley Stock	187	TQ4452
Goodnestone	178 179	TR0461
Goodnestone	179	TR2554
Goose Green	188	TQ6450
Goose Green	188	TQ8437
Gore	179	TR3055
Gore Street	179	TR2765
Goudhurst	188	TQ7237
Gover Hill	188	TQ6352
Grafty Green	189	TQ8748
Grain	178	TQ8876
Grange	178	TQ7968
Grantham Hall	188	TQ6737
Gravel Castle	179 189	TR2149
Graveney	179	TR0562
Graveney Hill	179	TR0563
Gravesend	177 178	TQ6574
Great Bower	179 189	TR0352
Great Chart	189	TQ9841
Great Cheveney	188	TQ7342
Great Grovehurst	178	TQ9066
Great Mongeham	179	TR3451
Greatness	188	TQ5356
Great Pattenden	188	TQ7344
Great Stonar	179	TR3359
Greatstone-on-Sea	189	TR0822
Greenhill	179	TR1666
Greenhithe	177	TQ5875
Green Street Green	177 188	TQ4563
Green Street Green	177	TQ5870
Greenwich	177	TQ3977
Grigg	189	TQ8544
Grove	179	TR2361
Grove Green	178 188	TQ7856
Grove Hill	179	TR2360
Grove Park	177	TQ4172
Grubb Street	177	TQ5869
Guilton	179	TR2858
Gun Green	188	TQ7730
Guston	179	TR3244

H

Hadlow	188	TQ6350
Hadlow Stair	188	TQ6047
Haffenden Quarter	189	TQ8840

Place	Sheet	Grid ref
Haine	179	TR3566
Hale	178	TQ7765
Hales Place	179	TR1459
Hale Street	188	TQ6749
Halfway Houses	178	TQ9373
Halfway Street	179	TR2547
Halling	178 188	TQ7064
Hall Place	179	TR1258
Halstead	177 188	TQ4861
Hamden	189	TQ8940
Ham Green	178	TQ8468
Hammill	179	TR2955
Hampton	179	TR1667
Hamptons	188	TQ6252
Hamstreet	189	TR0033
Hanging Bank	188	TQ4851
Harbledown	179	TR1358
Harbour, The	188	TQ8148
Hareplain	188	TQ8339
Harman's Corner	178	TQ8862
Harrietsham	189	TQ8752
Hartley	177	TQ6067
Hartley	188	TQ7534
Hartley Green	177	TQ6067
Hartlip	178 188	TQ8364
Harvel	177 188	TQ6463
Hassell Street	179 189	TR0846
Hastingleigh	179 189	TR0944
Haviker Street	188	TQ7246
Hawkenbury	188	TQ5938
Hawkenbury	188	TQ8045
Hawkhurst	188	TQ7630
Hawkinge	179 189	TR2140
Hawkwood	177	TQ4369
Hawley	177	TQ5471
Hawley's Corner	187	TQ4356
Hawthorn Corner	179	TR2167
Hayes	177	TQ4066
Haysden	188	TQ5645
Hazel Street	188	TQ6939
Hazel Street	178	TQ8559
Hazelwood	177 187	TQ4461
Headcorn	188	TQ8344
Hearnden Green	188	TQ8246
Hearts Delight	178	TQ8862
Heath Side	177	TQ5172
Heaverham	188	TQ5758
Hempstead	178 188	TQ7964
Henley Street	177 178	TQ6667
Henwood Green	188	TQ6340
Herne	179	TR1866
Herne Bay	179	TR1767
Herne Common	179	TR1765
Herne Pound	188	TQ6554
Hernhill	179	TR0660
Hersden	179	TR2062
Hever	188	TQ4744
Hextable	177	TQ5170
Hicks Forstal	179	TR1863
Higham	178	TQ7171
Higham Wood	188	TQ6048
High Brooms	188	TQ5941
Highgate	188	TQ7630
High Halden	189	TQ8937
High Halstow	178	TQ7875
Highstead	179	TR2166
Highsted	178	TQ9161
High Street	188	TQ7430
Highstreet	179	TR0862
Hildenborough	188	TQ5648
Hilden Park	188	TQ5747
Hill Green	178 188	TQ8362
Hill Hoath	188	TQ4944
Hill Park	187	TQ4355
Hinxhill	179 189	TR0442
Hither Green	177	TQ3974
Hoath	179	TR2064
Hoath Corner	188	TQ4943
Hockenden	177	TQ4968
Hockley	178	TQ9855
Hodsoll Street	177 188	TQ6263
Hogbarn	178	TQ8855
Hogben's Hill	178 179	TR0356
Holborough	178 188	TQ7062
Hollingbourne	178 188	TQ8455
Holt Street	179	TR2551
Homestall	178 179	TR0360
Honey Hill	179	TR1161
Honor Oak Park	177	TQ3674
Hook Green	177	TQ6170
Hook Green	177	TQ6467
Hook Green	188	TQ6535
Hoo St Werburgh	178	TQ7872
Horns Green	188	TQ4558
Horn Street	177 178 188	TQ6860
Horn Street	179 189	TR1835
Horsalls	189	TQ8754
Horselees	179	TR0659
Horsmonden	188	TQ7040
Horton	179	TR1155
Horton Kirby	177	TQ5668
Hosey Hill	188	TQ4553
Hothfield	189	TQ9744
How Green	188	TQ4746
Howt Green	178	TQ8965
Hucking	178 188	TQ8458
Hungershall Park	188	TQ5738
Hunters Forstal	179	TR1866
Hunton	188	TQ7149
Hythe	179 189	TR1634

I

Place	Sheet	Grid ref
Ickham	179	TR2258
Ide Hill	188	TQ4851
Iden Green	188	TQ7437
Iden Green	188	TQ8031
Ightham	188	TQ5956
Igtham Common	188	TQ5855
Ileden	179 189	TR2052
Ingress Abbey	177	TQ5975
Istead Rise	177	TQ6370
Ivychurch	189	TR0227
Ivy Hatch	188	TQ5854
Iwade	178	TQ8967

J

Place	Sheet	Grid ref
Jeskyns Court	177 178	TQ6669

K

Place	Sheet	Grid ref
Kearnsey	179	TR2843
Kempe's Corner	179 189	TR0346
Kemsing	188	TQ5558
Kemsley	178	TQ9066
Kemsley Street	178 188	TQ8062
Kenardington	189	TQ9732
Kennington	189	TR0144
Kent Street	188	TQ6654
Keston	177 187	TQ4164
Keston Mark	177	TQ4265
Kettle Corner	188	TQ7253
Kevingtown	177	TQ4867
Keycol	178	TQ8764
Key's Green	188	TQ6539
Kidbrooke	177	TQ4176
Kilndown	188	TQ7035
Kingsdown	179	TR3748
Kings Farm	177 178	TQ6572
Kingsgate	179	TR3970
Kingsnorth	178	TQ8072
Kingsnorth	189	TR0039
Kingston	179 189	TR1951
Kingswood	188	TQ8450
Kipping's Cross	188	TQ6439
Kippington	188	TQ5254
Kit's Coty	178 188	TQ7461
Knatts Valley	177 188	TQ5661
Knockhall	177	TQ5974
Knockholt	188	TQ4859
Knockmill	177 188	TQ5761
Knowlton	179	TR2853
Knox Bridge	188	TQ7840

L

Place	Sheet	Grid ref
Laddingford	188	TQ6948
Lade	189	TR0820
Lady Margaret Manor	178	TQ9255
Ladywell	177	TQ3774
Lamberden	188 199	TQ8228
Lamberhurst	188	TQ6736
Lamb's Cross	188	TQ7948
Lane End	177	TQ5671
Langdon Abbey	179	TR3246
Langley	188	TQ8151
Langley	189	TQ8940
Langley Heath	188	TQ8151
Langton Green	188	TQ5439
Larkfield	178 188	TQ6958
Lark Hill	189	TQ9047
Lashenden	188	TQ8440
Leacon, The	189	TQ9833
Leadingcross Green	189	TQ8951
Leaveland	189	TR0053
Leaves Green	177 187	TQ4161
Lee	177	TQ3974
Leeds	188	TQ8152
Lee Priory	179	TR2156
Lees, The	189	TR0050
Leigh	188	TQ5546
Leigh Green	189	TQ9032
Lenham	189	TQ8952
Lenham Forstal	189	TQ9150
Lenham Heath	189	TQ9149
Lessness Heath	177	TQ4978
Lett's Green	188	TQ4559
Lewisham	177	TQ3875
Lewson Street	178	TQ9661
Leybourne	178 188	TQ6858
Leysdown on Sea	178 179	TR0370
Lidsing	178 188	TQ7862
Lilyvale	179 189	TR0839
Linkhill	188 199	TQ8128
Linton	188	TQ7549
Littlebourne	179	TR2057
Little Chart	189	TQ9446
Little Chart Forstal	189	TQ9545
Little Hermitage	178	TQ7270
Little Mill	188	TQ6548
Little Mongeham	179	TR3350
Little Preston	178 188	TQ7358
Littlestone-on-Sea	189	TR0724
Little Watersend	179	TR2744
Liverton Street	189	TQ8750
Locksbottom	177	TQ4365
Lodge Lees	179 189	TR2047
London Beach	189	TQ8836
Longfield	177	TQ6069
Longfield Hill	177	TQ6268
Longford	188	TQ5156
Longlands	177	TQ4472
Loose	188	TQ7652
Loose Hill	188	TQ7552
Lords Wood	178 188	TQ7762
Lower Bitchet	188	TQ5654
Lower Bush	177 178	TQ6967
Lower Cox Street	178 188	TQ8160
Lower Ensden	179	TR0755
Lower Eythorne	179	TR2849
Lower Goldstone	179	TR2961
Lower Green	188	TQ5640
Lower Green	188	TQ6241
Lower Halstow	178	TQ8667
Lower Hardres	179 189	TR1553
Lower Hartlip	178 188	TQ8464
Lower Heppington	179 189	TR1453
Lower Herne	179	TR1866
Lower Higham	178	TQ7173
Lower Island	179	TR1066
Lower Rainham	178	TQ8167
Lower Stoke	178	TQ8375
Lower Sydenham	177	TQ3571
Lower Twydall	178	TQ8067
Lower Upnor	178	TQ7671
Loyterton	178	TQ9560
Luddenham Court	178	TQ9963
Luddesdown	177 178	TQ6766
Lunsford	178 188	TQ6959
Luton	178	TQ7666
Luxted	177 187	TQ4360
Lydd	189	TR0420
Lydden	179	TR2645
Lydden	179	TR3567
Lymbridge Green	179 189	TR1243
Lyminge	179 189	TR1641
Lympne	179 189	TR1235
Lynsted	178	TQ9460

M

Place	Sheet	Grid ref
Mabledon	188	TQ5744
Macklands	178	TQ8166
Maidstone	178 188	TQ7655
Maltman's Hill	189	TQ9043
Manston	179	TR3466
Maplescombe	177 188	TQ5564
Marden	188	TQ7444
Marden Beech	188	TQ7343
Marden Thorn	188	TQ7542
Margate	179	TR3570
Marine Town	178	TQ9274
Markbeech	188	TQ4742
Marley	179 189	TR1850
Marley	179	TR3353
Marlpit Hill	187	TQ4447
Marshborough	179	TR3057

Place	Sheet	Grid ref
Marsh Green	187	TQ4444
Marshside	179	TR2266
Martin	179	TR3347
Martin Mill	179	TR3446
Matfield	188	TQ6541
Maxted Street	179 189	TR1244
Maxton	179	TR3040
Maypole	177 188	TQ4963
Maypole	177	TQ5173
Maypole	179	TR2064
Medhurst Row	188	TQ4647
Meopham	177	TQ6465
Meopham Green	177	TQ6365
Meopham Station	177	TQ6367
Meresborough	178 188	TQ8264
Mereworth	188	TQ6653
Mersham	179 189	TR0539
Mersham-le-Hatch	179 189	TR0640
Middle Quarter	189	TQ8938
Milebush	188	TQ7545
Mile Oak	188	TQ6843
Mile Town	178	TQ9174
Millbank	179	TR2065
Mill Hill	178	TQ9672
Mill Hill	179	TR3651
Mill Street	178 188	TQ6957
Milstead	178	TQ9058
Milton	177 178	TQ6574
Milton Regis	178	TQ8964
Minster	178	TQ9573
Minster	179	TR3064
Mockbeggar	178	TQ7372
Mockbeggar	178	TQ9762
Mockbeggar	179 189	TR1443
Modest Corner	188	TQ5742
Molash	189	TR0251
Monks Hill	189	TQ8641
Monkton	179	TR2865
Moon's Green	189 199	TQ8827
Moorstock	179 189	TR1038
Moor Street	178	TQ8265
Moor, The	188 199	TQ7529
Morehall	179 189	TR2036
Motney Hill	178	TQ8268
Mottingham	177	TQ4172
Mountain Street	179 189	TR0652
Mount Pleasant	179	TR3065
Mowshurst	188	TQ4547
Mundy Bois	189	TQ9045
Murston	178	TQ9164

N

Place	Sheet	Grid ref
Naccolt	179 189	TR0444
Nackington	179 189	TR1554
Nash	177 187	TQ4063
Nash	179	TR2658
Nash Street	177	TQ6469
Neames Forstal	179	TR0557
Nether Toes	178	TQ8965
Nettlestead	188	TQ6852
Nettlestead Green	188	TQ6850
New Ash Green	177	TQ6065
New Barn	177	TQ6268
Newbarn	189	TR0731
Newbarn	179 189	TR1539
New Beckenham	177	TQ3670
New Charlton	177	TQ4078
Newchurch	189	TR0531
New Cross	177	TQ3676
New Cross Gate	177	TQ3576
New Eltham	177	TQ4472
Newenden	188 199	TQ8327
New House	177	TQ6372
New Hythe	178 188	TQ7059
Newingreen	179 189	TR1236
Newington	178	TQ8564
Newington	179 189	TR1737
Newington	179	TR3666
Newland Green	189	TQ8945
Newnham	178	TQ9557
New Romney	189	TR0624
New Street	177 188	TQ6264
New Town	177	TQ5474
New Town	178 188	TQ6757
Noah's Arks	188	TQ5557
Nonington	179	TR2552
Northbourne	179	TR3352
North Cray	177	TQ4972
Northdown	179	TR3770
North Elham	179 189	TR1844
North End	177	TQ5176
Northfleet	177	TQ6274
Northfleet Green	177	TQ6271
North Foreland	179	TR4069
North Halling	178	TQ7065
North Leigh	179 189	TR1347
North Street	178	TQ8174
North Street	178	TR0158
Northumberland Heath	177	TQ5077
Northwood	179	TR3767

O

Place	Sheet	Grid ref
Oad Street	178	TQ8662
Oakhurst	188	TQ5450
Oare	178	TR0062
Offham	178 188	TQ6557
Old Bexley	177	TQ4973
Oldbury	188	TQ5856
Old Romney	189	TR0325
Old Wives Lees	179 189	TR0754
Old Wives Lees	179	TR0755
Orpington	177	TQ4565
Ospringe	178	TR0060
Otford	188	TQ5159
Otham	188	TQ7953
Otham Hole	188	TQ8052
Otterham Quay	178	TQ8366
Ottinge	179 189	TR1642
Out Elmstead	179 189	TR2050
Oversland	179	TR0557

P

Place	Sheet	Grid ref
Paddlesworth	179 189	TR1939
Paddock	189	TQ9950
Paddock Wood	188	TQ6744
Painter's Forstal	178	TQ9958
Palmarsh	179 189	TR1333
Palmer's Green	188	TQ6841
Paramour Street	179	TR2861
Parker's Green	188	TQ6148
Parkgate	189	TQ8534
Park Gate	179 189	TR1745
Park Hill	189	TQ9531
Park Langley	177	TQ3867
Park Wood	188	TQ7851
Park Wood	178 188	TQ8063
Patrixbourne	179	TR1855
Payden Street	189	TQ9254
Pean Hill	179	TR1062
Pearson's Green	188	TQ6943
Peckham Bush	188	TQ6649
Pedlinge	179 189	TR1335
Peene	179 189	TR1837
Peening Quarter	189 199	TQ8828
Pegwell	179	TR3664
Pembles Cross	189	TQ8847
Pembury	188	TQ6240
Penenden Heath	178 188	TQ7657
Pennypot	179 189	TR1434
Penshurst	188	TQ5243
Perry	179	TR2559
Perry Court	178	TR0160
Perry Street	177	TQ6373
Pested	189	TR0051
Petham	179 189	TR1351
Pett Bottom	179 189	TR1652
Petteridge	188	TQ6641
Pettings	177 188	TQ6163
Petts Wood	177	TQ4467
Pigtail Corner	178	TQ9672
Pigwell	189	TR0320
Pineham	179	TR3145
Pipsden	188	TQ7730
Pittswood	188	TQ6149
Pizien Well	188	TQ6753
Plaistow	177	TQ4070
Platt	188	TQ6257
Platt's Heath	189	TQ8750
Plaxtol	188	TQ6053
Pluckley	189	TQ9245
Pluckley Thorne	189	TQ9144
Plumstead	177	TQ4478
Plumstead Common	177	TQ4577
Plumtree Green	188	TQ8245
Pollhill	189	TQ8652
Pootings	188	TQ4549
Postling	179 189	TR1438
Potters Corner	189	TQ9944
Potter's Forstal	189	TQ8846
Poundsbridge	188	TQ5341
Poverest	177	TQ4668
Powder Mills	188	TQ5647
Pratling Street	178 188	TQ7459
Pratt's Bottom	177 188	TQ4762
Preston	178	TR0260
Preston	179	TR2561
Preston Street	179	TR2461
Printstile	188	TQ5543
Puddledock	177	TQ5170
Pullington	188	TQ8132
Pye Corner	189	TQ8548

Q

Place	Sheet	Grid ref
Quarter, The	189	TQ8844
Queenborough	178	TQ9172
Queen Street	188	TQ6845

R

Place	Sheet	Grid ref
Rabbit's Cross	188	TQ7847
Radfall	179	TR1364
Rainham	178	TQ8065
Ram Lane	189	TQ9646
Ramsden	177	TQ4766
Ramsgate	179	TR3864
Ramslye	188	TQ5638
Ratling	179 189	TR2453
Reading Street	189	TQ9230
Reading Street	179	TR3869
Reculver	179	TR2269
Red Hill	188	TQ6954
Reynolds Place	177	TQ5667
Rhodes Minnis	179 189	TR1543
Richborough Port	179	TR3361
Ridge Row	179 189	TR2042
Ridley	177 188	TQ6163
Ringlestone	178 188	TQ7557
Ringlestone	178	TQ8755
Ringwould	179	TR3548
Ripper's Cross	189	TQ9543
Ripple	179	TR3449
Riseden	188	TQ7035
River	179	TR2943
Riverhead	188	TQ5055
Riverview Park	177 178	TQ6671
Robhurst	189	TQ9134
Rochester	178	TQ7268
Rodmersham	178	TQ9261
Rodmersham Green	178	TQ9161
Rolvenden	188	TQ8431
Rolvenden Layne	189	TQ8530
Romford	188	TQ6441
Romney Street	177 188	TQ5461
Rooting Street	189	TQ9545
Roseacre	178 188	TQ7955
Rosherville	177	TQ6374
Rough Common	179	TR1259
Roughway	188	TQ6252
Round Street	177 178	TQ6568
Rowling Court	179	TR2754
Royal British Legion Village	178 188	TQ7257
Royal Tunbridge Wells	188	TQ5839
Ruckinge	189	TR0233
Rushenden	178	TQ9071
Rusthall	188	TQ5639
Ruxley	177	TQ4870
Ryarsh	178 188	TQ6759

S

Place	Sheet	Grid ref
St Johns	177	TQ3776
St John's	188	TQ5256
St John's	188	TQ5841
St Lawrence	179	TR3765
St Leonard's Street	178 188	TQ6756
St Margarets	177	TQ5770
St Margaret's at Cliffe	179	TR3644
St Mary Cray	177	TQ4667
St Mary in the Marsh	189	TR0627
St Mary's Bay	189	TR0827
St Michaels	189	TQ8835
St Nicholas at Wade	179	TR2666
St Paul's Cray	177	TQ4669
St Peters	179	TR3868
Saint's Hill	188	TQ5241
Salmans	188	TQ5143
Salmestone Grange	179	TR3569
Saltwood	179 189	TR1535
Sandgate	179 189	TR2035
Sandhurst	188 199	TQ7928
Sandhurst Cross	188 199	TQ7827
Sandling	178 188	TQ7558
Sandown Park	188	TQ6040

Place	Sheet	Grid ref
Sandwich	179	TR3358
Sandwich Bay Estate	179	TR3657
Sarre	179	TR2564
Satmar	179	TR2539
Sayes Court	178	TR0266
Scadbury Park	177	TQ4570
Scott's Lodge	188	TQ4557
Scrapsgate	178	TQ9474
Seabrook	179 189	TR1834
Seal	188	TQ5456
Seasalter	179	TR0965
Seaton	179	TR2258
Sellindge	179 189	TR1038
Selling	178 179	TR0456
Selson	179	TR3055
Selsted	179 189	TR2144
Sevenoaks	188	TQ5255
Sevenoaks Common	188	TQ5252
Sevenoaks Weald	188	TQ5250
Sevington	179 189	TR0340
Shadoxhurst	189	TQ9738
Shalmsford Street	179 189	TR0954
Sharnal Street	178	TQ7974
Shatterling	179	TR2658
Sheerness	178	TQ9175
Sheldwich	178	TR0156
Sheldwich Lees	178	TR0156
Shepherdswell or Sibertswold	179	TR2547
Shepway	188	TQ7753
Sherwood Park	188	TQ6040
Shipbourne	188	TQ5952
Shirkoak	189	TQ9436
Sholden	179	TR3552
Shooters Hill	177	TQ4376
Shoreham	177 188	TQ5161
Shorncliffe Camp	179 189	TR1935
Shorne	177 178	TQ6971
Shorne Ridgeway	177 178	TQ6970
Shortlands	177	TQ3968
Shottenden	179 189	TR0454
Shuttlesfield	179 189	TR1841
Sidcup	177	TQ4672
Silver Street	178	TQ8760
Singlewell	177 178	TQ6570
Sinkhurst Green	188	TQ8142
Sissinghurst	188	TQ7937
Sittingbourne	178	TQ9063
Sixmile	179 189	TR1344
Skeete	179 189	TR1341
Slade	189	TQ9354
Slade Green	177	TQ5276
Sly Corner	189	TQ9632
Small Hythe	189	TQ8930
Smarden	189	TQ8842
Smarden Bell	189	TQ8642
Smart's Hill	188	TQ5241
Smeeth	179 189	TR0739
Snargate	189	TQ9828
Snave	189	TR0129
Snipeshill	178	TQ9263
Snodland	178 188	TQ7061
Snowdown	179 189	TR2451
Sole Street	177 178	TQ6567
Sole Street	179 189	TR0949
South Alkham	179 189	TR2441
South Ashford	189	TR0041
South Barham	179 189	TR1948
Southborough	177	TQ4267
Southborough	188	TQ5842
South Darenth	177	TQ5669

Place	Sheet	Grid ref
South Downs	177	TQ5769
Southend	177	TQ3871
Southfleet	177	TQ6171
South Green	178	TQ8560
South Stour	179 189	TR0338
South Street	187	TQ4357
South Street	177 188	TQ6363
South Street	178 188	TQ8361
South Street	179	TR0557
South Street	179	TR1265
South Willesborough	189	TR0241
Spearpoint Corner	189	TR0244
Speed Gate	177	TQ5765
Speldhurst	188	TQ5541
Spendiff	178	TQ7574
Stalisfield Green	189	TQ9552
Standen	189	TQ8540
Standen Street	188	TQ8030
Stanford	179 189	TR1238
Stanhope	189	TQ9940
Stanstead	177 188	TQ6062
Staple	179	TR2756
Staplehurst	188	TQ7843
Staplestreet	179	TR0560
Starvecrow	188	TQ5949
Statenborough	179	TR3155
Stede Hill	189	TQ8753
Stelling Minnis	179 189	TR1446
Stick Hill	188	TQ4643
Stiff Street	178	TQ8761
Stockbury	178 188	TQ8461
Stocker's Head	189	TQ9650
Stockland Green	188	TQ5642
Stocks Green	188	TQ5547
Stocks, The	189	TQ9127
Stodmarsh	179	TR2160
Stoke	178	TQ8275
Stone	177	TQ5774
Stonebridge Green	189	TQ9147
Stone Cross	188	TQ5238
Stone Cross	189	TR0236
Stone Cross	179	TR3257
Stonehall	179	TR2645
Stone Hill	189	TQ9046
Stone Hill	179 189	TR0938
Stonehill Green	177	TQ5070
Stone in Oxney	189	TQ9427
Stone Street	188	TQ5754
Stonestreet Green	179 189	TR0637
Stour Centre	189	TR0142
Stowting	179 189	TR1241
Stowting Common	179 189	TR1243
Stowting Court	179 189	TR1141
Street End	179 189	TR1453
Strood	178	TQ7269
Strood	189	TQ8532
Stubb's Cross	189	TQ9838
Studdal	179	TR3149
Studd Hill	179	TR1567
Sturry	179	TR1760
Styants Bottom	188	TQ5756
Summerfield	179	TR2755
Sundridge	177	TQ4170
Sundridge	188	TQ4855
Sutton	179	TR3349
Sutton at Hone	177	TQ5570
Sutton Valence	188	TQ8149
Swalecliffe	179	TR1367
Swanley	177	TQ5168
Swanley Village	177	TQ5269
Swanscombe	177	TQ5974

Place	Sheet	Grid ref
Swanton Street	178	TQ8759
Swift's Green	189	TQ8744
Swingfield Minnis	179 189	TR2142
Swingfield Street	179 189	TR2343

T

Place	Sheet	Grid ref
Tanden	189	TQ9138
Tankerton	179	TR1266
Temple Ewell	179	TR2844
Temple Hill	177	TQ5575
Tenterden	189	TQ8833
Teston	188	TQ7053
Teynham	178	TQ9562
Teynham Street	178	TQ9663
Thamesmead	177	TQ4780
Thanington	179	TR1356
The Chart	188	TQ4652
The Down	188	TQ6735
Thong	177 178	TQ6770
Three Chimneys	188	TQ8238
Throwley	178	TQ9955
Throwley Forstal	189	TQ9854
Thurnham	178 188	TQ8057
Tickham	178	TQ9560
Tilmanstone	179	TR3051
Timberden Bottom	177 188	TQ5162
Tonbridge	188	TQ5946
Tonge Corner	178	TQ9365
Tong Green	189	TQ9854
Tovil	188	TQ7554
Tower Hamlets	179	TR3041
Townland Green	189	TQ9434
Toy's Hill	188	TQ4751
Trench Wood	188	TQ5948
Trottiscliffe	177 188	TQ6460
Trouts	178	TQ9972
Troy Town	187	TQ4247
Troy Town	179 189	TR0744
Tudeley	188	TQ6245
Tudeley Hale	188	TQ6246
Tunbury Wood	178 188	TQ7662
Tunstall	178	TQ8961
Tutt Hill	189	TQ9746
Twenties	179	TR3469
Twitton	188	TQ5159
Twydall	178	TQ7966
Tyler Hill	179	TR1460

U

Place	Sheet	Grid ref
Ulcombe	188	TQ8449
Underlining Green	188	TQ7546
Underriver Ho	188	TQ5652
Upchurch	178	TQ8467
Uplees	178	TQ9964
Upper Bush	177 178	TQ6966
Upper Deal	179	TR3651
Upper Elmers End	177	TQ3667
Upper Goldstone	179	TR2960
Upper Halling	177 178 188	TQ6864
Upper Harbedown	179	TR1158
Upper Hardres Court	179 189	TR1550
Upper Hayesden	188	TQ5644
Upper Hockenden	177	TQ4969
Upper Newlands	178	TQ9661
Upper Sydenham	176 177	TQ3471
Upper Upnor	178	TQ7570

Place	Sheet	Grid ref
Upstreet	179	TR2263
Upton	179	TR3867

V

Place	Sheet	Grid ref
Valley, The	189	TQ9553
Vigo Village	177 188	TQ6361

W

Place	Sheet	Grid ref
Wainscott	178	TQ7471
Walderslade	178 188	TQ7663
Walderslade Bottom	178 188	TQ7662
Walmer	179	TR3750
Walter's Green	188	TQ5140
Waltham	179 189	TR1048
Wanshurst Green	188	TQ7645
Warden	178	TR0271
Ware	179	TR2760
Warehorne	189	TQ9832
Ware Street	178 188	TQ7956
Warmlake	188	TQ8149
Warren Street	189	TQ9253
Warren, The	189	TR0044
Waterham	179	TR0762
Wateringbury	188	TQ6953
Waterman Quarter	188	TQ8342
Wayfield	178	TQ7565
Weavering Street	178 188	TQ7855
Weddington	179	TR2959
Weller's Town	188	TQ5044
Well Hill	177 188	TQ4963
Welling	177	TQ4675
Well Street	178 188	TQ6956
Wennington	177	TQ5480
Westbere	179	TR1961
Westbrook	179	TR3470
West Cliffe	179	TR3444
West Cross	188	TQ8331
Westenhanger	179 189	TR1237
Westerham	187	TQ4454
Westerham	188	TQ4554
Western Heights	179	TR3140
West Farleigh	188	TQ7152
Westfield Sole	178 188	TQ7761
Westgate on Sea	179	TR3270
West Heath	177	TQ4777
West Hougham	179	TR2640
West Hythe	179 189	TR1234
West Kingsdown	177 188	TQ5763
West Langdon	179	TR3147
West Malling	178 188	TQ6857
Westmarsh	179	TR2761
West Minster	178	TQ9173
West Peckham	188	TQ6452
West Stourmouth	179	TR2562
West Street	189	TQ9054
West Street	179	TR3254
Westwell	189	TQ9847
Westwell Leacon	189	TQ9647
West Wickham	177	TQ3865
Westwood	177	TQ5970
Westwood	179	TR3668
West Yoke	177	TQ5965
Wetham Green	178	TQ8468
Whatsole Street	179 189	TR1144
Wheelbarrow Town	179 189	TR1545
Whetsted	188	TQ6545
Whiteacre	179 189	TR1147

Y

CITY STORES
46
45
MACKESON'S
HYTHE
ALES
WHISKY
PHILPOT'S
CYCLE
DEPOT